ALSO BY ROGER D. MASTERS

The Nation Is Burdened: American Foreign Policy in a Changing World

The Political Philosophy of Rousseau

The Nature of Politics

Beyond Relativism: Science and Human Values

Machiavelli, Leonardo, and the Science of Power

ROGER D. MASTERS

FORTUNE IS A RIVER

Leonardo da Vinci and Niccolò Machiavelli's

Magnificent Dream to Change

the Course of Florentine History

THE FREE PRESS
New York London Toronto Sydney Singapore

THE FREE PRESS
A Division of Simon & Schuster Inc.
1230 Avenue of the Americas
New York, NY 10020

Copyright © 1998 by Roger D. Masters
All rights reserved,
including the right of reproduction
in whole or in part in any form.

THE FREE PRESS and colophon are trademarks
of Simon & Schuster Inc.

Manufactured in the United States of America

10 9 8 7 6 5 4 3 2 1

Library of Congress Cataloging-in-Publication Data

Masters, Roger D.
    Fortune is a river: Leonardo da Vinci
and Niccolò Machiavelli's magnificent dream to change
the course of Florentine history / Roger D. Masters.
    p. cm.
Includes bibliographical references and index.
    1. Florence (Italy)—History—1421–1737. 2. Water diversion—
Italy—Arno River—History. 3. Diversion structures (Hydraulic
engineering)—Italy—Arno River—History. 4. Leonardo da Vinci,
1452–1519. 5. Machiavelli, Niccolò, 1469–1527. I. Title.
945′.51—dc21   97-48447
                                                                        CIP

ISBN 0-684-84452-4

Credits for art reproduced in the text and insert appear
in the back matter, following the essay on sources.

For Sandy

Contents

❦

1. A Mysterious Friendship   1
2. The Arno   7
3. Leonardo Achieves Fame   23
4. Niccolò Achieves Power   49
5. The Meeting   75
6. The Collaboration Begins   93
7. The Arno Diversion Fails   109
8. The Aftermath   135
9. Leonardo in the Courts of Power   149
10. Niccolò's Struggle, Victory, and Defeat   163
11. The Legacy   193

Notes   213

Sources   249

Credits   259

Acknowledgments   263

Index   265

Amid all the causes of the destruction of human property, it seems to me that rivers hold the foremost place on account of their excessive and violent inundations. . . . A river which is to be turned from one place to another must be coaxed and not treated roughly or with violence.

—LEONARDO DA VINCI, *NOTEBOOKS*

I liken her [that is, Fortune] to one of these violent rivers which, when they become enraged, flood the plains, ruin the trees and the buildings, lift earth from this part, drop in another; each person flees before them, everyone yields to their impetus without being able to hinder them in any regard. And although [rivers] are like this, it is not as if men, when times are quiet, could not provide for them . . .

—NICCOLÒ MACHIAVELLI, *THE PRINCE*

Chapter 1

A Mysterious Friendship

⚜

Leonardo da Vinci and Niccolò Machiavelli probably first met in the town of Imola during 1502. Their paths crossed at the court of Cesare Borgia, where—for different reasons—each was in residence from October through the end of the year. Leonardo had taken a position as Borgia's military architect and engineer. Niccolò, second chancellor of the government of Florence, was on a diplomatic mission to keep an eye on the unscrupulous Cesare. By June of the next year, both were back in Florence, working together on what turned out to be a magnificent failure.

Few know about the mysterious and ill-fated collaboration between these two famous men. Leonardo da Vinci, creator of the *Mona Lisa* and the *Last Supper,* is one of the best-known artists in history. Niccolò Machiavelli, whose *The Prince* has been blamed for immorality and praised for introducing a science of politics, is one of our best-known political thinkers. In the first years of the sixteenth century, they conceived an ambitious project to direct the Arno River through a canal, at some points twenty miles away from its natural course.

A decade before, Leonardo da Vinci had first developed a plan to make the Arno River navigable, turning Florence into a seaport and irrigating the Arno valley. Niccolò Machiavelli, as an administrator responsible for Florentine military and foreign policy, tried to implement the first phase of this project in 1503–4 in order to divert the river from Pisa, deprive the city of water, and thereby win a war that had frustrated his fellow citizens for a decade. Had the diversion at Pisa succeeded, it was hoped to go ahead with Leonardo's larger scheme of moving the Arno into a canal through Prato and under Mount Serravalle, transforming the economic basis of Florentine power.

Between 1503 and 1506, Niccolò Machiavelli benefited from Leonardo's assistance on other projects in addition to this plan to divert the Arno. In June 1503, at Machiavelli's insistence, Florentine troops besieging Pisa captured a fort called La Verruca; Leonardo was immediately sent as a military architect to propose its reconstruction. In fall of 1504, Machiavelli needed to show Florence's good intentions to Jacopo IV d'Appiano, lord of Piombino; Leonardo was sent on a mission of technical assistance. Because previous attempts to storm the walls of Pisa had failed, Leonardo worked out a complex scheme for blowing up partial sections of the walls in a way that would reduce loss of life among the attacking forces.

For his part, Leonardo da Vinci benefited from Machiavelli's position in the government. Lacking income on his return to Florence in 1503, Leonardo received the commission to paint an immense fresco—*The Battle of Anghiari*—in the Great Council Hall of the Palazzo Vecchio. To help plan the work, Machiavelli's assistant Agostino Vespucci (cousin of the explorer Amerigo Vespucci) wrote a description of the battle scene, which has been found in Leonardo's *Notebooks*. When progress on the painting did not satisfy the political leadership, Machiavelli played a role in negotiating a contract that allowed Leonardo to continue receiving his pay. On other matters as well, including Leonardo's lawsuit over a disputed inheritance, Machiavelli and his assistant Agostino apparently were of assistance.

Most of the projects on which Leonardo and Machiavelli collaborated were failures. The ditches intended to divert the Arno at Pisa collapsed because of a combination of incompetence and bad luck. The project was abandoned amid recrimination and criticism of its cost, ending any hope of implementing Leonardo's broader plan to make Florence a seaport. The following year, Leonardo had another disaster with his Council Hall fresco. The preliminary drawing for the *Battle of Anghiari* was the wonder of all who saw it. But because Leonardo used an experimental technique on the wall, paint ran and dripped, work on it was abandoned, and eventually the partially completed fresco was destroyed.

At the time, these setbacks had very serious implications for both Leonardo and Machiavelli, putting into question their reputation, status, and income. This probably explains why neither wrote of their work together. Who likes to bring attention to a disaster that can be attributed to bad judgment or incompetence? Today, however, the story is worth knowing. We see the human side of these two men of genius by appreciating how and why their collaboration failed.

In the five years after the attempt to move the Arno, Niccolò's fortunes seemed to recover. He organized a popular militia that played an essential role in the defeat of Pisa in 1509, allowing Florence to regain control of the Arno as far as the Ligurian Sea. Three years later, however, Niccolò's militia was routed by the Spanish. The republican government he served was overturned and Niccolò himself removed from office. Early in 1513 he was arrested and tortured on suspicion of plotting to kill Giuliano de' Medici, even though Giuliano and Niccolò had been associated years before and Niccolò actively sought to work for the Medici. After over a decade of public service, Niccolò lost his powerful role in Florentine politics, suffering what he called "a great and continuous malignity of fortune."

In the years after the Arno diversion failed, Leonardo also confronted frustration and loss of power. Abandoning his work in Florence, he moved to Milan in 1506. When his stepbrothers challenged an inheritance, he returned to pursue the legal case through interminable delays; ultimately, the conflict was settled by his agreement to leave disputed wealth to his stepbrothers on his death. Although Leonardo achieved financial security and status while serving the French in Milan between 1508 and 1512, all this was lost when the French armies were defeated and retired from Italy. Leonardo then entered the patronage of Giuliano de' Medici and moved to Rome, but life in the entourage of the Medici popes was not congenial. In the last years of his life, from 1516 to 1519, Leonardo finally found relatively secure wealth and status in Amboise at the court of Francis I of France, but by then a stroke had limited his artistic abilities.

The unsuccessful collaboration of Leonardo and Niccolò between 1503 and 1506 was ambitious and foresighted. Yet their attempt to move the Arno has been lost in the mists of history. Because their joint projects failed, little is known of their work together. Both men, often attacked by political enemies, had reason to remain silent about the disastrous Arno diversion. Other factors also conspired to hide their friendship.

Leonardo da Vinci and Niccolò Machiavelli were among the most secretive figures in our intellectual tradition. Between 1498 and 1512, Niccolò learned deception the hard way as a government official and diplomat often involved in delicate negotiations in dangerous places. Late in his life, he said of himself that "for some time now I have never said what I believe nor ever believed what I said; and if indeed I do sometimes tell the truth, I hide it behind so many lies that it is hard to find."

Leonardo also had his reasons for secrecy. Among his works were many practical inventions he sought to keep to himself and scientific inquiries that contradicted orthodox Christian doctrine. Although we know many details of Leonardo's life from his *Notebooks*, the entries are mainly jottings in mirror writing (from right to left) for his private use.

Because letters were often intercepted and read by one's enemies, a written message often had to protect its author and recipient through indirection, silence, and subterfuge. Niccolò Machiavelli, as a powerful public servant, was frequently at the center of situations that called for diplomacy and discretion. Leonardo da Vinci, serving as artist, engineer, and advisor to rulers and governments, found himself in similar circumstances.

A Mysterious Friendship / 5

During the Renaissance, it could be dangerous to put everything in writing. As Niccolò's friend Francesco Vettori put it, "I wish I could write many things that I know cannot be entrusted to letters."

What was true of correspondence at the time was true of behavior more generally. Charges of religious heresy or political disloyalty could be a matter of life and death. Assassination of enemies was not infrequent. In 1478 Giuliano di Piero de' Medici—brother of Lorenzo the Magnificent—was murdered in a conspiracy led by one of the city's leading aristocratic families. A generation later, Savonarola, the reformist preacher who effectively ruled Florence for four years, was excommunicated after openly challenging the pope, and then arrested, convicted, and burned at the stake outside the Palazzo Vecchio.

Another factor was a Florentine law that allowed anonymous accusations. At different times in their careers, both Leonardo and Niccolò were subject to such accusations: Leonardo in 1476 on a charge of sodomy (legally punishable by death), Niccolò in 1509, when political enemies claimed he was not legally eligible to serve as second chancellor and should be forced to resign. As Niccolò's assistant wrote him after the accusation of 1509, "your adversaries are numerous and will stop at nothing. The case is public everywhere, even *in the whorehouses*." For both Leonardo and Niccolò, the possibility of such challenges remained a constant threat to status and political influence.

To understand the story of these two men, therefore, we have to look behind the usual textbook accounts. Documents exist that reveal private attitudes and remind us that famous men and women of the Renaissance were human beings with familiar passions and foibles. In the letter from Francesco Vettori quoted above, after lamenting the inability to write everything, Niccolò's correspondent explains why he has fallen in love. Vettori, serving as the Florentine ambassador to the pope, has little to do:

> *I wrote you that idleness made me fall in love and I reaffirm this to you, because I have practically nothing to do. I cannot read much, by reason of my eyesight, which has been diminished by age. I cannot go out and enjoy myself unless I am accompanied, and this cannot always be done:*

I do not have so much authority or such resources as to be sought out; if I spend my time in thought, most of them bring me melancholy, which I try my best to flee; of necessity one must endeavor to think of pleasant things, but I know of nothing that gives more delight to think about and to do than fucking. Every man may philosophize all he wants, but this is the utter truth, which many people understand this way but few will say.

Whatever the historical changes over the last five centuries, the protagonists in our story remain very much our contemporaries.

Leonardo and Niccolò were fascinating, amusing, talented men, sometimes tortured by despair and often surrounded by enemies. Both had ideas ahead of their times—and knew it. Both attracted admiring friends, exercised power—and ultimately failed to succeed in some of their most cherished projects. Both could be charming—or exasperating. And at times, both had unbelievably bad luck.

This is the story of two men and a river. Although the two men are well known, the river, beautiful and rich in history, has a role of its own. Rivers are means of transportation and energy, sources of water for crops as well as people—and when they flood, devastating in their destruction. The Arno was all of these. It also provided the principal reason Leonardo da Vinci and Niccolò Machiavelli worked together. The failure of their grandiose plans—and of the other projects they attempted—teaches a great deal about Leonardo, Niccolò, and an extraordinary moment in Western history.

Chapter 2

THE ARNO

⚜

The Arno River originates in a multitude of streams along the western slope of the Apennines, the mountains that form the backbone of the Italian peninsula. It forms a long loop to the south toward Arezzo before flowing westward, to be joined by the Sieve River. After a few miles, the river flows through Florence. Then it is joined by other confluents like the Ombrone, which runs southward past the town of Vinci before meeting the Arno about twenty miles below Florence. From that point, the river winds between steep hills before reaching the plains at Pisa and flowing on to the Ligurian Sea (Figure 2.1).

The valley watered by the Arno contains rich agricultural lands, forming the core of the region known as Tuscany, of which Florence is the economic and political capital. The river is the lifeblood of this region, but at times it is dangerous. Throughout the fourteenth and fifteenth centuries, the Arno was capricious: in 1333, 1466, and 1478, serious floods destroyed crops and damaged buildings in the towns along its banks. Despite these disasters, however, the valley and the hill towns overlooking it flourished.

By 1450, Florence had emerged as one of the major centers of the

FIGURE 2.1. Leonardo, Aerial view of the Arno (ca. 1502). This map was probably drawn while Leonardo was in the service of Cesare Borgia. Apparently, it was based on an earlier map in the library of Urbino, but Leonardo added numerous details, especially in the upper reaches and tributaries of the Arno. Inscriptions in mirror writing indicate that it was drawn for his own use.

Italian Renaissance. Nestled below the hills of Fiesole, the city was a center for art, commerce, and banking, with its public buildings on the north bank of the river linked by the Ponte Vecchio and other bridges to the quarter known as Oltr' Arno ("across Arno"), where Machiavelli was born. Paintings of Florence in the Renaissance remind us that the site, the river, and the city were as beautiful then as they are today (Figure 2.2).

Leonardo da Vinci probably knew the course of the Arno as well as any individual who had ever lived. In many places, the Arno winds among the Tuscan hills with memorable beauty. Leonardo captured one such site in his earliest known drawing, dated August 5, 1473 (Plate II).

Leonardo knew, however, that the river was not always tranquil.

Amid all the causes of the destruction of human property, it seems to me that rivers hold the foremost place on account of their excessive and violent inundations. . . . Against the irreparable inundation caused by swollen and proud rivers no resource of human foresight can avail; for in a succession of raging and seething waves gnawing and tearing away high banks, growing turbid with the earth from ploughed fields, destroying the houses therein and uprooting the tall trees, it carries these as its prey down to the sea which is its lair, bearing along with it men, trees, animals, houses, and lands, sweeping away every dike and every kind of barrier, bearing along the light things, and devastating and destroying those of weight, creating big landslips out of small fissures, filling up with floods the low valleys, and rushing headlong with destructive and inexorable mass of waters.

For Christian believers in the sixteenth century, floods were an act of God. In contrast, Leonardo sought ways to give humans control over them.

After moving to Milan in the 1480s, Leonardo began to study the flow of water as a scientific problem in order to prevent floods, irrigate fields, and develop river transportation. To use hydraulic science effectively, he realized that technological expertise was needed because

a river which is to be turned from one place to another must be coaxed and not treated roughly or with violence; and to do this a sort of dam should

FIGURE 2.2. S. Bonsignori, Map of Florence called "della Catena."

be built into the river, and then lower down another one projecting farther and in like manner a third, fourth, and fifth so that the river may discharge itself into the channel allotted to it, or by this means it may be diverted from the place it has damaged as was done in Flanders according to what I was told by Niccolò di Forzore.

While in Milan, Leonardo apparently met Luca Fancelli, a Florentine architect, who proposed a system of canals to make the Arno navigable and improve the valley. Employing his knowledge of hydraulics, Leonardo worked out a more ambitious plan, with a single long canal through Pistoia. For such a project, he needed to know the precise location of the river's course. One of his remarkable maps, which he based on the work of earlier cartographers, shows the entire valley (Figure 2.1). This map, amazing for its accuracy, probably dates from 1502–3, when Leonardo was authorized to travel through the area as Cesare Borgia's military architect and engineer.

Like Leonardo, Machiavelli was interested in rivers more generally as well as the particular problems associated with the Arno. Readers of *The Prince* are familiar with a famous passage in Chapter 25 that compares "fortune" (or human history) with a river:

I liken her [that is, Fortune] to one of these violent rivers which, when they become enraged, flood the plains, ruin the trees and the buildings, lift earth from this part, drop in another; each person flees before them, everyone yields to their impetus without being able to hinder them in any regard.

Most scholars assume this is merely a poetic metaphor. Now, however, we know it also reflects Niccolò's practical experience in the attempt to divert the Arno at Pisa during 1503–4.

In *The Prince*, immediately after the passage cited above, Machiavelli echoes Leonardo's practical concern for controlling the flow of rivers:

And although they [rivers] are like this, it is not as if men, when times are quiet, could not provide for them with dikes and dams so that when they rise later, either they go by a canal or their impetus is neither so wanton nor so damaging.

For Machiavelli, however, the "rivers" are history, the "trees and the buildings" are civilization, and the "dikes and dams" are "good laws and good arms," which can be established only by outstanding leaders. While Leonardo focused on improved technological projects to control actual rivers, Machiavelli drew a political lesson from the failure of the Arno diversion.

Human efforts to control rivers were, of course, hardly new. In ancient times, the Tigris and Euphrates in Mesopotamia, the Nile in Egypt, and the Yangtze in China had been tamed to control floods and irrigate crops, just as Roman cities had been supplied with water through immense systems of aqueducts. Since the twelfth century, especially in Lombardy, Italian rivers had been harnessed by a system of dikes and canals, much as the Dutch had controlled the flooding from the North Sea with similar techniques.

Even military uses of artificially controlling rivers were not unknown. In the *Divine Comedy*, Dante, who also speaks of the peaceful uses of hydraulic engineering, imagined a way to punish Pisa by moving two islands so they would dam the Arno and flood the city. Early in the fifteenth century, the architect Brunelleschi convinced the Florentine government to try this device in practice, unsuccessfully damming the nearby Serchio River to flood Lucca. But nothing in earlier experience can compare to the grandiose project of making Florence a seaport by moving the winding Arno into a canal through Pistoia (which is over twenty kilometers north of the river's natural course) and tunneling it under the mountain pass of Serravalle on the way to the sea. Beyond the competence of sixteenth-century technology, such vast transformations of nature have become commonplace only in our own time.

The history of public works that control rivers is thus a good summary of the process of civilization. Reliable supplies of water are essential for both agriculture and urbanization. Before the Neolithic revolution, humans formed relatively small bands of hunter-gatherer-scavengers, which traveled as game moved, water holes dried up, or floods came. With the domestication of animals and the discovery of agriculture came sedentary villages and larger tribes, but these developments were not enough to make possible cities and civilizations.

Even with agricultural settlements along rivers, food supplies were not certain. Too little water, and crops fail; too much water, and floods destroy everything. In good years, many rivers—including the Arno—flood just enough to enrich agricultural soil. Usually, however, it was risky to rely entirely on nature. The centers of early civilizations were usually cities along rivers, and those civilizations were typically marked by massive hydraulic projects that made possible the irrigation of fields as well as the transport of heavy goods and the control of floods.

Several examples from the Roman province of Gaul, still visible in southern France today, illustrate the extraordinary technology associated with controlling rivers and water in ancient civilizations. Well known as tourist monuments, these examples also remind us how completely Roman hydraulic engineering had been lost during the early Middle Ages.

Roman bridges across the Rhône River are a good example. Rivers can divide land or unite it, depending on the ability of the inhabitants to cross them as well as to use them as waterways. The Rhône, as a major artery, could easily be used to float objects from the center of Gaul to the Mediterranean. But for the purposes of trade, it was also sometimes necessary to cross easily from one bank to the other. The Romans solved this problem with bridges of considerable size, spanning the Rhône at Vienne and at Arles.

According to some, the memory of yet another Roman bridge is implied in the old children's song "Sur le Pont d'Avignon, on y danse, on y danse." Actually, the song is about dancing *under* the medieval bridge at Avignon (originally, the words were "*Sous* le Pont d'Avignon"). There was an island in the middle of the Rhône that partially supported the bridge linking the papal city of Avignon with the territories of the French king. Because the island was neutral territory, dancing was possible there while not permitted on the shore. But the story of the bridge itself is even more interesting than the dancing.

In the Middle Ages, the Rhône at Avignon had been impassable except by boat. In the twelfth century, a peasant claimed that God told him how to build a bridge across the river. At first, everyone thought the task impossible: medieval stonemasons knew of no way to sink the foundations for a bridge in a river of such size and power. According to one account, the peasant's solution was actually simple: he built the bridge on the ancient pilings of a Roman wooden bridge, long since destroyed and forgotten. Divine revelation had probably been assisted by underwater swimming.

In classical antiquity, extraordinary engineering skill was evident also in the provision of water to Rome and the cities it controlled. Rome's Acqua Claudia aqueduct—built in the fourth century B.C. and restored by Pope Sixtus V—still functions today. It is in the Roman province of Gaul, however, that ancient remains probably give the clearest indication of the extent of Roman hydraulic engineering.

The Roman city of Arelate—today the French city of Arles—stands at a sharp bend of the Rhône River. Its water supply came by aqueduct from many miles away. One segment of the system of water supplies still remains: the magnificent Pont du Gard. Because Arelate developed on both sides of the Rhône, lead pipes were necessary to bring water from the central part of the city to Trinquetaille, on the other bank. Within the old city of Arles itself, one can visit the Roman baths, which provided public facilities for both hygiene and pleasure. Even in this provincial city, Roman technology tamed and utilized water to make living conditions comfortable and "civilized."

By the third century A.D., the system of aqueducts serving Arelate was expanded to bring water to the first automated factory known in history—a mill with twenty water-powered millstones for grinding the wheat of Gaul prior to its shipment to Rome, where it became the bread accompanying the circuses. The site, known as Barbegal, can be visited today just outside of Arles. In Roman times, it was surrounded by marshes, which allowed the delivery of grain floated down the Rhône and, after milling, its shipment to storage granaries in Arles and ultimately, by boat, to the Roman port of Ostia.

Today, tourists in Provence often visit the Pont du Gard or the Roman baths in Arles—and if well informed, even picnic on the steps of Barbegal. But only in the last two hundred years has industrial technology become fully capable of feats that the Roman engineers accomplished throughout the Empire.

Although many early villages were formed on fortified hills for security, since antiquity large cities have usually developed at the confluence of trade routes. Such cities played a central role in Italy throughout the fifteenth century. Milan was a crossroads of land routes in the Lombardy plain. Naples, Venice, and Genoa were major seaports. And like Rome, Florence was a city on a river. Its site on the Arno helps explain the role of the city and its region throughout history.

In *Florentine Histories,* published in 1525, Machiavelli explained the origins of his native city:

> *since the city of Fiesole had been placed on the summit of a mountain, to make its markets more frequented and more convenient for those who might want to come to them with their merchandise it had ordered the place for them not on the hillside but in the plain between the foot of the mountain and the Arno River. . . . Afterwards, when the Romans had conquered the Carthaginians, rendering Italy safe from foreign wars, the buildings multiplied to a great number . . . thus the security that was born in Italy through the reputation of the Roman Republic enabled the dwellings, already begun in the mode stated, to increase to such number that they took on the form of a town, which from the beginning was named Villa Arnina.*

Before becoming the city we know as Florence, then, the site even took its name from the river. With the civil wars that ravaged ancient Rome in the first century B.C., Florence grew into a genuine city, called Florentia, whose inhabitants were known as Florentini.

The Roman Empire brought with its rule the skill of its engineers. In Roman cities, life was made comfortable by plentiful public water supplies using aqueducts and lead pipes; there were toilets with sewers, and public baths. Water was used for transport and as a source of mechanical power. The control of water supplies required for such civilized amenities depended upon governmental decisions, as Machiavelli noted when citing the Roman historian Tacitus:

For already in the time of Tiberius they [the people of Florence] governed themselves by the custom of the other Italian cities, and Cornelius [Tacitus] refers to Florentine spokesmen as having come to the emperor to beg that water from the [Val di] Chiana not be emptied onto their country.

With the establishment of Constantinople and the fall of the western empire, waves of barbarians from the north descended on Italy. Technological know-how was lost in the ensuing centuries of chaos, but eventually the engineers of the Renaissance improved their ability to tame rivers. Some of the first developments were aided by accidents. The Belgian city of Bruges rose to prominence in the twelfth century after a flood opened the six-mile stretch of the Zwyn River to the North Sea (though the city declined in power three centuries later after silting again blocked the channel). Seeking to control these events, hydraulic engineers in the late thirteenth century developed techniques to prevent floods, keep harbors open, and use water. In Italy, rivers that had long been clogged by silt began to be improved. Engineers started to think of draining marshes and building canals, of using waterways again as a mode of transport and a source of energy. Better ships were built, most notably in Venice, where the technology used in the shipyards of the Arsenale was such a highly guarded secret that an unapproved visitor would be put to death.

The historical development of Florence would always be intimately incorporated with the river from which it first took its name. After the floods of 1333, there was much discussion of the problems of controlling the Arno. As early as 1347, the government of Florence considered the project of making the river navigable to the Ligurian Sea. In the Po valley and Lombardy, the building of dams and canals was even more advanced. Whereas the annual flooding of the Arno in good years provided natural irrigation, the drier plains to the north were not as fertile. Around Milan, a network of canals was developed from the twelfth century onward, linking the lake region around Como to the north with the Adda, Lambro, and Bembro Rivers. Milan's prosperity at the center of the Lombard plain depended in no small part on the irrigated fields and water-powered mills made possible by progress in hydraulic engineering.

The rediscovery of engineering and the development of trade provided an important foundation for art and philosophy. After a long period of instability between 1180 and 1350—associated with rapid population growth, persistent inflation, famine, plagues, and warfare—scholars have described the period from around 1400 to 1470 as the "equilibrium of the Renaissance." Particularly in Italy, agriculture flourished and harvests improved, populations stabilized, and political conflict moderated. These transformations were slower to come to northern Europe, particularly in regions where the technology of water control was not as well developed as in Italy.

Commerce developed along with banking houses (like that of the Medici of Florence), which helped make it possible. Technology spread more rapidly than ever before. A striking example is provided by printing. Schoolchildren know that Gutenberg invented movable type and used it to print the Bible in the middle of the fifteenth century. Within a decade, Gutenberg's invention was in use in Strassburg and Basle; within twenty-five years, it had spread throughout Italy and to France, Poland, England, and central Europe. Similar changes took place in military technology, as gunpowder and cannon were developed and used in Europe for the first time to destroy medieval fortresses.

Political institutions in Italy favored such technological and economic development. With no single ruler in command of the entire peninsula, different cities were open to entrepreneurship and rivalry, sometimes without the constraints of feudal lords (who frequently taxed and restricted commerce for short-term benefits). The relative social mobility and openness of the Italian cities, like those of Greece in antiquity, fostered a spirit of enquiry and innovation. These trends were particularly evident in Florence, a republic governed by elected assemblies and officials quite unlike the hereditary kings of France, Spain, England, or Germany. As the great humanist Leonardo Bruni wrote in 1428, "equal liberty exists for all—the hope of gaining high office and to rise is the same for all." Though he exaggerated a bit, the city on the Arno did achieve a measure of republican self-government.

Major decisions in Renaissance Florence were made by an executive committee called the Signoria. Two members of the Signoria were chosen from each of the four quarters into which the city was divided, with the ninth being the head of government, or standard-bearer of justice *(gonfaloniere)*, representing the city as a whole. The eight members of the Signoria representing quarters of the city (called priors) were elected by lot; names were pulled from a bag containing the names of eligible male citizens who had paid their taxes. Their term of office lasted only two months.

Decisions of the Signoria were also referred to two councils, the Twelve Good Men *(Buonomini)* and the Sixteen Standard-bearers *(Gonfalonieri)*, representing the four flag companies in each quarter. Also elected by lot, these officers served for three or four months. Specialized committees, like the Ten of War *(Dieci)*, responsible for military affairs, were also appointed. Finally, before making an important decision, the Signoria often convoked a special consultative meeting *(practica)* of citizens to discuss alternatives in public.

Under Lorenzo the Magnificent, who controlled the city from 1476 to 1492, the system was manipulated by putting only Medici supporters' names in the bags from which officials' names were drawn. After Savonarola became the effective leader of Florence in 1494, the popular element underlying the city's institutions was strengthened. To prevent the abuses of the Medici, a Great Council was formed, based on lists from all citizens whose parents or grandparents had been eligible for office. This body elected the Signoria and the colleges of the Twelve Good Men and the

Sixteen Standard-bearers by picking names from a leather bag into which all eligible names were placed. Other positions were filled by a Council of Eighty on the basis of nominations made and seconded in the Great Council. Among these elective officials were administrators: the chancellors and secretaries, like Niccolò Machiavelli, who served the Signoria and other government committees.

On paper this sounds very democratic, but the reality was quite different. First of all, not everyone could vote. The total population of Florence in the fifteenth century has been estimated as between forty and ninety thousand. Of these, only taxpaying resident male citizens over thirty could vote. Of the roughly eight thousand men of age, only around fifty-six hundred had the taxable wealth required to be on the voting rolls. The actual electorate was further restricted by the need to be a member of a guild, to have actually paid taxes, and to be in Florence at the time of the vote.

Second, political practice was a matter of patronage, cliques ("sects"), and personal alliances rather than individual voting. Wealthy or aristocratic families formed the core of the system. The leaders of a family provided favors for friends and neighbors in return for support. In the words of one historian, Florentine politics resembled "a league of Mafia families."

Personal connections were based also on confraternities. Originally associated with religious activity and based in churches, some of these associations came to link leading aristocrats and voters of specific quarters or in specific trades. In the middle of the fifteenth century, these adult confraternities were supplemented by youth groups, often associated with a family of wealth and preeminence in a particular quarter. For example, both the Vangelista youth confraternity (named for Saint John the Evangelist) and the adult Confraternity of Saint Paul were based in Niccolò's parish church of Santa Trinità, and both were supported by Lorenzo de' Medici, whose son Giuliano was a member of Vangelista until he reached the age of twenty-four (when young men were supposed to leave the youth groups). Although some confraternities stressed religious devotion, with rituals of flagellation and prayer, others focused on assisting the poor or running hospitals, while providing a network of social contacts (not entirely unlike Rotary, Kiwanis, or other American service clubs today).

While far from perfectly democratic, Florence still provided a highly diverse environment in which economic initiative, artistic ability, humanistic scholarship, and political astuteness could flourish. Artisans—and artists—took renewed interest in novelty. A few, like the architect Brunelleschi, began to study natural science and applied themselves to such technological questions as flood control along the Arno. More often, change took the form of an increased willingness to experiment. Travel, whether by land or water, became easier. Innovation was applied to military strategy as well.

Praising his native city, Leonardo Bruni claimed that "Florence harbours the greatest minds: whatever they undertake, they easily surpass all other men, whether they apply themselves to military or political affairs, to study or philosophy, or to merchandise." In Florence as elsewhere, however, there was still a profound gap between the scientists and humanists, who studied theory, and the artisans and technicians, who made things work. In philosophy and science, the Renaissance of ancient pagan thought was the work of scholars who were far removed from technology and practice. Although the humanists sometimes played a role in politics, they came from a different world than the first generations of inventors and engineers whose practical know-how fueled the economic developments of the thirteenth and fourteenth centuries.

Pico della Mirandola expressed the spirit of many fifteenth-century humanists in his *Oration on the Dignity of Man*. In a revealing point in the work, God admonishes Adam:

You may have and possess whatever abode, form and functions that you might desire. The nature of all other beings is limited and constrained within the bounds of law prescribed by us. But you, constrained by no limits, in accordance with your own free will, in whose hand we have placed you, shall ordain for yourself the limits of your nature.

This stirring manifesto, far removed from practical technology or natural science, broke with medieval traditionalism without embracing either empirical research or political activism.

In Florence as elsewhere in Italy, the doctrines of the Catholic Church were still generally honored, but popes increasingly acted as secular rulers, competing with kings, dukes, and republics for political power and earthly prestige. Despite the pragmatism of fifteenth-century engineers, artisans, bankers, or political leaders, Renaissance humanists were often more concerned with astrology than with natural science. And through it all, the life of the common man was often little different than it had been hundreds of years before.

Leonardo da Vinci and Niccolò Machiavelli grew up and worked together in this exciting world along the Arno. In some ways, however, these two men were different from those around them. Leonardo was angered by the humanists of Florence, who disdained him because he did not speak Latin and his scientific theories were based on experimentation and mathematics rather than quotations from the ancient authors. Machiavelli, taught by those humanists, came to view their thought as contrary to the lessons of classical antiquity and an obstacle to the beneficial exercise of political authority. Both sought to develop theories of nature and human nature that could be used in practice to benefit society.

Leonardo created a science of hydraulics and imagined a comprehensive transformation of the Arno River valley into an irrigated flood-control system generating wealth and security for Florence and all of Tuscany. Niccolò, as a public servant, found himself responsible for gaining control of the rebellious city of Pisa, which blocked the free use of the Arno for Florentine commerce. To this end, Niccolò supervised an attempted diversion of the river, intended both to defeat the Pisans by depriving them of water and to realize the first stage of Leonardo's larger scheme.

To many of their contemporaries, even the diversion at Pisa (the initial phase of this project) was a foolish waste of time and money. The first time the government debated the proposal, some criticized it as "little more than a fantasy." Both the Florentine field commander and the commissioner in charge of the siege of Pisa tried vigorously to stop it. Two years after the project failed, the field commander wrote Machiavelli: "Certainly, as far as human judgment can see, we cannot hope for anything but ill, if He that saved the people of Israel from the hands of Pharoah does not open up for us in the midst of this tossing sea an unexpected road to salvation, as that one once was." For most people in the early sixteenth century, only God could part the Red Sea or manipulate the Arno for human benefit.

Leonardo and Machiavelli tried, through scientific engineering, to do what God did for Moses. Despite their failure, the ideas behind the project were to have a lasting impact. Leonardo developed, in outline, scientific theories and technical inventions that were not fully realized for three centuries. Niccolò presented a theory of politics that ushered in modern nation-states and taught leaders a new attitude toward action. Working together in Florence between 1503 and 1506, the two sought to turn knowledge into power. But to understand why they were attracted to each other, it is necessary to describe how Leonardo da Vinci and Niccolò Machiavelli came to be in Imola in October 1502.

Chapter 3

LEONARDO ACHIEVES FAME

(1452–1499)

⚜

Vinci, a small hill town in Tuscany above one of the Arno's tributaries, gave its name to a family of lawyers and thrifty landowners—and thus a world-famous artist. In the middle of the fifteenth century, Ser Piero da Vinci, local notary and twenty-three-year-old son of this well-established family, had an affair with Caterina, a peasant girl. When Caterina became pregnant, a wedding was out of the question: though an illegitimate child was no longer a permanent disgrace, her class and lack of dowry were an insuperable barrier to marriage. And so, not long after Leonardo da Vinci, the child of Caterina and Ser Piero, was born on April 15, 1452, Piero da Vinci was married to Albiera di Giovanni Amadori, a sixteen-year-old from a more appropriate family.

Leonardo was at first sent to live with his mother, Caterina, who had been conveniently betrothed to a young farmer from the nearby hamlet of Campo Zeppi. Albiera remained childless, however, and by 1457, tax records show that Leonardo was living in his father's house in Vinci. Ser Piero often went to Florence, where business interests led to his partnership with a local notary in an office across the street from the Bargello (the famous prison in the center of the city). After his wife, Albiera, died, Ser Piero married Francesca Lanfredini in 1465, choosing a wife from one of the most prominent commercial families in Florence. Meanwhile, Leonardo was raised in Vinci by his paternal grandparents and their youngest son, Francesco, only sixteen years Leonardo's senior.

Sometime before 1468, in his teens, Leonardo moved to Florence, where he was apprenticed to Verrocchio, well known as a painter, sculptor, and goldsmith. Under Verrocchio's tutelege, he learned many skills. In 1472, at the age of twenty, Leonardo was enrolled as a member of the painters' guild. But Leonardo was not to be just an artist.

Leonardo's extraordinary skills were soon apparent. The architect and art historian Giorgio Vasari, in his influential *Lives of the Artists,* called him "specially endowed by the hand of God," the universal—or, as we now say, Renaissance—man, who could apparently do everything well. In virtually every field, from physics, anatomy, and engineering to music, architecture, and city planning, Leonardo was an innovator whose ideas, spread by word of mouth and example in an age when printing was still something of a rarity, foreshadowed and influenced developments in coming centuries.

Genius often seems to spring up in a miraculous way, without regard to circumstances. For Leonardo, however, the circumstances of birth did have at least one lasting effect. Had he been the legitimate heir of Ser Piero growing up in Florence, he would more likely have gone to school, learned Latin, and become a humanist. As it was, Leonardo was not accepted by the humanistic scholars at the university and the Platonic Academy in Florence. This rejection galled Leonardo so intensely that, as a man over forty, he learned Latin and spent hours recording vocabulary-building exercises in his *Notebooks.*

Painters and artisans—often one individual was both—usually came from a different social class than scholars, or humanists. For example, the father of Marsilio Ficino, perhaps the most famous philosopher in Florence, was a doctor; Angelo Poliziano, another leading classicist associated with the Medici court, came from a family of jurists. By contrast, Perugino—Leonardo's fellow apprentice in Verrocchio's studio—came from a peasant background. For such artists, a living wage was often more important than formal status. Not so for Leonardo, whose manner, dress, and aspirations were those of his father's class rather than of his contemporaries in the world of art.

Leonardo's frustration at the rejection of his work by humanist scholars is epitomized by a draft Introduction for his *Treatise on Painting:*

> *I am fully conscious that, not being a literary man, certain presumptuous persons will think that they may reasonably blame me; alleging that I am not a man of letters. Foolish folks! do they not know that I might retort as Marius did to the Roman Patricians by saying: That they, who deck themselves out in the labours of others will not allow me my own. They will say that I, having no literary skill, cannot properly express that which I desire to treat of; but they do not know that my subjects are to be dealt with by experience rather than by words; and [experience] has been the mistress of those who wrote well. And so, as mistress, I will cite her in all cases.*

Most Renaissance artists established a studio, taught apprentices (who often had to pay for the right to work), and undertook commissions for artisanal products. Verrocchio's *bottega* produced the enormous bronze ball to mount on the cupola of Florence's Duomo, costumes and decorations for Lorenzo de' Medici's pageants, and a suit of armor for presentation to the duke of Milan, as well as statues and paintings for Florence's churches, guilds, and wealthy patrons. Leonardo could contribute to making all these things with amazing skill, but he also sought to discover and teach the fundamental principles underlying them. To explain the art of painting, for instance, he engaged in experimental and observational studies of vision, an analysis of optics, and—to ensure that the dynamics of bodily movement was accurately portrayed—anatomical studies of humans as well as other animals.

Perhaps as a result of his father's social class, Leonardo brought an intellectual or scientific approach to activities that were often based on tradition, individual hunches, imitation, and trade secrets. In personal terms, Leonardo also sought a degree of public recognition that was long denied him. Not only did his ambition transcend the horizon of most painters; he also sought greater political and social influence than most of the humanists and scientists.

Leonardo developed from the illegitimate son of a notary into *l'uomo universale* in three main stages. The first was in Vinci from 1452 to around 1467, where as a child he discovered his artistic skill. During the second, working with Verrocchio in Florence between 1467 and 1482, Leonardo explored the diverse and remarkably free life of that city and realized that his genius transcended art. In the last stage, after moving to Milan, from 1483 to 1499 Leonardo further trained his many talents, working at first in partnership with the de Predis brothers (competent but not outstanding artists) and then as a member of Duke Ludovico Sforza's court. When Milan fell to the French in 1499, Leonardo was famous not only as an artist but as an engineer, scientist, architect, and musician.

We know little of the childhood of most famous men. Although Leonardo is unusual in the amount of information on his life embedded in his voluminous *Notebooks,* many of the entries are elliptical, private jottings for his own memory and pleasure. Still, the combination of this treasure with other written sources gives us a good idea of Leonardo's youth.

Because the rules of his father's guild did not allow an illegitimate son to become a magistrate or notary, Leonardo did not learn to read and write at a formal school. Perhaps this explains why, when he did acquire these basic skills, Leonardo—being left-handed—developed a practice of noting personal information in mirror script, written from right to left. Educated in Vinci, he never studied Latin and the classic authors in the fashion of the middle-class children of Florence.

With his father in Florence, the young Leonardo had time to wander alone in the hills around Vinci. As an inquisitive child, he discovered nature. Blessed with both a retentive memory and artistic ability, he was free to observe and to wonder.

Leonardo's *Notebooks* contain several passages that probably reflect these early experiences. One concerns a storm, which Leonardo describes in the draft of a chapter entitled "Of the Movement of Air Enclosed in Water":

> *I have seen motions of the air so furious that they have carried, mixed up in their course, the largest trees of the forest and whole roofs of great palaces, and I have seen the same fury bore a hole with a whirling movement digging out a gravel pit, and carrying gravel, sand and water more than half a mile through the air.*

In the *Florentine Histories*, Machiavelli describes such a storm, on August 24, 1456, in the Val d'Arno—and since there are no records of such a twister in Florence itself, it is possible the passage records a childhood memory that Leonardo shared with Niccolò.

A second passage describes an equally intense experience, though this time with a focus on Leonardo's own emotions as an observer of nature.

> *Unable to resist my eager desire and wanting to see the various and strange shapes made by formative nature and having wandered some distance among gloomy rocks, I came to the entrance of a great cavern, in front of which I stood some time, astonished and unaware of such a thing. Bending my back into an arch I rested my left hand on my knee and held my right hand over my down-cast and contracted eye brows: often bending first one way and then the other, to see whether I could discover anything inside, and this being forbidden by the deep darkness within, and after having remained there some time, two contrary emotions arose in me, fear and desire—fear of the threatening dark cavern, desire to see whether there were any marvellous thing within it.*

That eager desire to see and understand any marvellous thing in nature would never leave him.

Leonardo had an uncanny ability to remember visual images. At some point, he must have begun to draw. Ser Piero, looking for a place for his illegitimate son, obviously noticed his skill. As a notary and businessman in Florence, moreover, Ser Piero had contacts with the world of artists and artisans. In 1465, Ser Piero signed the contract for an important commission with Verrocchio. Shortly thereafter, Leonardo became his apprentice in Florence.

The *bottega,* or workshop, of Andrea Verrocchio was, in many respects, a microcosm of the artistic and artisanal world of the Italian Renaissance. At various times, among his apprentices were Perugino, Botticelli, Ghirlandaio, and Lorenzo di Credi. Verrocchio's assistants worked on the varied commissions he received from churches, merchant guilds, and the Medici. Together, they formed the nucleus of a generation of artists whose work is now taught in every introductory course in art history.

In this environment, Leonardo soon realized he surpassed others in artistic talent. Vasari describes an event that must have been a lesson in how much his skill could be worth. Ser Piero had been asked by one of his tenants to have a wooden shield decorated by a painter, and gave the job to his son, Leonardo. The young artist collected "lizards great and small, crickets, snakes, grasshoppers, bats, and other strange creatures," dissected and combined them, and painted a monster "emerging from a cleft in a dark rock, vomiting fire from its gaping jaws, its eyes blazing, and poisonous vapors emanating from its nostrils." When Ser Piero came to get the finished shield, Leonardo had set it in a darkened room, with only a ray of light from the partly closed shutters illuminating his creation. On seeing his father's reaction of shock and fear, Leonardo opened the shutters to reveal his artistry, adding: "That is what a shield ought to do. Take it." Ser Piero was so impressed that he bought an ordinary substitute for the tenant and sold his son's work to an art collector for one hundred ducats. The shield in turn was sold to the duke of Milan for three hundred ducats.

Around 1472, when Leonardo formally registered in the painters' guild, he assisted his mentor, Verrocchio, on a *Baptism of Christ* commissioned by the Monastery of San Salvi. Art historians are generally agreed that the angel at the lower left of this painting (and much of the background) is the earliest known painting by Leonardo. According to Vasari's biography, Leonardo's skill in painting the angel so astonished and dumbfounded his master that Verrocchio swore never to paint for the rest of his life.

Vasari's story is probably an exaggeration, but three things are beyond doubt. First, Leonardo quickly gained a reputation for unusual artistic skill; second, he was clearly aware of his own abilities; finally, in addition to the friendship and confidence of Verrocchio, he began to encounter not only painters but the poets, writers, and scholars who made up the lively intellectual world of Florence in the 1470s.

Enjoying the company of others, Leonardo at this time engaged in a good deal of frivolity. From contemporary accounts and self-portraits, he was a young man of astonishing beauty. His musical talent and fine voice attracted note. His pleasure in practical jokes amused his fellows. According to one of his biographers, Leonardo's main occupations were probably "dressing up, taming horses, and learning the lute."

Being extremely attractive can have disadvantages. In 1476, a personal disaster struck. Under the Florentine system of anonymous denunciation, one could accuse another of illegal or immoral behavior by putting the charge on an unsigned paper in boxes set up for the purpose. This was not unlike Victorian England's practice of placing anonymous items in newspapers to spread rumors of scandal. In Leonardo's case, the consequences were frightening. Along with three others, he was accused of committing sodomy on a known prostitute. The penalty, though rarely carried out, was death at the stake.

A first hearing, on April 9, 1476, produced no evidence. The case was adjourned, and a second hearing held on June 7. No evidence was forthcoming and the charges were dismissed. Some have suggested that the real target was another of the accused, Lionardo de' Tornabuoni (a relative of Lorenzo de' Medici's mother), that the entire affair was politically motivated, and that Leonardo was included merely to "augment the lineup."

Whatever the truth of the charges, Leonardo was apparently terrified by the threat to his precarious status. Biographers suggest the charge contributed to his obscure but complex attitude toward sexuality. Some think that Leonardo was repelled from all forms of sexuality, while others deduce from Leonardo's attraction to handsome young men that he was homosexual. At least one conclusion is generally accepted: "There is no record of any woman in his life—not even a female friendship."

During the years following this public accusation, Leonardo more fully revealed his artistic skill. From this period can be dated the portrait of Genevra de' Benci (now in the National Gallery in Washington—the only painting by Leonardo in an American museum); the *Benois Madonna* (now in the Hermitage, St. Petersburg); and the haunting but unfinished *Saint Jerome* (now in the Vatican). Each of these paintings reveals elements of precision, of daring novelty, and of powerful emotion rarely attempted prior to Leonardo.

Leonardo also began to explore technological inventions and scientific inquiries of a remarkable variety. To be sure, there were other artists (like Brunelleschi) interested in a scientific approach to perspective or anatomy. Leonardo, however, extended his inquisitive search for knowledge and technical skill further, and in more varied directions, than anyone at the time.

Unlike most artists, he sought out scientists and university professors. As early as the 1470s, Leonardo may have attended lectures on Aristotle's natural philosophy by John Argyropoulos, a Greek scholar who taught temporarily in Florence. After 1480, Leonardo apparently made the acquaintance of other scholars, including Benedetto Aritmetico (a specialist in engineering and mechanics) and Paolo del Pozzo Toscanelli (the astronomer whose map of a westward route to India was to guide Columbus in 1492). Among Toscanelli's maps of the world was one (made in 1474) in the shape of a globe; among Leonardo's notes are references to "a globe" and to "my map of the world which Giovanni Benci has."

While studying with Toscanelli, Leonardo apparently met another young Florentine interested in geography and science: Amerigo Vespucci, member of one of the city's leading families and the future explorer whose name would be given to the New World. Leonardo's connection with this family, of which we will hear more, is recorded in his *Notebooks:* "Vespuccio will give me a book of Geometry." Amerigo's uncle, the monk Giorgio Antonio Vespucci, was a famous scholar and humanist who donated his library to the Monastery of Saint Mark, where Toscanelli worked; Leonardo's notes also contain references to "the library at St. Mark's" and "the library at Santo Spirito" (the quarter where the Vespucci family—not to mention the Machiavelli—lived).

Leonardo also sought practical applications for his ingenuity. In the years after 1480, if not before, he began to draw designs for various machines and to explore the problems of controlling the flow of rivers like the Arno. Probably stimulated by a war in which Florence seemed besieged by Naples and the papacy, Leonardo also turned to military technology. He imagined a number of technical devices, such as a system of sliding beams that could be used to knock down the ladders of forces besieging a citadel (Figure 3.1). Often his agile mind would alight on a technological problem in the midst of work on a painting, so that a single sheet of his *Notebooks* shows one of his inventions along with the preliminary sketches for a work of art.

Although Leonardo doubtless met the humanist intellectuals who played a central role at the Medici court, these scholars championed Neoplatonic metaphysics and quotations from books rather than observation, experimentation, and practical know-how. Leonardo's approach to scientific theory and invention was thus at odds with the views of the most influential scholars and intellectuals of the day.

In art as well, Leonardo's conceptions were not conventional. At Lorenzo's court, artists like Botticelli and Pollaiuolo flourished. Leonardo was critical of their poor sense of perspective and casual approach to landscapes. Instead of major commissions, Leonardo seems to have done little more than decorations for Lorenzo's state pageants. In 1481, a number of Florence's leading artists—including Botticelli, Signorelli, Ghirlandaio, and Perugino—received commissions to decorate the Sistine Chapel in Rome for Pope Sixtus IV. Leonardo was not among those chosen.

That year, at the age of twenty-nine, Leonardo finally received a major commission, an *Adoration of the Magi* for the monastery at San Donato. Perhaps the contract was due to his father, since Ser Piero did legal work for the monks. Certainly, Leonardo approached the task with great intensity and care, as can be seen from the extensive preparatory sketches that survive. As always, Leonardo sought perfection—and in this case, he achieved an astounding emotional intensity by breaking radically with the traditional iconography for the scene (Figure 3.2).

After completing the cartoon and beginning to paint the work, Leonardo abandoned it. Although such eminent artists as Botticelli,

FIGURE 3.1. Leonardo, Defense against ladders attacking a wall. For the offensive counterpart, see Figure 3.4. Note how Leonardo includes the human figures operating his proposed equipment. In later years, Leonardo realized that artillery radically changed the appropriate design and technology of fortifications (see Figures 5.3, 7.2, and 7.3).

Filippino Lippi, Ghirlandaio, Raphael, and even Michelangelo were amazed and influenced by what Leonardo completed, the *Adoration* was left unfinished. The reason remains a mystery. Some assume Leonardo stopped work due to his perfectionism and caprice, as with other commissions he failed to complete, or because his artistic solution was so difficult to execute. Others, however, suggest that it was the monastery that terminated the project, judging the painting too radical to accept.

In addition, there may have been another reason: money. The contract Leonardo signed with the monks was most unusual, offering title to a property rather than payment in money. The situation was quite disad-

FIGURE 3.2. *Adoration of the Magi* (ca. 1481-82). Although the radical iconography and powerful emotion displayed in this work are said to have astounded contemporary artists, Leonardo soon abandoned it and moved to Milan, where he eventually entered the service of the ruler, Ludovico Sforza.

vantageous in the short run, since Leonardo found himself without the cash to meet the contract's provisions or even to pay for his paints. Why sign such an agreement?

Leonardo sought the independence to continue his studies of nature and technology. To have a studio of his own, he also needed money to support assistants. Routine painting commissions could not ensure that he would avoid the poverty and uncertainty that had often confronted his master, Verrocchio. This was an especially serious problem because Leonardo's wealthy patrons often misunderstood and rejected his work as too radical. If Leonardo could complete the *Adoration,* the income-producing property that the monks were to transfer would ensure his financial independence.

Later in life, Leonardo was to show the importance he attached to becoming a property owner in the family tradition by fighting fiercely to gain his disputed inheritance from his father and uncle. The odd contract was thus a gamble that Leonardo probably took (and lost) in the hopes of gaining a steady income. After Leonardo abandoned the *Adoration of the Magi,* without money and support, he left Florence for Milan.

Leonardo went to the Milanese court of Ludovico Sforza not as a painter, however, but as a musician. Lorenzo de' Medici counted music among his many avocations. Leonardo, whose beautiful voice and musical ability were widely admired, had invented a silver lute in the shape of a horse's head. To cement a politically useful alliance between Florence and Milan, Lorenzo de' Medici decided to give the lute to Sforza. Leonardo seems to have leapt at the chance to take it to Sforza's court himself. He was to stay there for over eighteen years. They may have been the happiest years of his life.

Leonardo arrived in Milan in 1482 or 1483, accompanied by a young singer named Atalante Migliorotti. As his *Notebooks* make evident, by this time Leonardo knew his talent extended to engineering and science as well as music and painting, to the invention of weapons as well as sculpture and architectural design. He knew that his true worth had never been appreciated in Florence. And he sought not only artistic commissions and wealth, but personal access and influence with the regent and de facto ruler, Ludovico Sforza (nicknamed Il Moro—"the Moor").

It apparently took some time for Leonardo to make progress toward these goals. Because he did not at first gain a formal position at Sforza's court, Leonardo joined the studio of the de Predis brothers. With Ambrogio and Evangelista de Predis, Leonardo received the commission for an altarpiece for the Confraternity of the Immaculate Conception: the *Virgin of the Rocks*. Once again, Leonardo broke sharply with traditional iconography. Whether due to Leonardo's unconventional treatment of the theme or for other reasons, the friars refused to pay him in full. Leonardo protested.

In the years that followed, Leonardo worked in an astounding variety of areas. He continued to study vision and analyze painting as a science, writing what we now know as the *Treatise on Painting* (published only in the seventeenth century). He worked with the mathematician Luca Pacioli, illustrating his *De Divina Proportione*, finished in 1498 and published in 1509. He studied anatomy, completing dissections and exploring the precise structure of the human body. He developed skill as an architect, planning buildings of many types. He invented dozens of machines for both industrial and military purposes. And finally, he succeeded in gaining a position at Ludovico Sforza's court.

Leonardo was eager if not desperate for public recognition, influence, and security. Because the Milanese were known for their suspicion of outsiders, he was limited in what he could achieve while working with the de Predis brothers. His *Notebooks* contain the draft of a letter to Ludovico Sforza, explaining the skills he could offer the ruler of Milan. This letter is not an advertisement for Leonardo's services as a musician, nor even as a painter. Rather, it is focused on his abilities as a military engineer.

At the time, Milan was at war, particularly threatened by Venice until 1484 (when a treaty between the two cities was signed). Sforza, a proud and often devious man, generally preferred local talent to foreigners, and often pitted one "expert" against another. Leonardo, a Florentine artist in partnership with the de Predis brothers, had come to the Milanese court to present a musical instrument as a gift from Lorenzo de' Medici. During the preceding decade in Florence, Leonardo had begun to reflect on military technology, but no one would have reason to believe his ideas were superior to those of experts. And Leonardo did not have a secure, independent source of income that could support not only his household but his scientific and technical research.

The text in Leonardo's *Notebooks* is clearly a draft. The first paragraph suggests a previous conversation with Il Moro, in which Leonardo—probably perceived by Sforza as a court musician and artist—had offered his services as a military engineer and was asked to compare his inventions with those available from others at the court. Whereas Leonardo's letters asking a favor from an unknown man of power and status start with a salutation, this draft begins like a report to someone with whom Leonardo was already associated. The first sentence begins: "Having, my most illustrious Lord, now sufficiently seen and considered the specimens of all those who are reputed masters and inventors of military technology..." This implies that Leonardo has been asked to look at the existing proposals for technological innovation in military affairs; the letter immediately gives his assessment "that the inventions of the operations of the said instruments are in no way different from those in common use."

Competing with experts whose inventions contain nothing really new, Leonardo made an offer of service. In his letter, he promised a bewildering array of military technologies, including "light and strong bridges" that were movable, siege machines, "methods for destroying every rock or other fortress," mortars, naval vessels, mines, "covered chariots" (tanks), heavy cannon, and catapults. Also included were skills useful "in time of peace": architecture, hydraulic engineering, sculpture, and painting. As if it were an afterthought, Leonardo added that "the bronze horse" that had been projected to honor Francesco Sforza "may be taken in hand." In other words, he offered to create a large equestrian statue of the duke's father. While some say that this was the prime objective of the letter, it was not a project of the highest priority, and several years would pass before

Leonardo Achieves Fame / 37

Leonardo's offer to create an equestrian monument to the Sforza family was taken seriously by Il Moro.

As this letter shows, Leonardo sought to establish a *personal* relationship with the ruler of Milan (offering to "explain myself to Your Excellence, showing you my secrets"). That is, Leonardo wanted to be a technical advisor who would not replace any current official or member of Ludovico Sforza's court (he offered his services "without prejudice to anyone else"). Leonardo was not just seeking a job—he was after a position as an influential, personal advisor whose primary responsibilities would be military technology and civil engineering as well as sculpture and painting.

Ultimately, Leonardo's attempt to gain employment from Ludovico Sforza was successful, and he became a member of the court, with a room in the ducal palace and a salary (which was not always paid). In Milanese documents, he is often listed as an engineer or architect—which suggests that his letter to Sforza had the desired effect. In fact, however, for some time his main functions were those of a kind of court jester and producer of festivals. During festivities, such as the Masque of the Planets performed in 1490 to celebrate the wedding of Gian Galeazzo Sforza (the legitimate heir to power) and Isabella of Aragon as well as Ludovico Sforza's own marriage to Beatrice d'Este, Leonardo designed and built scenery, pennants, costumes, and the pageantry Sforza used to astonish and please the assembled populace. Often Leonardo was engaged as a poet, storyteller, and singer: his *Notebooks* contain riddles from games played at the court and fantastic tales he apparently used to regale Beatrice and the other members of the court. Leonardo was frustrated by this frivolity: his *Notebooks* include entries complaining of the time-consuming chores of amusing the court, not to mention drafts of letters to Sforza asking that his long-overdue salary be paid as soon as possible.

In addition to these activities, Leonardo continued his scientific studies and worked on projects that reflected the abilities he advertised to Il Moro. Leonardo had promised to show Ludovico Sforza techniques for building bridges (Figure 3.3), for various kinds of siege equipment (Figure 3.4), for "mortars" resembling today's machine guns that fire shrapnel (Figure

3.5), for naval armaments of both offense and defense (Figure 3.6), for sapping and mining enemy fortifications, for constructing self-propelled armored vehicles like the modern tank (Figure 3.7), and other innovative ways to propel weapons. Interestingly enough, he also worked on "a method of letting a flood of water loose on an army, and bridges and walls of cities" by using a sort of "mobile lock." From the drawings in his *Notebooks*, Leonardo seemingly fulfilled his promise to "contrive various and endless means of offence and defence."

Although there is no evidence that Ludovico Sforza commissioned any of these devices, Leonardo's images and technical notes show that he was deeply engaged in military technology and strategy. This interest was to persist. Some have said that Leonardo produced some prototypes while serving as Cesare Borgia's military architect and engineer in the fall of 1502. The following year, he advised the Florentine government on ques-

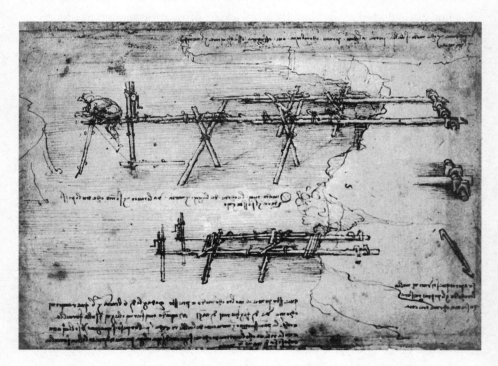

FIGURE 3.3. Leonardo, Wooden bridges. These easily constructed structures would provide a means to get soldiers across a river at a point dictated by military circumstances.

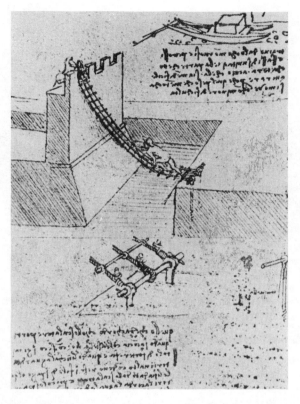

FIGURE 3.4. Leonardo, Siege equipment. This rope ladder for scaling a wall across a moat shares the simple technology of Leonardo's early defensive technologies (as in Figure 3.1).

tions of military fortification. Although the diversion of the Arno to deprive Pisa of water and force its capitulation was not part of Leonardo's original scheme for the river, this application of hydraulic engineering to warfare had been foreshadowed by his designs for a movable lock for Ludovico Sforza's defense of Lucca, and by his later proposal that the Venetians flood the Friuli as a defensive measure against the Turks.

In the letter to Ludovico Sforza, Leonardo also offered to "give perfect satisfaction and to the equal of anything in architecture and the composition of buildings public and private." During his early years in Milan, there were several major architectural projects for which there was vigorous competition. Foremost among these was the crossing dome to surmount the cathedral of Milan. When it became apparent that the tempo-

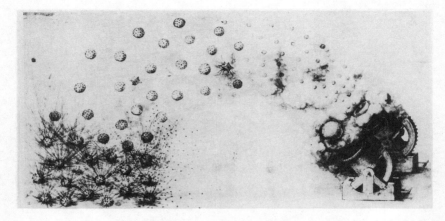

FIGURE 3.5. Leonardo, Shrapnel-firing cannon. Artillery of this design was ultimately introduced in the American Civil War. Leonardo imagined many other types of firearms, including something like a machine gun.

rary dome on the cathedral might collapse, Ludovico Sforza consulted Luca Fancelli, a Milanese architect. An open competition for designs to complete and repair the cathedral was announced in 1487. Leonardo submitted a full model based on extensive designs (Figure 3.8).

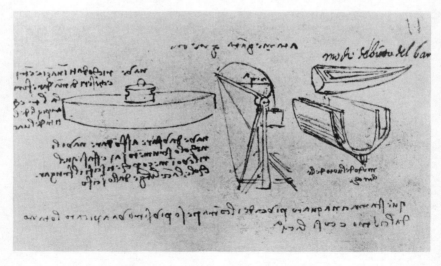

FIGURE 3.6. Leonardo, Double-hulled structure and mysterious vessel for sinking enemy ships. Leonardo also designed underwater swimming equipment that would allow a diver to sink enemy ships by drilling holes in their hulls, but expressed fears at the consequences of using such devices.

FIGURE 3.7. Leonardo, Scythed chariot and covered armored car. Although scythed chariots had been used in antiquity, the amored tank did not revolutionize warfare until World War II.

There were numerous hesitations and many consultations. Three years later the commission finally went to Milanese architects—though Leonardo may have served as a consultant to those who completed the work. As the *Notebooks* reveal, Leonardo also drew plans for numerous buildings, including symmetrical churches, palaces, and fortresses.

Leonardo's interest in architecture was not limited to individual buildings. In 1484, the plague hit Milan and ravaged the city for two years. Ludovico Sforza and the court—including Leonardo—fled to the country. Reflecting on the health risks associated with urban garbage and filth, Leonardo drew plans for an entirely new kind of city.

Leonardo's urban planning was audacious. He conceptualized a city on multiple levels (like recently built shopping malls), with service functions on a lower level while the upper classes moved on special walkways at a higher level (Figure 3.9). These designs provided for watercourses, like modern sewers, to carry waste and drain rainwater in a healthy manner. To prevent the pressures of population from creating the conditions he

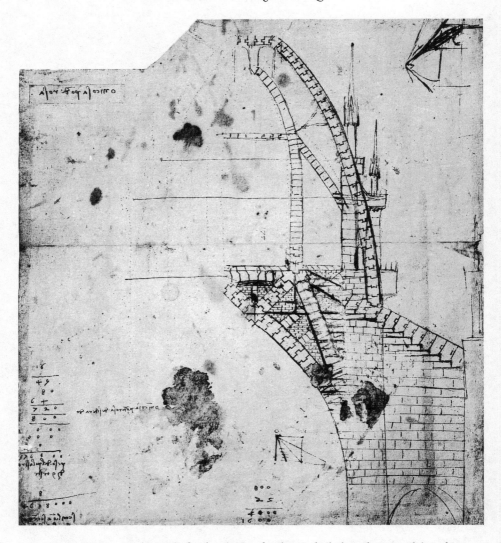

FIGURE 3.8. Leonardo, Study for the tiburio of Milan Cathedral. Both Leonardo's architectural skills and his interest in making the Arno navigable developed in Milan, where he (in competition with other famous architects) submitted a proposal for completing and repairing that city's cathedral duomo. It was probably in working on his design for the cathedral's tiburio that Leonardo met Luca Fancelli and discussed Fancelli's plan for a canal on the Arno between Florence and Signa (near Empoli).

associated with the plague, Leonardo proposed a series of such planned towns, each limited to ten thousand inhabitants.

This view of urban and regional planning combined civil and domestic architecture with economics and politics. Leonardo saw the need to main-

FIGURE 3.9. Leonardo, Communications and buildings of city with raised streets. Leonardo's conception of urban planning included the functional separation of road levels and water canals for both convenience and public health.

tain the canals and watercourses on which the health of the new cities would depend. For that purpose, on the sheets with his architectural drawings, he proposed specific legislation requiring property owners along the shores of urban canals to provide maintenance. That is, Leonardo imagined a total reorganization of the way entire populations live "in time of peace." In the words of a leading twentieth-century theorist of urban planning, Leonardo was the first person who "tried to survey and organize the natural forces of a whole region so as to serve human purposes."

Although controlling the flow of water through a city was a component in Leonardo's urban planning, it was listed separately in his draft to Ludovico: "I can give perfect satisfaction . . . in guiding water from one place to another." There was no novelty in the attempt to control the flows of rivers, but Leonardo promised to be "the equal of any other," if not to surpass the established hydraulic engineers.

Leonardo's *Notebooks* from the 1490s show extensive reflection on redirecting rivers in order to reduce the dangers of floods and increase agricultural output. In his youth, Florence had repeatedly been flooded. Elsewhere, including Milan, floods occasionally did untold damage. Moreover, undrained swamps and shallow lagoons—particularly close to the sea—were areas known for poor health, due (as we now know) to malaria, among other things.

The rivers north of Milan, like the Adda, were the focus of some of Leonardo's plans for canalization. Although these projects for "guiding water from one place to another" were not carried out by Sforza's regime, many were ultimately financed by the French king Francis I in 1516.

While in Milan, Leonardo also began to consider the idea of moving the Arno. He worked on maps showing an extensive project to transform the Arno valley between Florence and the sea (Plates IV, V). Why, when working in Milan, would Leonardo develop a plan to straighten the channel of the Arno in order to create a rich agricultural valley and open Florence directly to the sea and therewith to naval commerce?

The answer may be related to Leonardo's proposals for repairing and completing the Cathedral of Milan. In thinking about the structural problems involved, it is likely that Leonardo consulted with Luca Fancelli, the Florentine architect who had discussed the cathedral with Il Moro in 1487. In August of that year, Fancelli wrote to Lorenzo de' Medici in Florence, proposing canals that would make the Arno navigable. Some suspect that these conversations led Leonardo to do extensive research on the problem during the following decade. Evidence for this view is found on a later map by Leonardo (Plate V) that indicates both Fancelli's suggested canal from Florence to Signia (parallel to the winding course of the Arno immediately below the city) and several alternative routes for a much longer route through Pistoia. Whatever the inspiration, Leonardo was to pursue projects in hydraulic engineering as a professional expert for the rest of his life.

Leonardo's projects for urban and regional planning were based on considerations that went beyond mere technology. In the 1490s, his *Notebooks* reveal an increasing commitment to write comprehensive scientific treatises on matters as diverse as the art of painting, human anatomy, the motion of water, physics, and geology. Among these manuscripts is a notebook with the entry "On the 2nd of April 1489, book entitled 'Of the human figure.'" Elsewhere in this same notebook, Leonardo wrote: "And so may it please our great Author that I may demonstrate the *nature of man and his customs*, in the way I describe his figure."

In addition to technology and science, Leonardo completed many paintings during his years in the Sforza court, including the *Lady with an Ermine* (now in Cracow), *Madonna Litta* (now in the Hermitage of St. Petersburg), *La Belle Ferronière* (now in the Louvre), and the *Musician* (now in Milan's Ambrosiana). Among his last works in Milan, started in 1498, were decorations for the Salle delle Asse in Sforza's castle. But most important of all, Duke Ludovico sponsored a large fresco in the refectory of a Dominican church, Santa Maria delle Grazie: the *Last Supper*.

Leonardo received the commission for the *Last Supper* in 1493. For several years he drew preparatory sketches while working on his many other projects. Once the cartoon was completed, Leonardo set up scaffolding in the refectory. To the annoyance of the prior, however, the painting progressed slowly. It is said that Leonardo would arrive in the hall, look intently at the painting for as much as two hours, add a single stroke, and leave again. In 1497, a memorandum by Ludovico ordered one of his subordinates to urge Leonardo to finish the painting so that he could work on another wall of the refectory.

Leonardo paid special attention to the faces painted for each of the apostles, seeking features appropriate to each character while he walked the streets of Milan, and then inserting the image into the painting. According to one account, when all that remained to complete the *Last Supper* was the face of Judas, the prior of Santa Maria delle Grazie lost patience and asked Ludovico to order Leonardo to finish. Leonardo supposedly explained to the duke that he was still seeking the perfect face for Judas, but that if not allowed to find it, he would have to use the second best he had seen—the prior himself. Il Moro let Leonardo finish as he wished.

Leonardo was not particularly known for sculpture before going to

Milan, even though his master, Verrocchio, was among the leading sculptors of the age. In promising Ludovico Sforza that "the bronze horse may be taken in hand, which is to be the immortal glory and eternal honour of the prince your father of happy memory, and of the illustrious house of Sforza," Leonardo was relying in part on skills he had learned as an apprentice but had not fully exploited as a mature artist.

The story of the commission for this statue shows that the connection between art and politics was often very close. After many other artists had been consulted, Leonardo finally received the commission in 1489. His first designs for *Il Cavallo*, as he came to call the project, were for a life-size statue. Then it was decided to make a truly grandiose monument. The largest known equestrian statue cast in bronze since antiquity was Verrocchio's monument to Colleoni, the Venetian condottiere. That statue was thirteen feet high (horse and rider combined). Leonardo imagined an equestrian statue in which the horse alone was *twenty-four feet* in height.

At first, to make the statue more imposing, Leonardo conceived of a rearing horse (Figure 3.10). Because his design would require that the huge weight of the statue be supported only by its hind legs, with a foreleg supported by the body of a fallen warrior, Leonardo ultimately chose a less difficult path. Even so, the design presents a trotting horse of amazing vitality and force. The conception of such a statue and its realization in full-scale clay was—as Leonardo complained—delayed by Ludovico's insistence on other tasks in the court.

Finally completed in 1493, the clay statue of *Il Cavallo*, ready for casting, was put on display in the courtyard of the duke's palace. It would be an understatement to say that this statue astounded those who saw it. Based on Leonardo's extensive studies of anatomy, the form seemed to be in lifelike motion. Yet its gigantic scale, surpassing anything that contemporaries had seen, made an even greater impression. But even after he overcame the obstacles to such a grandiose sculpture, Leonardo's problems were not over.

No one knew how to cast a bronze statue of this size. In the end, about 158,000 pounds of bronze were set aside for the monument. Leonardo set

FIGURE 3.10. Leonardo, Study for the monument to Francesco Sforza (ca. 1488–89). This sketch of a rearing horse corresponds to Leonardo's original conception for *Il Cavallo*, later changed to a walking stance because of the difficulty of supporting a massive monument in this pose.

about to solve the technical problems posed by both size and weight, inventing a radically new way of casting a large statue. Then the bronze designated for the statue was diverted for the casting of cannon to defend Milan against the French. Perhaps the clay statue merely crumbled with age. But according to one story, when the forces of King Louis XII under Charles d'Amboise captured Milan in 1499, French troops camped in the ducal castle. Bored but in high spirits, as troops can be after victory, they began using *Il Cavallo* for target practice. Before Leonardo's eyes, the story goes, they destroyed what many thought was the most extraordinary statue of the age.

Il Cavallo is a fitting symbol of Leonardo's stay in Milan, where he perfected his genius in many fields and gained—for the first but not the last time—the experience of working directly for a powerful ruler. The goal of combining art, science, and technology in the service of political influence was never to be absent for the remainder of Leonardo's career. In the short run, however, most of these projects were failures. Between 1502 and 1506, both the ambitious goals and the failure were to be evident in the mysterious friendship between Leonardo and Niccolò Machiavelli.

Chapter 4

NICCOLÒ ACHIEVES POWER
(1469-1501)

The baptismal register of the Church of Santa Reparata—today called the Duomo of Florence—reports for May 4, 1469: "Niccolò Piero Michele son of messer Bernardo Machiavelli, p[arish] of S. Trinità, born on the 3rd at 4 o'clock, baptized on the 4th." According to one story, the boy's father, Bernardo Machiavelli, was the illegitimate son of Niccolò di Buoninsegno Machiavelli, a bachelor who—on his deathbed—had legitimized his son. It is probable that this was a scurrilous tale invented in later years by the younger Niccolò's enemies, who at most could say that his father, Bernardo, had been on the debtors' list. From all other evidence, Niccolò di Bernardo Machiavelli, future second chancellor of Florence, was (unlike Leonardo) the eldest legitimate son of the family and legally a citizen of his place of birth.

Like Ser Piero da Vinci and his family, the Machiavelli were property-owning citizens of Florence. Trained as a lawyer, Bernardo had an income derived from the labors of tenants but was far from wealthy. Although the Machiavelli had political connections and several relatives held offices in the government, they were not among the leading aristocratic clans with power in Florentine society.

Under its Latin name of Maclavellorum—or the Tuscan equivalent, Machiavegli—the family had a long history among the politically active minor Florentine nobility, tracing its lineage to a fief in Montespertoli. That history had been checkered. Many members of the family held minor posts in the city. Alessandro Machiavelli died during a pilgrimage to the Holy Land; Guido Machiavelli was one of the seventy-four representatives of the wool workers in their uprising in 1378; Girolamo Machiavelli had been exiled to Avignon for his opposition to the political oppression under Cosimo de' Medici—and died in prison around 1458 after returning illegally to the city. While not among the leading families, the Machiavelli had a family chapel along the nave of the Church of Santa Croce (until, a generation after Niccolò's death, a confraternity displaced them and took control of the coveted altar).

Bernardo had title to property in the hills of San Casciano, as well as the house in the Santo Spirito quarter in Florence, just across the Arno from the center of Florence. He married Bartolomea Nelli, whose family had property outside the city in Mugello. She was also literate; happy to have a son after two daughters, she composed hymns to the Virgin Mary dedicated to the newborn. "Niccolò" was a common name among the Machiavelli: three years later it was given to a relative who became a banker in Rome, and another cousin Niccolò was to be one of the governing council, or Signoria, in 1499 and a commissioner in negotiations with Pistoia the following year.

Bernardo Machiavelli was a careful manager. He kept a book of accounts that records that Niccolò was first sent to a teacher at seven. At eleven, Bernardo records, his son was being taught by a "*maestro* of abacus"—and a year later was learning Latin from a priest with connections in the Chancery. During Niccolò's youth, Bernardo recorded either borrowing or purchasing books of many famous authors: Aristotle *(Ethics, Topics)*, Cicero *(Philippics, Offices, On Oratory)*, Ptolemy *(Cosmography)*, Boethius *(On Divisions)*, Justinian, Macrobius *(Dream of Scipio, On the Saturnalia)*, Flavio Biondo *(Italy Illustrated*, the *Decades)*. In return for compiling an index to an edition of the *Decades* of Titus Livy, Bernardo received a set of printer's sheets and asked Niccolò, seventeen at the time, to take them to a binder.

Niccolò's political education was not confined to books. When he was nine, on Sunday, April 26, 1478, the city was convulsed by a conspiracy of the Pazzi, a leading family deeply hostile to the ruling Medici. With the tacit support of the pope himself, the Pazzi decided to assassinate both Lorenzo de' Medici, who had become the effective ruler of the city, and his younger brother Giuliano di Piero de' Medici. In later years, Niccolò would summarize the event in the *Discourses on Titus Livy*:

> *The conspiracy of the Pazzi against Lorenzo and Giuliano de' Medici is known. The order given was that they give a breakfast for the cardinal of San Giorgio and kill them at that breakfast, in which it had been assigned who had to kill them, who had to seize the palace, and who had to run through the city and call the people to freedom. It befell that when the Pazzi, the Medici and the cardinal were in the cathedral church in Florence for a solemn office, it was understood that Giuliano was not breakfasting there that morning. That made the conspirators assemble together, and what they had to do in the house of the Medici they decided to do in church. That came to disturb the whole order because Giovambatista da Montesecco did not wish to share in the homicide, saying that he did not wish to do it in church. So they had to change new ministers in every action, who did not have time to firm up their spirits and made such errors that in its execution they were crushed.*

In the *Florentine Histories*, Niccolò gave a more detailed account, describing the murder of Giuliano de' Medici in the cathedral, the capture of the Pazzi conspirators, and the outpouring of popular support for Lorenzo: "there was no citizen armed or unarmed who did not go to the houses of Lorenzo in that necessity, and each one offered himself and his property to him."

Was Bernardo Machiavelli one of these citizens among the crowd who went to the Medici palace? Was the nine-year-old Niccolò himself in the Church of Santa Reparata earlier that day? Did he see the hanging of the conspirators? Even more tantalizing, a year later—after the assassin Bernardo Bandini had been captured, returned from his flight to the Turks, and executed—did Niccolò cross paths with Leonardo while the young artist was sketching the hanging body (Figure 4.1)?

In May of 1479, the plague broke out in Florence. Bernardo prudently

FIGURE 4.1. Leonardo, Bernardo di Bandini Baroncelli (1479). Leonardo's sketch of the execution of Giuliano de Medici's assassin, who had been captured and returned to Florence a year after the Pazzi conspiracy. Notations of the color and material of Baroncelli's clothing suggest that Leonardo hoped for a commission to paint the hanging body (as Botticelli had painted the hanging bodies of the other conspirators, who had been captured and executed immediately after the assassination).

sent the family to his wife's family property in Mugello. On June 10, Bernardo recorded that he was ill and had returned to town. Papal troops allied with the king of Naples descended on Tuscany. On September 7, 1479, they defeated the Florentines in the battle of Poggio Imperiale. To protect Florence itself, as Niccolò later put it, a Florentine army that "had been successful around Perugia . . . was brought to San Casciano, a fortified town eight miles from Florence." For most of the following month, one of the Florentine captains and his troops were lodged at the family property in Sant' Andrea, several miles from San Casciano. Bernardo again sent his family away to safety.

Because friends and contacts were especially important in the shifting cliques of Florentine politics, two additional facts about Bernardo Machiavelli were relevant to the future of his son Niccolò. First, Bernardo was a member of the Confraternity of San Girolamo sulla Costa, a religious society more popularly known as La Pietà. One of the foremost flagellant societies, La Pietà brought together over 140 men from various walks of life for religious ceremonial, for social service and charity—and sometimes for political scheming. Associated with it was a youth group, the Confraternity of Sant' Antonio da Padova.

Assuming Bernardo followed the custom, young Niccolò would have entered this youth confraternity as a teenager and have been expected to compose an oration on a religious theme. That this happened is suggested by "An Exhortation to Penitence" found in Niccolò's works. Conforming to the requirement that members of a youth confraternity join the adult confraternity at or soon after reaching the age of twenty-four, Niccolò himself joined La Pietà in 1495. Niccolò's membership in the religious confraternity of his father may well explain the many letters he received in later life from otherwise unknown correspondents, who often referred to him as *compare* ("brother" or "buddy") when asking for favors.

Another fact about Bernardo Machiavelli probably explains even more about the circle of contacts and political connections that young Niccolò was to establish. From 1464 to 1497, the first chancellor of Florence—the administrator responsible for the secretarial functions of the government—was a humanist named Bartolomeo Scala. Bernardo Machiavelli was his best friend, as is confirmed by one of Scala's works, a dialogue between the author and Niccolò's father. Since Scala was responsible for the administrative correspondence of the Florentine Signoria during the rule of Lorenzo the Magnificent and remained in office under Savonarola, it has even been suggested that the young Niccolò may have been given small commissions in the Chancery before his own election as second chancellor in 1498.

Niccolò received a humanist education befitting the status and friendships of his father. At the time, intellectual life along the Arno was dominated by three figures: Marsilio Ficino, Angelo Poliziano, and Giovanni Pico della Mirandola. Ficino, the son of Cosimo de' Medici's physician, was best known for his translations of Plato and his attempt to show the harmony of Christianity with Platonic (or Neoplatonic) thought. At the Medici court, Ficino presided over the intellectual milieu of verbal jousting and textual citation that—along with such superstitions as Ficino's belief in astrology—had often outraged the young Leonardo.

A second major figure at Lorenzo de' Medici's court was Angelo Ambrogini, known as Poliziano or Politian. Born in Montepulciano in 1454 to a family of jurists, Poliziano had studied Latin and Greek with the best-known teachers of the day. In 1470, he translated four books of the *Iliad* into Latin hexameter, earning the title *Homericus juvenis*. At eighteen, he edited Catullus. Soon brought to the Medici court as tutor, he was known for courses in Ovid, Statius, Quintilian, the younger Pliny, and the *Pandects* of Justinian. His publications included not only essays and poetry in Latin, but verse and a play, *Orfeo*, in Italian.

Perhaps the most famous humanist of the time, however, was Giovanni Pico della Mirandola. Born in 1463, Pico was the youngest son of the count of Mirandola. Having learned Hebrew, he came to believe that the Kabbala contained proof of Christian mysteries. In 1486, he published a monumental work of nine hundred *Questions* and theological answers, and in 1491, the mystical *Heptaplus*. A friend of both Ficino and Poliziano, he visited Florence, was influenced by Savonarola, and shortly before his death, in 1494, had decided to give up his worldly goods to travel the world as a mendicant.

Such famous men were part of the day-to-day world of both Leonardo and Niccolò. In the *Florentine Histories,* Niccolò refers to these scholars explicitly, connecting their careers with the fortunes of the Medici:

> *Cosimo was also a lover and exalter of literary men; he therefore brought Argyropoulos to Florence, a man of Greek birth and very learned for those times, so that Florentine youth might learn from him the Greek language and other teachings of his. He took into his home Marsilio Ficino, second father of Platonic philosophy, whom he loved extremely; and that Ficino might pursue his studies of letters more comfortably and that he might be able to use him more conveniently, Cosimo gave him a property near his own in Careggi.*

Later, according to Niccolò, Lorenzo de' Medici showed the same enthusiasm for intellectuals:

> *He [Lorenzo the Magnificent] loved marvelously anyone who was excellent in an art; he favored men of letters—of which Messer Agnolo da Montepulciano [Poliziano], Messer Cristofano Landino, and Messer Demetrio [Chalcondylas], a Greek, can give firm testimony. Hence, Count Giovanni della Mirandola, a man almost divine, left all the other parts of Europe where he had traveled and, attracted by the munificence of Lorenzo, made his home in Florence. Lorenzo took marvelous delight in architecture, music, and poetry; and many poetic compositions not only composed but also commented on by him are in existence. And so that the Florentine youth might be trained in the study of letters, he opened in the city of Pisa a school to which the most excellent men in Italy then were brought.*

It is not clear whether Niccolò himself attended this school. Apart from hints based on the life of Bernardo Machiavelli, we have little direct evidence of Niccolò himself prior to 1494, when he was appointed as his father's representative in negotiations for the dowry of his sister Primavera. His early studies can, however, be discerned by reading his correspondence and published works with care. He was trained primarily in poetry, literature, and history rather than theology, philosophy, or law. He knew Latin well, but had a more limited knowledge of Greek. More important, he was thoroughly familiar with the work of the two leading poets of Florence, Dante and Petrarch.

The influence of long study of Dante is particularly apparent throughout his correspondence and writings. Many other poets that Niccolò studied in his youth can be inferred from his literary references immediately after losing office. In 1513, when he was forced to retire to his villa and began writing *The Prince*, Niccolò wrote a famous letter to his friend Vettori, then Florence's ambassador to Rome. In describing his daytime activities, Niccolò describes reading "Dante or Petrarch, or one of the minor poets like Tibullus, Ovid, or some such." This letter also contains a quotation from Petrarch and references to Dante's *Inferno,* Lucretius, Virgil, Juvenal, Plautus, and a modern novella based on Plautus.

Niccolò also knew from his youth such classical writers as Xenophon and Plutarch, not to mention Tacitus and Livy. More important, as a student Niccolò learned how to write poetry. During his term as second chancellor, he composed verses to be set to music, as well as a history of Florence's foreign affairs in the form of a rhymed poem (the *First Decennale*). After the fall of the republic, when he was imprisoned and tortured, he wrote poems to Giuliano de' Medici complaining that his torture and "other miseries" were "the way *poets* are to be treated" in the new regime. Years later, he was to write *La Mandragola,* sometimes called the greatest comedy in the history of Italian theater.

Under these circumstances, it should not be a surprise that Niccolò thought of himself as a poet. For example, after his fall from power, Niccolò was writing a poetic fable, *The Golden Ass* (ultimately left unfinished), when he wrote a friend in Rome:

> *Lately I have been reading Ariosto's* Orlando Furioso; *the entire poem is really fine and many passages are marvelous. If he is there with you,*

give him my regards and tell him that my only complaint is that in his mention of so many poets he has left me out like some prick and that he has done to me in his Orlando *what I shall not do to him in my* Ass.

While Niccolò thought of himself as a poet, he was more ambitious than most literary men.

The oldest surviving fragment in Niccolò's hand is the draft of a letter in Latin written when he was twenty-eight, less than a year before he took office. The purpose of this text is not clear, though its date (December 1, 1497) is said to connect it with a second letter, dated the following day. The powerful Pazzi family (rehabilitated after the botched conspiracy against the Medici) had contested the appointment of a relative named Francesco Machiavelli to a church property and convinced Cardinal Lopez to annul it. In the second of these letters, dated December 2, 1497, Niccolò wrote out a letter to the cardinal that was then signed by several of his relatives.

The letter of December 2 is a formal appeal to the cardinal, whereas the draft of December 1 is a personal plea for help to someone whom Niccolò knows well. The draft of the first letter tells us something of young Niccolò's view of himself in the world of Florence in the last years of the fifteenth century:

Yet beset by ill health I did not have the strength to write back to you. Now, however, with my health recovered, I shall write nothing other than to encourage, beg, and pray that you do not cease until our efforts have a happy outcome. Toward this end I ask that you show your might, and use all your might; for if we, mere pygmies, are attacking giants, a much greater victory is in store for us than for them. For them, inasmuch as it is base to compete, so it will be a very base thing to give in; we, on the other hand, shall consider it not so ignominious a thing to be beaten, as it is honorable to have competed, especially having a competitor at whose nod everything is done immediately. Wherefore, whatever outcome Fortune may reserve for us, we shall not regret having failed in such endeavors.

Niccolò, as a young man, thought of himself as among the "mere pygmies," without power or high status comparable to a family like the Pazzi. He considered it "honorable to have competed" with those having more power. By the age of twenty-eight, he had learned that, in competition for honors and wealth, if "our efforts" are to produce "victory . . . for us," allies are needed. And he wrote in Latin, which suggests that his correspondent was an educated man, probably a professor.

This early letter indicates that by 1497 Niccolò was already accustomed to negotiations that could be called political. Having served as the representative of the family's interests in his sister's dowry, a delicate negotiation because without a large dowry marriage was often impossible, Niccolò was already acting as a responsible agent in dealing with others. And as the family letter of December 2 confirms, both powerful aristocratic families and the church, or at least some of its representatives, were sometimes threats to Niccolò and his family.

Three years earlier, in 1494, Niccolò had witnessed the sudden ascent to power of Savonarola, the intense friar who chastised both Florence and the church for sinful behavior. After Lorenzo the Magnificent had invited Savonarola to Florence, the fiery preacher embarked on a moralistic campaign against the corruption of the Medici court and Florentine society. Then Lorenzo was succeeded by his son Piero, a weak and ineffective leader who was soon deposed. By 1494, Savonarola had engineered the enactment of a republican constitution for the city, combining populist rhetoric with religious fervor and an attack on excessive wealth and vice in the church. The temper of his dominance of Florentine life was epitomized by the "bonfire of the vanities" he organized in 1497, as enthusiastic followers hurled objects of luxury into the flames. The next year, Savonarola would be excommunicated and burned at the stake. A secular government took power, in which Niccolò, an unknown poet and humanist of twenty-nine, was elected second chancellor and secretary. Nothing seems to have prepared the way for this election, which some have called a "mystery."

⚜

The second chancellorship was an influential administrative post, with a salary of about 128 gold florins. Most of the officials of the Florentine republic were amateurs who served very short terms. The two chanceries provided them with administrative support. According to tradition, the First Chancery was focused primarily on foreign affairs, while the Second—subordinate to the First—was nominally responsible for domestic issues. In practice, the activities of these government bodies overlapped. Moreover, Niccolò also came to occupy a position with the committee of the Ten of War, with responsibility for correspondence with foreign governments (with the First Chancery) and defense of Florentine territory (with the Second).

Members of the chanceries, like bureaucrats everywhere, had to read correspondence, summarize issues, and draft letters or state papers for the political leadership, including the eight members of the Signoria as well as the *gonfaloniere*, or head of state. In twentieth-century terms, the system had a prime minister *(gonfaloniere)*, advised by the cabinet of eight members (the Signoria), both of which were elected by the Great Council, and assisted by the secretaries in the chanceries. As second chancellor, therefore, Niccolò would be responsible for directing a staff as well as for responding to the demands of political officials.

Under Savonarola's reforms, governmental positions were filled by election rather than lottery, with the Great Council sometimes choosing other officials from a slate of nominees established by the Council of Eighty. The first and second chancellors had to be reelected each year (though the first election was for a two-year term). While reelection in settled times was often routine, there could be a bitter contest over the choice of a new incumbent.

In practice, these elections were dominated by rich and powerful families who created alliances with groups of clients through various forms of patronage and favors. As in today's politics, rivalries were partly based on principle, but even more on contacts and personalities. Historians studying Renaissance Florence can even reconstitute which families were allied by examining who was nominated by—or nominated—the leading citizens. For example, by this means we know some members of the

Machiavelli family were allied with several powerful men who were highly critical of Machiavelli's superior, Piero Soderini, after the latter was elected to a lifetime term as *gonfaloniere* of justice, or head of state, in 1502. By this same means we have a hint that, in the last years of his life, Ser Piero da Vinci may have been associated with the Soderini family.

Niccolò's election to the powerful post of second chancellor cannot be understood without reference to this web of power and personalities, based on wealth, family, confraternities, and other social connections, that surrounded all elections in the Florentine republic. Then as now, politics was often a matter of patronage. But even granted that Niccolò had political pull, no one seems to have minded that the new second chancellor had not reached the age of thirty, which, before Savonarola's reforms, had traditionally been required for voting and election to office in Florence. What happened to change the rules of the game?

Niccolò became a powerful official at a moment of political and economic crisis in Florence. The years of Savonarola's power coincided with epidemics and poor harvests. Parties ("sects") formed, each with sharply different attitudes to the friar's blend of religious fervor and popular politics. Aristocrats were strongly critical of both the Medici and Savonarola. Republicans sought to remove the radical friar but keep the popular institutions he had created after the overthrow of the Medici. Some were supporters of a return of Medici rule, others freedom-loving enemies of the puritanism of Savonarola with little else on their political agenda. And there remained a fervent group who continued to support Savonarola and his religious prophecy.

Even within the Medici family and its allies there was division. Piero de' Medici (Lorenzo the Magnificent's son), who had been deposed after giving up Pisa to the French in 1494, still had supporters among those hostile to Savonarola's creation of a Great Council of all eligible voters. Another branch of the family, descended from Pierfrancesco de' Medici (Lorenzo the Magnificent's cousin), combined hostility to Savonarola's puritanism with a more populist stance in politics. Immensely wealthy in commerce, the two sons in this branch—Lorenzo and Giovanni di

Pierfrancesco—took the name de' Popoleschi and openly distinguished themselves from the haughty and tyrannical Piero.

The violent events leading to the overthrow of Savonarola involved shifting coalitions among these competing groups. In 1497, supporters of the deposed Piero de' Medici—impatient with the increasing power of the clergy and its supporters—threatened a coup d'état. Piero imagined that, by coming to the gates of the city with a band of Spanish soldiers, he could trigger a spontaneous rising against Savonarola and his puritanical policies. Nothing happened, and Piero returned to Venice.

The Signoria, led by Francesco Valori, reacted violently. Five leading supporters of the Medici were arrested, tortured, and sentenced to death for complicity in the supposed plot. When the families of the convicted plotters exercised the legal right to appeal the death sentence, Valori demanded the law be changed retroactively. A first vote was five to four against this proposal. One of Valori's supporters grabbed the leading opponent and threatened to throw him out the window (five stories above the public square). Violence was barely averted—and a second vote against clemency carried, six to three. The plotters were promptly executed.

With Valori and his party in control of the Florentine government, Savonarola and his partisans sought to purify the city of its corruption. For example, convictions and punishments for sodomy rose markedly in number and severity, with ten offenders being sentenced to death after 1494 and others subjected to public humiliation, branding, exile, or fines. In place of traditional Carnival revelry, processions of white-robed boys symbolized a movement to rid Florence of gambling, homosexuality, and other vices. Public opinion, soon tiring of Savonarola's persistent puritanism and angered by the high price and scarcity of food, began to turn.

These domestic conflicts were further complicated by the hostility of Pope Alexander VI to Savonarola, who was seen in Rome as a threat to the balance of power in Italian politics as well as a challenge to papal authority. The pope ordered Savonarola to Rome. The preacher refused. The pope ordered him to stop preaching. Savonarola found a surrogate who gave equally explosive sermons condemning both secular and religious corruption. In 1497, Alexander VI issued a bull excommunicating Savonarola. By preaching again early in 1498, Savonarola was in open rebellion against the pope.

Early in 1498, the annual elections for the posts of first and second chancellor were held. On February 18, as Savonarola's power was wavering, Niccolò—then a twenty-eight-year-old unknown—was among the seven candidates for the post of second chancellor, nominated in the Council of Eighty. Two days later (February 20), in one of the last meetings of the Great Council in which Savonarola still had a majority, Alessandro Braccesi (or Bracci)—already a secretary in the chancery and a known supporter of Savonarola—was elected. Niccolò was among those identified as suspect by Savonarola's allies.

That young Niccolò Machiavelli was associated with those committed to Savonarola's removal and the establishment of secular political institutions is confirmed by one of his earliest surviving letters, written several weeks after his unsuccessful candidacy. The situation was confused at this time because, while many in Florence were hostile to Savonarola, the friar still had considerable public support and some of his opponents dared not act for fear of causing papal interference in Florentine politics. Niccolò's correspondent was Ricciardo Becchi, a secretary in the Vatican who represented the interests of Florence at the papal court. Becchi was in an awkward position, serving a pope hostile to Savonarola while being unable to attack the rebellious friar openly (since to do so would appear to undermine Florentine political independence).

A great deal can therefore be inferred from Niccolò's long and detailed letter to Becchi of March 9, 1498. The letter begins, "In order to give you, *in accordance with your wishes,* a full account of matters here concerning the friar": the young Niccolò has been asked by Becchi to provide this report. The letter is not merely concerned with what Savonarola said, since Niccolò adds that "you have already received copies" of the sermons. Rather, while summarizing the preacher's exhortations, Niccolò provides a careful and accurate account of Savonarola's behavior in response to the election of a new Signoria with a majority hostile to the friar.

Niccolò does not pretend to judge "the condition of the times and the people's minds concerning our affairs," leaving such an analysis to Becchi. But Niccolò makes his own position quite clear by asserting that "in my judgment, he acts in accordance with the times and *colors his lies accordingly*." Whatever else could be said about this letter, it proves that by March 1498, Niccolò was up to his ears in politics.

The elections of the spring of 1498 brought to power a majority of the Signoria hostile to Savonarola. Contemporaries attributed this outcome to the manipulations of the young Popoleschi, Lorenzo di Pierfrancesco de' Medici and his brother Giovanni, though other powerful men were also behind the scenes. Before the election, the puritanical friar and his allies had dared critics to a trial by fire in the Piazza della Signoria. A Franciscan monk now took up the challenge. On the appointed day, the fire was prepared and rivals met—but Savonarola insisted that his champion carry the sacred host through the flames. His challengers denounced this as sacrilege. The entire test was called off amid mutual recrimination.

Riots followed. A mob stormed Francesco Valori's house, killing both the leader of the pro-Savonarola faction and his wife. Savonarola and his fellow preachers were arrested. Savonarola was tortured, tried, and burned at the stake. Committed republicans opposed to the friar's religious passions and principles took power.

After Savonarola's execution, several of the friar's allies were removed from their offices, and special elections held to replace them. On June 15, 1498, the pro-Savonarola Braccesi was dismissed as second chancellor; Niccolò was among those nominated in the Council of Eighty to replace him. Three days later, on June 18, he was elected by the Great Council. At the same time, another post—that of chancellor in charge of public records—was filled by Antonio Vespucci on the basis of a highly irregular nomination, which indicated that leaders in the assembly were intent on finding reliable men for key administrative offices. In the official election register, as if to underscore the political maneuvers involved, the results of June 18 are added in the margin in an incomplete form.

Of the three other candidates for second chancellor, one was in the party of Savonarola's supporters and two were in the party of his extremist enemies; Niccolò was apparently the only candidate acceptable to the remaining political factions.

Niccolò thus gained office as the agent of those hostile to Savonarola, including—though by no means limited to—allies of the Medici. This is confirmed by the connections of those who came to office at the same time. Antonio Vespucci, who had served in high office before Savonarola's rise to power, was Amerigo Vespucci's brother—and Amerigo was by this time in charge of the business interests of the Popoleschi, Lorenzo and Giovanni di Pierfrancesco de' Medici. Another member of the Vespucci family, Agostino, was named coadjutor, or assistant, to the second chancellor. Niccolò's election to office seems to have been part of a concerted political effort of Savonarola's enemies to regain control of the government.

Before 1498, who were Niccolò's patrons and allies? His personal connections were to a network of families hostile to Savonarola and friendly to those members of the Medici family with "popular," or republican, views. In addition to Agostino Vespucci, Niccolò had another assistant in the Chancery, Ugolino de Martelli, from a family of merchants associated with the Medici who were useful on different occasions to both Niccolò and Leonardo. Even before his election as second chancellor, Niccolò seems to have been widely connected, with many friends—and not a few enemies—in Florentine politics.

The evidence suggests that his election as second chancellor was assured by connections with some of the Medici and their friends. Nothing indicates that, early in his career, Niccolò was an ally of Piero Soderini before the latter's election as *gonfaloniere* for life, in 1502. In contrast, Niccolò had ties to the Medici that can be traced to the early 1490s and were to have lasting effects on his career.

The key document is not explicitly connected with politics. It is a manuscript of Carnival poems copied in the beautiful handwriting of Biagio Buonaccorsi, who was to become Niccolò's fellow secretary and closest friend in the Florentine chanceries. On the cover of this manuscript is an illustration that has been attributed to Sandro Botticelli (Figure 4.2).

Apart from some later additions, the contents of this booklet include one poem each by Lorenzo di Pierfrancesco de' Medici and Angelo Poliziano, three by Niccolò Machiavelli, and ten by Lorenzo de' Medici. Because Botticelli died in 1510, the manuscript has been traced to the Medici court in the years immediately preceding Savonarola's rise to power. Assuming the poetry was copied during the lifetime of Poliziano, the copy cannot be later than 1494; if it was written when Lorenzo the Magnificent was alive, it antedates 1492.

One of the three poems by Niccolò Machiavelli is a "Pastorale," apparently dedicated to the adolescent Giuliano de' Medici (who was between thirteen and fifteen in 1492–94). Niccolò, as a young poet in the Medici court, was apparently seeking Giuliano's patronage. Even before this date, Niccolò may have known Giuliano de' Medici through contacts in the world of Florentine confraternities.

Since the leading scholars of the day came together in the Medici court, it is also possible that Niccolò—obviously a bright student—was introduced to this circle by one of his teachers or by his father's friend, first chancellor Bartolomeo Scala. The assumption that Niccolò was a client of the Medici by 1494 explains his letter to Ricciardo Becchi four years later. Becchi's family had long been linked to the Medici, since Gentile Becchi had been Lorenzo the Magnificent's tutor when the Medici ruler was a boy. In 1498, to communicate by a separate channel to a Florentine representative in the pope's service, leaders of the Medici faction in Florence may have used the young Niccolò as a reliable observer and reporter of Savonarola's behavior.

Corroborating evidence is provided by an exceptionally warm letter of December 23, 1502, from Alamanno Salviati, Piero de' Medici's son-in-law and one of the leaders of a powerful faction linked to the Medici. At the time of this letter, Niccolò was traveling with the court of Cesare Borgia. After predicting that the second chancellor would be reelected in the forthcoming elections, Salviati concluded: "I am very happy about

FIGURE 4.2. Poem by Machiavelli with sketch attributed to Botticelli, in a pamphlet of poems copied by Biagio Buonaccorsi (ca. 1492–94?). In addition to three poems by Niccolò, this manuscript contains courtly poems by Lorenzo de' Medici, Poliziano, and Lorenzo di Pierfrancesco de' Medici.

[Niccolò's likely reconfirmation] for the reason I have stated, and *we should do everything necessary* and make every effort, and *I in particular, who could not desire our entire welfare any more than if it affected myself.*" The "we" would seem to be the group that had supported Niccolò since he entered the chancery in 1498.

Although Piero Soderini had been elected *gonfaloniere* for life in September 1502, there is little evidence that Niccolò was close to him before the election. The new *gonfaloniere* originally had support from the Salviati family, but within two years Alamanno and his faction became vigorously hostile to Soderini and his policies. Despite this fact, Niccolò dedicated his *First Decennale* to Alamanno Salviati in the fall of 1504, perhaps in hopes of assuring Alamanno's faction of continued friendship. And even though the enmity between the Salviati and Piero Soderini was well known, it was apparently news when—in October 1506—Niccolò's close friend Buonaccorsi wrote in code that "when Alamanno was in Bibbona, dining with Ridolfi, where there were also a lot of young people, speaking of you, he said: 'I never entrusted anything at all to that rascal since I have been one of the ten.'" The second chancellor, often indifferent to criticism, did not take this lightly, later trying to mend fences with Salviati by writing a long letter addressing Alamanno as "Honored Patron."

Many puzzles in Niccolò's career are illuminated by the likelihood of an early association with the Medici and a faction favorable to them, later associated with the Salviati. For example, Niccolò's correspondence records the Machiavelli family's extensive efforts to locate profitable church properties for his brother Totto, who ultimately became a priest. On November 3, 1503, a relative wrote of the discovery of two abbeys that were potentially suitable because Cardinal Giulio de' Medici had the right to repossess them. The suggestion that Niccolò contact the cardinal about these church properties makes sense if the second chancellor has personal relations with some of the Medici and their allies.

Niccolò's attitude to Piero Soderini was more complicated. After Soderini had been elected for life, in the fall of 1502, the second chancellor—who had to be reelected each year—had little choice if he was to remain in government service. Outwardly, he worked energetically with Soderini. But some letters and texts suggest Niccolò's private reservations toward Soderini for his frequent compromises and cautions. Conversely, when Soderini fell from power, Niccolò actively sought to reestablish close ties with the Medici family—and persisted in so doing until he was successful.

A chancellor needed to be well trained in the classics. Diplomatic correspondence was often couched in Latin. More important, the job required an ability to write rapidly and accurately, not only from dictation by political superiors, but also whenever governmental affairs required a report or summary of a problem. In twentieth-century terms, the government of Florence was run by men of letters rather than specialists in public policy.

The position of chancellor also normally required experience or seniority. Niccolò's sponsor, the first chancellor and soon his immediate superior, was Marcello Virgilio Adriani, a professor of humanistic studies at the university who continued to teach while in office. Niccolò's most serious rival for appointment as second chancellor was a teacher of rhetoric at the university. Such positions were thus usually held by professors or lawyers with extensive experience, not by unknown young men.

From the first, many established leaders in the government were highly pleased by Niccolò's ability to write a clear, insightful, and politically valuable analysis of complicated matters. After taking office, Niccolò quickly gained the trust of figures in the government outside the circle associated with the Medici and their allies. As a highly placed correspondent wrote Niccolò after reading one of the second chancellor's dispatches, "Your essay and the description could not have been more appreciated, and people recognize what I in particular have always recognized in you: a clear, exact, and sincere account, upon which one can rely completely."

At one point while in office, he wrote Bartolomeo Vespucci, professor of astronomy at Padua, on the practical importance of studying astronomy and the absurdity of astrology. Machiavelli's letter to Vespucci is lost, but Vespucci answered him (in Latin) that "I can scarcely express with my tongue or inscribe with my pen the great joy I conceived in my mind just now when I received your utterly delightful letter. For your culture, well known to all, shone in it brighter than the sun."

During his first two years of service, Niccolò was particularly occupied by two ongoing challenges facing the new regime in Florence: first, the revolt of Pisa, which blocked Florentine merchants' access to the sea; second, diplomatic relations with France, a major factor in the city's conflicts with other Italian powers. The issues were intertwined by the complicating and rapidly shifting chaos of European foreign politics in the closing years of the fifteenth century.

One of the principal issues of the day concerned the long-standing hostility between Florence and Pisa. As a commercial center far inland, Florence had a long history of seeking to control the Arno all the way to the sea. Pisa had an equally long tradition of stubborn independence. Not surprisingly, many Florentines expressed a traditional hatred for the Pisans that was cordially reciprocated.

After many conflicts, Florence had finally acquired control over Pisa in 1406. Florence's enemies, notably Venice and Milan, had long sought to take over Pisa or at least deny the Florentines control over the route to the Mediterranean. In 1494, at the invitation of Ludovico Sforza in Milan, Charles VIII of France invaded Italy, seeking to establish claims to the Kingdom of Naples. At first he was opposed by Piero de' Medici, who had succeeded his father, Lorenzo the Magnificent, two years earlier. In the resulting battle, the French captured Pisa, allowing it to reclaim its independence.

Furious at Piero de' Medici's inability to hold Pisa, the Florentines removed Piero from power, ending Medici rule. After the interlude of Savonarola, the recapture of Pisa was a major focus of public attention. By 1498, the French had temporarily withdrawn their troops from Italy. At this time, with the support of Milan, a Florentine army under the condottiere Paolo Vitelli began a campaign against Pisa. The Venetians sought to come to the aid of the Pisans, but eventually gave up that effort in order to send their troops elsewhere. The Florentines then renewed their moves against Pisa, hopeful of taking the city now that it was abandoned by Venice and not protected by the French.

Niccolò, as secretary to the Ten of War, was absorbed in the endless details of these actions. In May 1499, he wrote his first state paper, the *Discourse on the Pisan War*. Soon thereafter, he was sent on his first mission, to Jacopo IV d'Appiano, the lord of Piombino and one of Florence's military captains. In July, a second and more important mission led him to negotiate with Ludovico Sforza's illegitimate daughter, Countess Caterina Sforza. One of Caterina's sons was a condottiere whose services were needed by more than one rival. It was not clear whether the condottiere would fight for Florence (as the countess claimed to want) or come to the aid of Duke Ludovico, at the time threatened by the oncoming French troops.

Niccolò went to Forlì, where he successfully handled the difficult negotiations with the wily countess and the Milanese envoy. Astutely, Niccolò secured favorable relations without having to pay for the condottiere's services. Just as Niccolò returned home, the Florentine army under Paolo Vitelli defeated the Pisans and seemed on the verge of taking the city. However, Vitelli unaccountably failed to follow up on his victory—some claiming it was treason, others blaming undue caution. The Signoria decided the next step in secret, apparently with Niccolò present: Vitelli, the unsuccessful captain general, was captured, returned to Florence, tortured, and put to death.

At this moment, the troops of French King Louis XII arrived in Italy and drove Duke Ludovico Sforza from power in Milan. Immediately thereafter, with the assistance of the notoriously corrupt Pope Alexander VI, King Louis made more trouble by helping the pope's illegitimate son, Cesare Borgia, conquer Imola and Forlì. Now Florence had a potential threat from Cesare (to the east) as well as a war with Pisa (to the west).

The Signoria of Florence managed to hire the French troops for a campaign to retake Pisa. The threat from Cesare was thereby somewhat reduced while Pisa was directly engaged. By June 1500, an army of French and Swiss mercenaries moved on the besieged city. Since the Florentines were paying for the war, two commissioners were sent to the camp outside Pisa. Niccolò was attached to the commissioners, sometimes joining them with the French army and sometimes returning to his office in the Palazzo Vecchio. Then one of the commissioners fell ill and left, increasing young Niccolò's responsibilities.

Once again a mercenary army in the pay of Florence seemed to have defeated the Pisans, who offered to surrender on condition that the occupation of their city be delayed a month. But despite Niccolò's advice that the terms be accepted, the remaining commissioner in the field rejected them. The French troops hesitated, then alleged they had not been paid, and abandoned the campaign; the Swiss mercenaries mutinied, holding the Florentine commissioner captive until he produced a ransom of thirteen hundred ducats. Niccolò, ordered to return to Florence by the commissioner, had to inform the Signoria of the ignominious failure of yet another attempt to take Pisa.

It was necessary to renew negotiations with the French king in hopes of fulfilling the promised military campaign and thereby at last secure Florence's access to the sea. The Signoria named two envoys—Francesco della Casa and Niccolò Machiavelli. On July 18, 1500, a little over two years after beginning his career, Niccolò left Florence on his first major diplomatic mission to a royal court (and his first trip outside Italy). In August, the envoys first met Louis XII and his foreign minister (an encounter described in *The Prince*); Niccolò was not to get back to Florence until January 14, 1501.

The negotiations were difficult. The French demanded more money for a new campaign. The Florentine envoys did not have authorization for such payment. The fear was that the French would denounce their alliance with Florence, leaving the commercial republic without troops and at the mercy of other forces in Italy. The Florentines were especially worried about

Cesare Borgia, who was establishing control over one town after another in the Romagna, to the east of Tuscany. Worse, Cesare was said to envisage a restoration of Piero de' Medici as ruler in Florence. And by astute negotiations, Niccolò kept Louis XII from abandoning the alliance with Florence until the Signoria agreed to resume payments for military protection.

At all costs it was necessary to keep the impatient French from denouncing their long-standing support of Florence. Louis XII moved his court repeatedly; the envoys followed; della Casa claimed illness and left for Paris, leaving Niccolò alone. In the negotiations, Niccolò found himself with few resources and a need to temporize. Throughout the six months of this mission to the French court, it was Niccolò who wrote the dispatches to the Signoria and the Ten of War. These reports were widely praised in Florence. And by astute negotiation, Niccolò kept Louis XII from abandoning the alliance with Florence until the Signora agreed to resume payments for military protection.

Looking back on his mission to France when he wrote *The Prince*, Niccolò makes it clear that by this time he had already learned a good deal about politics:

> *Thus, King Louis lost Lombardy for not having observed any of the conditions observed by others who have taken provinces and wished to hold them. Nor is this any miracle, but very ordinary and reasonable. And I spoke of this matter at Nantes with Rouen [the king's foreign minister] when Valentino (for so Cesare Borgia, son of Pope Alexander, was called by the people) was occupying Romagna. For when the cardinal of Rouen said to me that the Italians do not understand war, I replied to him that the French do not understand the state, because if they understood they would not have let the Church come to such greatness.*

Niccolò returned to his native city early in 1501 as a seasoned diplomat. He had been on a series of difficult missions, negotiating under extremely trying circumstances with Countess Caterina Sforza, with the French and Swiss before Pisa, and in the royal court of France. In these missions, he

Niccolò Achieves Power / 73

had acquitted himself well both in face-to-face encounters with powerful leaders and in detailed reports to the government in Florence.

Niccolò's selection as second chancellor may have been a stroke of luck; now, as he went back to his office in the Palazzo Vecchio, some in the Signoria saw him as a valuable and respected official. In 1498, he had been a poet in search of political office. In 1501, Niccolò was an established secretary of the Florentine republic. But the security of the republic was highly uncertain. The Arno still flowed through Pisa, and Pisa remained independent.

Chapter 5

THE MEETING

(1501-1503)

❖

In January 1501, as Niccolò returned to the Palazzo Vecchio after his mission to France, there was cause for worry. With neither its own army nor money in the treasury, what could the Signoria do to preserve Florence and her independence? Savonarola had left the city more or less bankrupt and defenseless. Wealthy aristocrats and businessmen tried to block government actions that they felt were against their interests. And the populace was helpless without leadership, but shy of trusting anyone after what happened under Savonarola.

To secure military forces, Florence had either to hire a condottiere, who could recruit and lead troops, or to ally with a foreign ruler, who would have his own army—and his own agenda. Neither was reliable and both cost money. In April 1502, for example, the city signed an agreement with the French, who were to provide an army to capture Pisa for Florence at a price of forty thousand ducats a year for three years.

Many Florentines wanted above all to capture Pisa and ensure commercial access to foreign markets, but did not want to pay taxes to support the war. In the years from 1498 to 1502, direct taxes from customs, tax stamps, the salt monopoly, and gate tolls raised on the average under 140,000 ducats a year. Special taxes and forced loans were required to fund military operations and other government expenses—and when revenue fell short, the government had recourse to unsecured loans. The rich aristocratic families resented taxes aimed at them; other citizens claimed that the tax system crippled them while benefiting the wealthy (who received interest on government loans).

By 1501, the situation became critical. In addition to the war in Pisa, there were serious challenges to Florentine control of Pistoia to the north and Arezzo to the east. The city seemed helpless to defend itself. Within Florence, things also reached a critical point. The Great Council refused to vote new taxes. Treasury officials resigned, asserting that they could not meet their legal obligations to raise public funds. Over four hundred thousand ducats were on loan from wealthy citizens, with little prospect of retiring the debt. Conflicts between the leading aristocratic families and the less affluent citizens were paralyzing the government.

The principal external threat came from Pope Alexander VI, who was if anything more ambitious than his predecessors. And his ambitions were neither pious nor otherworldly. He was using his son, Cesare Borgia, as an instrument to control the Romagna, thereby giving the papacy unquestioned political dominance throughout central Italy. Aided by papal support, young Cesare—like many other condottieri bold and cruel, but also inordinately ambitious, unpredictable, and scheming—was collecting an army with units from France, Germany, and numerous petty rulers in Italy. Few wanted to say no to the pope, and the result was an army controlled entirely by Alexander and his son.

After the Romagna, the next target for Cesare Borgia's army could well be Tuscany. Among Florence's leaders, this fear was reinforced by the presence of the deposed Piero de' Medici among Cesare's supporters. A defeat by Borgia would probably lead to the overthrow of the republic and the restoration of Medici rule in Florence.

As one citizen told a consultative assembly in January 1502, "The illness of the city is so severe that we do not have much time to look for medicine." The chanceries were buried with work in these difficult times.

Niccolò—who had married Marietta Corsini in August 1501—was dispatched on brief missions to Pistoia (in revolt), Cascina, Siena, and again to Pistoia. In the summer of 1502, he would be sent on the first of two diplomatic missions to the court of Cesare Borgia.

Meanwhile, after the fall of his former patron Duke Ludovico Sforza, Leonardo had been seeking a job without success. In 1500, Leonardo sent his money to Florence for safekeeping and left Milan with the mathematician Pacioli and his ward, Salai (who had joined his household as a beautiful boy of ten in 1490). Leonardo had been offered a position by Cesare Borgia, but turned it down. He visited Mantua, but his stay there was brief despite the invitation of Isabella d'Este, Sforza's sister-in-law: Isabella's importuning requests for a portrait confirmed her reputation as an overly demanding patron of the arts. After his years at the court in Milan, Leonardo needed more—more money to support the style of life appropriate to his genius, more contact and influence with people who mattered, more opportunity to continue his scientific studies.

Venice beckoned, opulent, powerful, and independent of the papacy. Under threat from the Turks, the Venetians might well need Leonardo's services as a specialist in military technology. A visit there did not work out well, however. Venice was a republic governed by a Senate of powerful families, and neither the senators nor the doge seemed likely to understand his independent genius. So, after proposing plans for the Venetians to improve their defenses, lagoons, and water supplies, Leonardo came back to Florence in the spring of 1500. There he found himself without powerful patronage, living from "day to day," studying mathematics with Pacioli and casting about for a stable situation.

Leonardo was given lodging and food by the Servite monks of Santissima Annunziata, where in April 1501 he finished a cartoon, or basic drawing, for the *Virgin and Child with Saint Anne*—the famous painting now in the Louvre (Figure 5.1). Vasari claimed, in his *Lives of the Artists*, that when the cartoon for the painting was put on display for several days, all who saw it were "stupefied by its perfection." Even so, Leonardo did not

FIGURE 5.1. Leonardo, Cartoon, *Virgin and Child with Saint Anne* (ca. 1501?). This cartoon differs in some respects from the famous painting now in the Louvre. Vasari says that the cartoon of this subject astounded those who first saw it, but his description corresponds more closely to the version in the Louvre.

find the income, status, and influence he sought in Florence. Given the political uncertainties in the city, perhaps this should not have been a surprise.

In the spring of 1501, Cesare Borgia took Faenza, controlling the route from Florence northeastward to Ravenna on the Adriatic (see map, Plate I). Having expanded his power in the Romagna, Cesare demanded that the Florentines form an alliance, paying him for military services. Without waiting for an answer, his troops advanced almost to the walls of Florence. Rumors circulated that aristocratic families were in league with Cesare to overthrow the city's popular government.

The French, still allied with Florence, demanded that Cesare leave, and the city paid him handsomely to do so. Borgia moved his army around to the southwest of the city, besieging Piombino on the Ligurian coast. In September, Cesare took control of Piombino and deposed its ruler, Jacopo IV d'Appiani. Meanwhile in Arezzo, to the southeast of Florence, Cesare's lieutenant, Vitellozzo Vitelli, had engineered a revolt against Florentine control. A Florentine force attacking the Pisan countryside was quickly withdrawn, but this did not prevent Cesare's forces from gaining one town after another in the Val di Chiana, the area of the headwaters of the Arno.

At this time, for unknown reasons, Leonardo changed his mind and accepted the position of architect and general engineer in the service of Cesare Borgia. Some say that he did this for status and potential influence with the pope's son. Others think that powerful men in Florence may have suggested that Leonardo take the position to convince Cesare to expand in directions other than Tuscany and perhaps to work covertly on Florence's behalf as an informant, if not a spy. Money is a third possibility, since Leonardo had not had a stable income since he left Milan. Leonardo's *Notebooks* show that he traveled through Cesare's territories in the summer and fall of 1502: in July, Leonardo was in Piombino; then in Siena, Arezzo, Urbino, Pesaro, Rimini, and Cesena.

Cesare Borgia's successes frightened the Signoria of Florence. After he had captured Urbino in June of 1502 and been given the title of duke by his father, the pope, Cesare asked the Florentines to send him an official emissary. Francesco Soderini, bishop of Volterra, was dispatched with Niccolò as his secretary. The mission was brief and, because Florence could not make a permanent alliance with Borgia without offending France, necessarily inconclusive. (It seems the secretary more than satisfied the ambassador because, several months later, Bishop Soderini wrote to him as a "very dear friend.")

Because Leonardo was traveling widely throughout the summer, it is not clear whether he was in Urbino when Bishop Soderini and Niccolò were on their brief mission to Cesare's court. In Leonardo's travels, his typically inquisitive behavior may well have caused difficulties with Cesare's captains (some of whom were difficult to control). On August 18, 1502, Cesare Borgia signed a document formally confirming Leonardo's position and giving him permission to continue to travel without hindrance:

> *To all our lieutenants, castellans, captains, condottieri, officers, soldiers, and subjects who read this document: We order and command this: that to our most excellent and dearly beloved architect and general engineer Leonardo da Vinci, bearer of this pass, charged with inspecting the places and fortresses of our states, so that we may maintain them according to their needs and on his advice, all will allow free passage, without subjecting him to any public tax either on himself or his companions, and to welcome him with amity, and allow him to measure and examine anything he likes. To this effect, provide him with the men he requests and give him any aid, assistance, and favor he asks for. We desire that for any work to be executed within our states, each engineer be required to confer with him and to conform to his judgment. Let no man act otherwise unless he wishes to incur our wrath.*

Once again, Leonardo was in the position of advisor to a powerful, ambitious—and in this case, ruthless—leader.

Back in Florence, to address the governmental crisis, a major constitutional reform was adopted: the election of a *gonfaloniere* of justice (head of state) for life. In September 1502, Piero Soderini was chosen from a field of 236 candidates. Patrician and moderate, Soderini's father had been associated with the Medici regime. Originally supported by many aristocrats—including some, like the Salviati family, who were to become implacable enemies—Soderini sought to reconcile competing interests while opening many issues to broad public discussion (a method strongly opposed by many of the wealthy aristocrats).

The choice seemed to be good news for Niccolò. Given his relations with Piero's brother, Francesco Soderini, Niccolò could expect to be in a position of influence. Niccolò hastened to write a "charming letter" of congratulations to the new *gonfaloniere*. Bishop Francesco replied for his brother, thanking the chancellor for his "affection for the fatherland and for my family." Bishop Soderini added that Niccolò's support was all the "more welcome" because he was "second to none in ability and affection."

In October, Cesare Borgia took up residence in Imola, to be joined by Leonardo. This small city, on the main road from Bologna to Rimini, was to be fortified, thus giving Cesare a powerful position between Florence and the Adriatic Sea. For Florence, the strategic threat of military encirclement was combined with the increased vulnerability of overland trade, previously compromised to the west by the Pisans and now to the east by Borgia. For Cesare, Imola—particularly if its fortress, La Rocca (Figure 5.2), were to be made impregnable—could be a central location for a court.

In addition to proposing architectural renovations for the fortress of La Rocca (Figure 5.3), Leonardo set to work to map Imola precisely. From his sketches (Figure 5.4), we can see that Leonardo paced the distances of streets to gain absolute precision. The result (Plate VI) is one of the most accurate and beautiful maps drawn in the Renaissance, with a detail that resembles the aerial reconnaissance photographs made possible only when, in the twentieth century, Leonardo's dream of the airplane was finally realized.

As we can see from Leonardo's map, Imola was a relatively small town. In October 1502, the Florentine government again sent an envoy to Cesare's court. Would it have been possible for two inquisitive

FIGURE 5.2. La Rocca, the fortress at Imola, where Cesare Borgia made his headquarters in the fall of 1502.

Florentines, one very famous and the other on an official government mission, to spend several months in a place of this size without meeting each other?

The historian Francesco Guicciardini later explained the mission as follows: "so as to keep [Cesare Borgia] on our side with some sort of favorable actions, the Ten sent Niccolò Machiavelli, chancellor of the Ten, to [Borgia] in Imola." Niccolò did not particularly want to go on this mission. And given the known dangers of Cesare Borgia's volatile personality, he did not want to stay in Borgia's court for any length of time. But the mission was of the highest importance if Cesare was to be persuaded to leave the Florentines in peace until they received military support from the French king and resolved the chaotic financial and political situation of their city. As it turned out, Niccolò was to remain with the duke of Urbino until January of the following year, distracting Cesare by the promise of an alliance without actually committing himself.

The importance of Niccolò's mission to Imola was underscored in a letter Piero Soderini wrote him shortly after taking office in November 1502. As the newly elected *gonfaloniere* emphasized, ensuring that Cesare Borgia not attack Florence was especially critical given the city's domestic crisis.

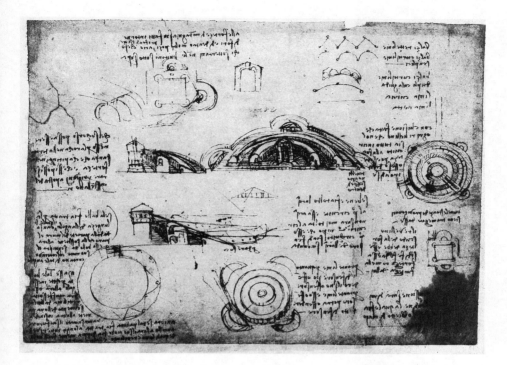

FIGURE 5.3. Leonardo, Sketch of La Rocca and fortification designs. While in Imola working on Cesare Borgia's fort of La Rocca (upper left), Leonardo considered the radical changes in fortification required by the development of artillery. Combined with dry defensive ditches, the innovative low, rounded walls would allow defenders to fire at attacking forces, and would cause incoming cannonballs to ricochet. Such designs were later endorsed in Machiavelli's *Art of War*.

As Piero Soderini put it: "We have found the city very disorganized in respect to money, allotments and many other things, as must be very well known to you."

Piero Soderini and the Signoria wanted Niccolò in Imola specifically because of his skill in reporting complex diplomatic situations. One highly placed correspondent, whose letter of October 1502 praised Niccolò's ability to produce "a clear, exact and sincere account," added: "Your judgment is desired here about affairs over there, and your description of the French ones, and the hopes the Duke has about them." When Niccolò again indicated to his colleagues his desire to return home, Piero Soderini

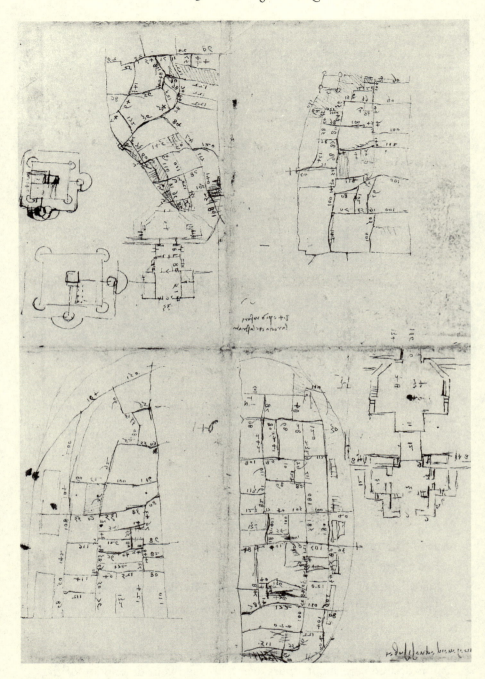

FIGURE 5.4. Working sketches for map of Imola (ca. 1502). Folded in four, this sheet apparently records Leonardo's own paced measurements of Imola; the upper left image quadrant also shows two sketches of La Rocca. For the final version, see Plate VI.

wrote personally to encourage him to stay longer and continue his careful reports of Cesare Borgia's behavior and intentions.

While in Borgia's court, Niccolò had to be careful what he wrote. He noted that: "it's part of my assignment to write you [the Signoria] how many visitors are at this nobleman's court, where they are staying, and many other local particulars." His letters were indeed full of references both to Cesare's leading lieutenants and "secretaries" (including one named Messer Agobito) and to "visitors" to his court (including, in a letter dated November 3, "Monsignore di Montison . . . Baron di Bierra, Monsignore Lo Grafis et Monsignore di Borsu, luoghitenenti di Fois, Miolans et Dunais").

Although such intelligence was highly valued by the Signoria, in all his dispatches and letters from Imola, Niccolò never mentioned Leonardo by name.

By 1502, Leonardo was a famous man, though this reputation was based primarily on his artistic abilities, whereas less was known of his expertise in architecture, military technology, and natural science. In a small town like Imola, such a figure was unlikely to be invisible as he paced the streets making measurements for his detailed map. Having been officially "charged with inspecting the places and fortresses of [Cesare's] states," Leonardo was engaged in reinforcing the fortress at Imola. He would thus have been among the most important people for Niccolò to interview. As soon as Leonardo's presence in Imola was known, even an emissary not as efficient and inquisitive as Niccolò Machiavelli would have tried to seek him out.

More tantalizing, in the first days of November, Niccolò's official reports to the Signoria depart sharply from the practice of naming everyone of importance with whom he speaks. Suddenly, in writing to his superiors, Niccolò frequently refers to a nameless figure in Cesare's court. On November 1, Niccolò reported that after talking to Cesare's aide Messer Agobito, he verified that conversation by talking "to another who is also acquainted with the Lord's secrets." On November 3, Niccolò reported on a "long" discussion with "one of the first Secretaries [of Cesare] who confirmed everything I wrote in my other letters." By November 8, Niccolò wrote of an anonymous "friend" whose analysis of Cesare is worthy of attention.

Sometimes, the most important clue in a criminal investigation is the evidence that a dog did *not* bark, especially if the dog typically barks at strangers and the leading suspect is well known in the household. Could there be a good reason for Niccolò to be silent about meeting Leonardo in Imola? One plausible explanation arises from the behavior of Cesare Borgia during the fall of 1502. Readers of *The Prince* have long been struck by Niccolò's apparent praise of Cesare in chapter 7. There, after asserting that "Cesare Borgia . . . did all those things that should be done by a prudent and virtuous man to put his roots in the states that the arms and fortune of others had given him," Machiavelli describes the actions of Alexander VI and his son in the first years of the century:

> *Once the duke [Cesare Borgia] had taken over Romagna, . . . he judged it necessary to give it good government, if he wanted to reduce it to peace and obedience to a kingly arm. So he put there Messer Remirro de Orco [Lorqua], a cruel and ready man, to whom he gave the fullest power. In a short time Remirro reduced it to peace and unity, with the very greatest reputation for himself. Then the duke judged that such excessive authority was not necessary, because he feared that it might become hateful; and he set up a civil court in the middle of the province, with a most excellent president, where each city had its advocate. And because he knew that past rigors had generated some hatred for Remirro, to purge the spirits of that people and to gain them entirely to himself, he wished to show that if any cruelty had been committed, this had not come from him but from the harsh nature of his minister. And having seized this opportunity, he had him placed one morning in the piazza at Cesena in two pieces, with a piece of wood and a bloody knife beside him. The ferocity of this spectacle left the people at once satisfied and stupified.*

Niccolò knew whereof he spoke, since he was in Cesena with the court and saw the "spectacle" firsthand. Cesare himself had written that his "wrath"

Plate I. Northern Italy in the fifteenth century. As the map shows, the Republic of Florence controlled a large region, as did the papacy, Milan, Venice, and Naples (the main contenders for power within the Italian peninsula). Boundaries shown as of 1454.

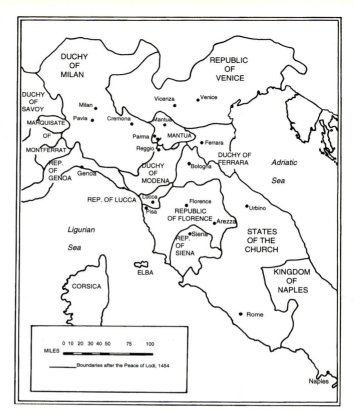

Plate II. Leonardo da Vinci, Sketch of the Arno (1473). Leonardo's earliest known drawing captures a view of the Arno valley from the hills. He grew up seeing views like this around his native Vinci. The writing in the upper left, in Leonardo's habitual mirror-image, left-to-right notation, gives the date of the drawing (August 5, 1473).

Plate III. Leonardo, Bird's-eye view of the Arno (ca. 1502–3). This extraordinary map uses an imagined aerial view to present topography for the entire Arno valley, the setting of both the military diversion of the river at Pisa and the more ambitious plan to open navigation to Florence. There are traces of wax on the back, and names are written from left to right, indicating that this map was among those used for a public presentation.

Plate IV. Leonardo, Arno from Empoli to Pisa (ca. 1503–4?). A preliminary sketch of the course of the Arno, apparently from the early phase of Leonardo's plans for the river. Pisa is at the bottom of the sketch; Empoli is at the top. Leonardo's measurements of distance indicate his concern for exact scale. Vinci is noted at the upper left.

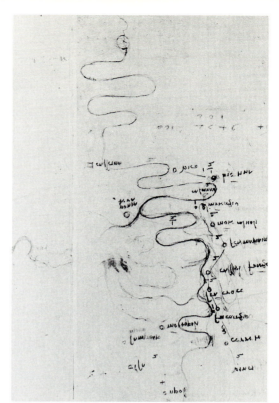

Plate V. Leonardo, Two routes of canal from Arno to the sea (ca. 1503–4?). A sketch of possible routes to make the Arno navigable, probably for the peaceful development of the valley. In addition to two different routes north through Pistoia, the map (at A) indicates the shorter canal between Florence and Signa that Fancelli had proposed in 1487. Beside the map Leonardo wrote this fragment: "The law which establishes that those who want to make mills can conduct water through any land, paying twice its value."

Plate VI. Leonardo, Map of Imola (ca. 1502). Dating from the months when both Leonardo and Niccolò were in Imola, Leonardo's finished work has been called "the most accurate and beautiful map of its era" (Martin Clayton, *A Curious Vision*, p. 94). For the working sketches of this map, see Figure 5.4.

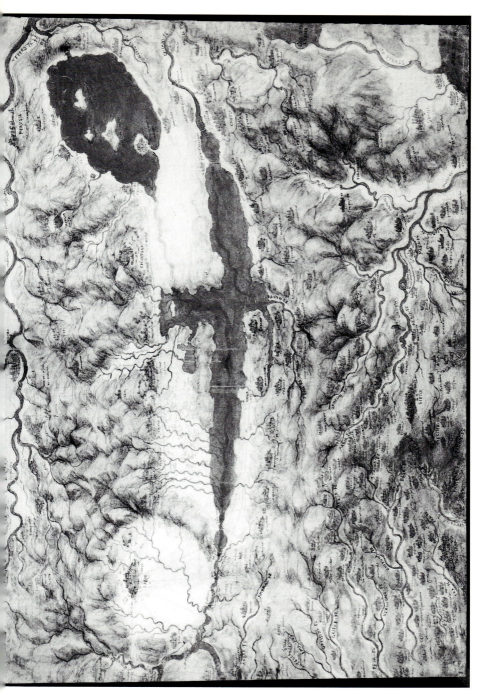

Plate VII. Leonardo, Val di Chiana (ca. 1502–3). Traces of wax on the back of this sheet, and the careful writing from left to right, show that this map was used for a public presentation. The distortions, unusual for Leonardo's maps, permit a view of the complex relationship between the headwaters of the Arno and the Tiber.

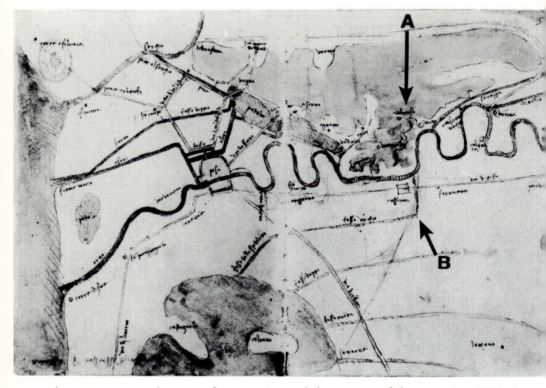

Plate VIII. Leonardo, Map of Pisa region and the estuary of the Arno (ca. 1503–4). Leonardo's map shows the site of the Arno diversion, with place names written from left to right; La Verruca ("Verrucola") is noted (at A). In this map, there is a single canal joining the Arno (at B), draining the river into the Stagno by two possible routes, not the twin ditches joining the Arno to the Stagno that were dug to implement the plan (see Figure 7.4).

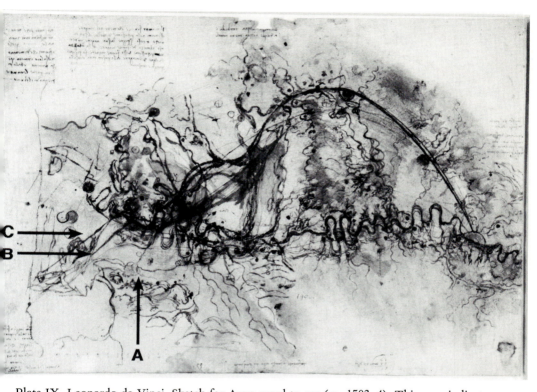

Plate IX. Leonardo da Vinci, Sketch for Arno canal to sea (ca. 1503–4). This map indicates alternate routes for the diversion at Pisa, showing both the route of the military project and two possible routes below Pisa consistent with his earlier peacetime project. In the margin, Leonardo wrote: "Prato, Pistoia, and Pisa, as well as Florence, will gain 200,000 ducats a year, and will lend a hand and money to this useful work." A denotes the route to Stagno di Livorno for military diversion; B and C denote routes directly to the sea, west of Pisa.

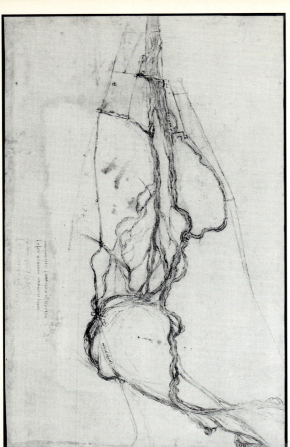

Plate X. Leonardo, A stretch of the Ar[no] (1504). Leonardo's preparatory drawing [of] the river just west of Florence, showing h[is] plans for improving the flow as part of t[he] broader project of making the river navigab[le]. A close inspection of the original shows t[he] compass holes Leonardo used to make t[he] presentation copy.

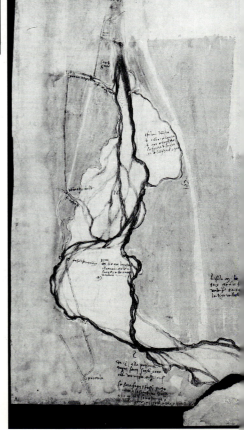

Plate XI. Leonardo, A stretch of the Arno (1504). The polished version of Plate X, with places named in left-to-right script. This map shows not only that Leonardo's plans for hydraulic engineering along the Arno included nonmilitary improvements at Florence itself, but that they were prepared for presentation to decision-makers.

could be dangerous for subordinates—and as we know, Leonardo was one of those subordinates.

Later that fall, it was the turn of Cesare's military captains—who had temporarily united in hostility to the young duke—to discover how dangerous. Confronted with open disloyalty by Vitellozzo Vitelli, Oliverotto da Fermo, and his other condottieri, Cesare officially pardoned them and invited them to a conference in Sinigaglia. There, on December 31, "with a small escort and a smile on his lips, he went out to meet them at the city gates. . . . He invited them to meet informally in his rooms, then had them arrested and strangled, ignoring their pleas, without further form of trial." Or, as Machiavelli puts it more delicately in *The Prince*, "their simplicity brought them into the duke's hands at Sinigaglia. So, when these heads had been eliminated . . ."

Niccolò's reports from Imola during the fall of 1502 appear in a different light when Borgia's ruthlessness and impetuosity are kept in mind. In the Italian Renaissance, letters were frequently intercepted and never secure. Many passages in Niccolò's reports were written in code. His correspondence frequently makes mysterious allusions to "onions," "cloth" of various sorts, and items of clothing ("a cloak," "the mantle," "the velvet hat," "the hat . . . of several colors," a "doublet").

In a situation where such precautions were necessary, Niccolò's unnamed "friend" and informant would have been in mortal danger were his name to be divulged. One obvious explanation is that Niccolò's contact was Leonardo, who came from Florence and hence might easily have been viewed by Cesare as a spy.

By the summer of 1503, documentary evidence shows, Leonardo and Niccolò were working together on highly important military projects in the war against Pisa. The circumstantial evidence that they first met in Cesare's court during the fall of 1502 helps to explain why they started collaborating so quickly after Leonardo's return to Florence. The first project on which the second chancellor was to consult Leonardo in 1503 concerned the renovation of a fortress outside of Pisa, a job that utilized

Leonardo's skills as a military architect (largely unknown in Florence, but seen at first hand by Niccolò while he was in Imola). Moreover, the project of redirecting the Arno river and making Florence into a seaport, which also was initiated in 1503, depended on Leonardo's observations of the river's headwaters during his service as Cesare's architect and general engineer.

Mentioned by Vasari but long neglected, Leonardo's plans to alter the course of the Arno were sketched on maps discovered in Madrid only in the last thirty years (for example, Plates V, VIII). On the basis of a project he had first imagined while in Milan a decade earlier, Leonardo drew a detailed but puzzling map of the Val di Chiana, the area containing the headwaters of both the Arno and the Tiber, while in Cesare's service.

This map (Plate VII) is unusual because, unlike most of Leonardo's maps, it is oddly distorted. Commentators have not been sure why it was drawn. In the center is the large marshy pond out of which the headwaters of two major river systems flow—the Arno to the west and the Tiber to the east. The map is clearly not a sketch but a carefully finished image: towns are labeled in Leonardo's hand, with writing from left to right (unlike in his private notes). It shows both the Mediterranean and the course of the Tiber, even though to squeeze them in Leonardo had to foreshorten the distance to the sea and twist the Tiber's riverbed. In the famous map of the Arno (Plate III) and other maps intended for display, none of these distortions is present.

Some have claimed that the Val di Chiana map was drawn for Cesare Borgia on the occasion of an uprising in Arezzo that threatened the duke's control over the Romagna. But nothing in the map directs attention to this town. On the contrary, what is notable is Leonardo's insistence on showing the location of all of the major water systems flowing out of the valley. This makes sense if the map was related to the idea of developing the Arno.

Leonardo elsewhere notes that to execute his dream of moving the Arno, the river's flow would have to be controlled to ensure sufficient water depth throughout the year, including times of reduced rainfall. The technology of his project had a political prerequisite: the government that controlled Tuscany would have to control the Val di Chiana. To demonstrate this fact, a map would have to show both the complex flows of the two river systems flowing through the valley and their relationship to the sea. The distortions could therefore be explained if the map was drawn to convince someone in power of the prerequisites of a vast technological initiative.

The extraordinary map proves that during 1502–3, Leonardo spent a considerable amount of time surveying the water system of the headwaters of the Arno. As architect and general engineer to Cesare Borgia, Leonardo's principal responsibilities were the design of fortifications, urban architecture, and military technology. Work for Cesare does not explain the extensive observations needed to produce this map, and there is little evidence that Cesare Borgia had the slightest interest in the Val di Chiana's waterways.

Events during Niccolò's embassy in Imola, however, suggest why important people in *Florence* would have been very interested in Leonardo's map. While at Cesare's court in September of 1502, Niccolò received an urgent letter from his kinsman Lorenzo: a mule train carrying the goods of two Florentine merchants had been seized by Cesare's troops. Lorenzo Machiavelli wrote: "I beg you with all my might and for all the love that has ever been between us that, in any way you can assist the above-mentioned Marco [the mule driver], you do it with all diligence." About six weeks later, on October 22, Piero Soderini, the *gonfaloniere*, wrote personally about the same case, urging Niccolò to speak with Cesare Borgia and "beseech him" for their return *"over and over again."* The negotiations seem to have been protracted, however, because Soderini wrote of the these mules again on November 14, this time asking Niccolò to "make recommendations."

Marco the mule driver and his cargo symbolized a common problem for Florence. Shipments of goods by Florentine merchants were often intercepted and goods stolen. To get them back, money had to cross greedy palms. It was difficult to negotiate with roving armed men loosely controlled by freelance condottieri. The threat that Cesare's armies might encircle Florence, cutting off access to both the Ligurian Sea to the east and the Adriatic to the west, made the problem even more serious.

Such problems would disappear if Florence could gain a permanent naval outlet to the sea. Leonardo's Arno project would have exactly that result. Having profited from his freedom of movement as Cesare's engineer to map in detail the Val di Chiana, Leonardo was in a position to work intensively with Niccolò to implement such a plan when, after the spring of 1503, both found themselves back in Florence.

In the early months of 1503, the situation of Florence remained dangerous. After voting to allow the Signoria to borrow twenty-five thousand ducats to pay interest on the debt, from January to April the Great Council rejected tax bills. In an attempt to gain consensus for a solution to the financial crisis, Soderini called a consultative meeting with representatives of every flag company from the four quarters of the city.

Among the speeches was a violent denunciation of the government by a member of the Scala flag company named Luigi Mannelli. He charged that taxes were "being used by the rich to crush the poor," while the city was not defended against Borgia and his allies. Three days later, other representatives of this flag company were summoned and asked if Mannelli's speech had been authorized by the group as a whole; several said it was not. Soderini agreed with the advice of other magistrates and had Mannelli arrested. He was tortured, convicted, and sentenced to be deprived of political office for life and forbidden to enter the city for ten years. Republican government in Florence did not extend to unlimited free speech.

Such tension reflected the vulnerable foreign situation. The French, seeking to establish Louis XII's dynastic claim to the Kingdom of Naples, sustained a series of reverses in the south of Italy. Pope Alexander VI, supposedly allied with the French, began dallying with shifting his alliance to Spain.

Throughout the past fall, Niccolò's stalling tactics in the negotiations with Cesare had succeeded. By offering a promise of alliance without delivering an agreement, the secretary had kept an eye on the unpredictable Borgia, whose court and army kept moving, from Imola to Fano through the Romagna to Perugia. Although the French gave Borgia some troops, they too sought to keep him in check. For the security of Florence, the French alliance was still of the highest importance to the Signoria. And even so, if Louis XII were to be defeated and forced to leave Italy, the Venetians, the Spaniards, and the emperor might well combine with the pope to deprive Florence of her territories and her freedom.

These long-term strategic considerations were less pressing, however, than the persistent issue of Pisa. Florentine merchants needed an outlet to the sea. The new government needed a victory for prestige. Florence needed an army if it was to bring the besieged Pisans to their knees—not to mention defend itself from Cesare should he change his mind yet again.

In the early months of 1503, both Niccolò and Leonardo returned to Florence. The second chancellor was the first to return. By January of 1503, Piero Soderini and the Signoria were apparently convinced that little more could be gained by leaving Niccolò as an emissary in Cesare's court.

Sometime in the spring (probably in March), Leonardo also returned to Florence. Why he left Borgia's service has never been made clear. Fear of suffering the fate of Remirro Lorqua and the condottieri? Frustration from working with a suspicious, secretive, and brutal young man (Cesare was only twenty-seven), who gave Leonardo even less influence or attention than Duke Ludovico Sforza in Milan? Or—as a few have wondered—the end of his mission as a Florentine agent?

In the spring and summer of 1503, Leonardo was living on his own resources, drawing on savings from his accounts at Santa Maria Nuova. At this time, Niccolò's prestige had been enhanced by the departure of Borgia's army toward the south. Leonardo, without an income, was seeking new challenges. Niccolò was administratively responsible for the Pisan campaign, which was not showing signs of success. In the months that followed, Leonardo and Niccolò would bring their interests together in a stunning way.

Chapter 6

THE COLLABORATION BEGINS

(1503)

After the failure of the last two campaigns against Pisa, Soderini saw the advantage of Niccolò's suggestion to raise a citizen militia so the city would not have to depend on a foreign army or condottieri. There were, however, strong objections. To finance the recruitment, after much discussion a tithe was proposed that would fall on the clergy as well as the ordinary citizens. That would, of course, require papal approval, but first the Florentines themselves needed to agree to the idea. Niccolò wrote a speech in support of the proposal, apparently to be given by a member of Signoria before the assembly.

Negotiations with Pope Alexander VI required an emissary to Pandolfo Petrucci, the ruler of Siena, who was suspicious that Florence was seeking to remove him from power. To reassure Pandolfo that the main purpose of discussions with the pope was permission to tax the clergy, Niccolò left Florence on April 26, 1503. Pandolfo was reassured, but the negotiations with the papacy came to little beyond the purchase of a cardinal's hat for Bishop Francesco Soderini, Niccolò's friend, at the moment the Florentine ambassador to France. The price was twenty thousand gold ducats. The benefit was a vote in the College of Cardinals when the next pope was elected.

Meanwhile, since early March, if not before, Leonardo had been back in his native city. After he drew money from his account in Santa Maria Nuova on March 4, the direct evidence of his activity refers to a loan of four ducats to Attavante, painter of miniatures (April 8), purchases for his ward, Salai (April 8 and 20), and correspondence with a monk at Santa Croce (April 17). For Leonardo's other occupations, we have no unquestionable written evidence until early summer.

In the late spring, Niccolò was focusing his attention on the Pisan campaign now that Cesare Borgia's troops no longer threatened the city. In May, Niccolò wrote to the field urging actions to prevent the people of Lucca from providing aid to the Pisans. After the civil commissioner reported the capture of Librafatta, a strategic site between Pisa and Lucca (Plate VIII, top), Niccolò expressed his pleasure. On June 14, he wrote the commissioners responsible for the camp besieging the city on the need to follow up their military advance by taking the Pisan fortification, called La Verruca or Verrucola, on a rocky site to the east of Pisa (Plate VIII, center right). Because this stronghold (Figure 6.1) had been "always a continuous nuisance and impediment" to Florentine armies, Niccolò insisted that the army "act quickly, without losing an hour of time," to take the site.

The orders were followed. On June 19, word reached Florence that La

FIGURE 6.1. Ruins of La Verruca (or La Verrucola), the fort just outside Pisa. Leonardo's *Notebooks* (Codex Madrid II, folio 17, recto) contain a sketch of these fortifications drawn at the time of his visit in 1504, and accompanied by his calculations on work to be done at the site.

Verruca had been taken on the preceding day. On June 21, Leonardo was at the site, analyzing the existing fortification and proposing how it could be used by the armies of Florence. The field commissioner of the Pisan campaign, Pier Francesco Tosinghi, reported as follows:

> *Leonardo da Vinci, himself and company, came here and we showed him everything, and we think that he likes La Verruca very much, being well fitted to his taste. Afterwards, he said that he was thinking of having it made inexpugnable. But this is something to be set apart for the time being, for the main need is at Librafatta, which is not a small undertaking, nor one to be underestimated. This [La Verruca] ought to be repaired now to provide sufficient protection, and then it can be furnished to the required perfection.*

Leonardo's *Notebooks* contain a sketch of the site, on which he made many calculations, proving that he had carefully examined La Verruca in preparation for advising the Florentine government on its repair and fortification. On June 26, a master builder named Luca del Caprina was sent to carry out Leonardo's proposed repairs.

Whoever asked Leonardo da Vinci to undertake this mission knew his ability in advance, since he was on the site within two days of its capture. But Leonardo's principal experience as a military architect was in the service of Cesare Borgia during the preceding two years, and most of those who knew of him from his youth in Florence or his reputation in Milan would have had little reason to employ him as an architectural expert in fortifications. Did others in the Florentine government know that while Leonardo was in Imola in the fall of 1502, he worked on renovating La Rocca, the fort at Imola? Niccolò, who was there, would obviously have been aware of this—and as we know, his reports to the Signoria do not mention Leonardo.

Other military architects were available. Officially, the chief military architect of Florence was Antonio da Sangallo the Elder, who along with his brother Giuliano, also a well-known expert, may also have been consulted with regard to La Verruca. Leonardo's role is therefore hard to explain without assuming that Niccolò, the second chancellor, responsible for the capture and renovation of La Verruca, was already closely acquainted with Borgia's former architect and general engineer. Oddly enough, the only reference to La Verruca in Machiavelli's published writings occurs in the comedy *Mandragola* as a remark by the ridiculous Messer Nicia.

Leonardo's role as an advisor to the Florentine government was not limited to his architectural consultation on La Verruca. A month later, on July 24, 1503, Leonardo visited the camp of Pisa once again, this time as a hydraulic engineer *(maestro di acque)*. The report from the field reads:

> *Ex Castris, Franciscus Ghuiduccius, 24 July 1503. Yesterday one of your Signoria, Alexandro of the Albizi, was here together with Leonardo da Vinci and some others, who examined the plan in the presence of the governor and, after many discussions and doubts, they concluded that the work was very appropriate, whether Arno turned there or remained with a channel; in any case, it would provide that the hills could not be attacked by the enemies; they will tell you everything in person.*

What was this plan? Two days later, an entry in the account books of the Signoria of Florence gives us part of the answer:

> *Leonardo's trip to the camp below Pisa. Extra expenses, of the amount of 50.56 "soldi," must be paid for the 26th of July, 13 of them to Giovanni Piffero. This money has been spent to provide six-horse coaches and to pay the board expenses for the expedition with Leonardo in the territory of Pisa to divert Arno from its course and take it away from Pisa.*

Confronted with the failure of two military attacks on Pisa by mercenary troops, and lacking a large army of their own, the Signoria were discussing a plan to use technology instead, diverting the Arno River to deprive the Pisans of water and thereby forcing them into submission. Once proposed, the plan was strongly supported by both Soderini and Niccolò against strong opposition both within the government and at military headquarters outside Pisa.

Critics who viewed the plan to divert the Arno as fantasy doubtless had in mind Brunelleschi's fiasco seventy years earlier. The result of that attempted use of a river for strategic purposes had been recorded in 1440, soon after the fact, by Giovanni Cavalcanti:

> *[In Florence] there were some capricious people (among whom was Filippo di ser Brunellesco) who advised, and with their false and deceitful science of geometry (not in itself, but in the ignorance of others) demonstrated, that the city of Lucca could be flooded, and therefore with their arts which were not well learned they devised a scheme and the foolish people cheered that it had been done.*

Perhaps with this example, opponents of the new plan at first carried the day in the Signoria.

Despite this opposition, Niccolò and Soderini continued to urge the project. Niccolò probably had been thinking of using the river as a weapon even before Leonardo's second trip to the camp at Pisa. On July 1, he wrote the commissioners, urging them to convince the people of Lucca not to help the Pisans "with *so much as a glass of water*" and threatening them that if the Lucchese did so, the Florentine army would "have to pursue them within the walls of Lucca." The capture of Librafatta was part of a coherent strategy to isolate Pisa from aid from the north and west, and then deprive the city of water by diverting the Arno to the east of the city.

There were good reasons to believe that the projected diversion could prove successful. One was the strategic difference between flooding a city into submission (as Dante had imagined and Brunelleschi attempted) and diverting a river to deprive the besieged population of water.

We know that, later in life, Niccolò was aware of this difference because of the way he described Brunelleschi's failure in his *Florentine Histories*:

> *In those times [1434] there was a most excellent architect in Florence, called Filippo di ser Brunelleschi, of whose works our city is full.... He*

showed how Lucca could be flooded, considering the site of the city and the bed of the river Serchio; and so much did he urge it that the Ten commissioned the experiment to be made. But nothing came of it other than disorder in our camp and security for the enemy, for the Lucchese raised the earth with a dike on the side where the Serchio was being made to come and then one night they broke the dike of the ditch through which the water was flowing. Thus, the water found the way toward Lucca blocked and the dike of the channel open, and it flooded the plain so that not only could the army not get near the town but it had to draw off.

When Brunelleschi had tried to flood Lucca, Machiavelli implies, Florentine soldiers could not patrol the riverbank nearest the target city; to defeat the strategem, the besieged had merely to come out to their side of the river, build a dike to protect their city—and then breach the dike on the other bank, thereby turning the tables and flooding the Florentine camp.

In contrast, the plan discussed by Leonardo and others on July 24 was militarily defensible as long as Florentine soldiers could be stationed between the point of diversion and Pisa itself (Plate VIII). Presumably this is what is meant by Francesco Guiducci's report that Leonardo and the others "concluded that the work was very appropriate, whether Arno turned there or remained with a channel; in any case, *it would provide that the hills could not be attacked by the enemies.*" One of the hills was, of course, La Verruca, taken and refortified at Niccolò's insistence (Figure 6.1).

Assuming Niccolò was already aware of this strategic factor in 1503, Soderini could have dismissed comparisons with the earlier disaster. But how could he be sure that the Arno would flow in the predicted manner? There were "many discussions and doubts" raised by those visiting the site of the proposed diversion on July 24, later reinforced by the objections by the military commander and civil commissioner in the field. Even today, some experts say the plan was "utopian from the beginning."

The selection of the experts to design and assess the project in Pisa was obviously of particular importance. On July 24, when a member of the governing Signoria was sent to the site to determine the feasibility of the diversion, Leonardo da Vinci was the only hydraulic engineer in the group who was indicated by name. Several weeks before, he had been sent to the field as a military architect, but who in the government would have known and trusted Leonardo's expertise as a hydraulic engineer?

At this time, Leonardo was known more for painting, sculpture, or music than for science and technology. Even three years later, when Charles d'Amboise, the French governor of Milan, wrote the Signoria asking that Leonardo be allowed to stay in that city rather than return to Florence, he noted that "Master Leonardo da Vinci, your fellow citizen, . . . already famous for painting, remains comparatively unknown when one thinks of the praises he merits for his other gifts." When d'Amboise wrote this, in 1506, Leonardo was engaged—among other things—in the redesign of the canals around Milan. It would seem that, in 1503, only someone who had extensive contact with Leonardo would have known of his deep knowledge of the flow of rivers and his studies of the Arno valley. The most likely person was Niccolò.

The diversion of the Arno was not an isolated military action to defeat Pisa, but merely the first step in Leonardo's grandiose plan to create a seaport for Florence. Leonardo's drawings provide direct evidence of this. Among many maps associated with projects to change the flow of the Arno, the most important is a rough pen-and-wash sketch of the entire Arno valley, showing the bold project to make the river navigable from Florence to the sea (Plate IX). Among other things, the route in this plan involved going under or over a mountain pass called Serravalle. Leonardo's notes indicated he opted for the tunnel. The difficulty of the military diversion pales in comparison to a plan for a canal of the Arno running north through Pistoia, and requiring a tunnel through a mountain!

The map sketching this project coincides with many new sketches dating from 1503–4 that show how to straighten the course of the Arno at Florence itself, design locks, and use the Arno's water for mills and irrigation while making the river navigable. It also shows three different solutions for altering the course of the Arno at Pisa:

- The canal farthest to the east (Plate IX, at A) brings the Arno from a point above the city into the Stagno di Livorno, a large pond and marsh—

since drained—to the south of Pisa. This site corresponds to the military diversion discussed on July 24, 1503, and approved by the Signoria the following month.

• The middle canal and the one farthest to the west (Plate IX at B and C) lie below Pisa, and draw the Arno directly to the sea. These alternative sites would be suited for the pacific project of rendering the Arno navigable, but useless in the military project.

Another feature of the map is visible only if one has the opportunity to inspect it with care. It was Leonardo's practice, when making a map for public display, to sketch a draft and then, using a pin to prick out the lines of crucial landmarks, use the draft to prepare a finished, colored drawing of exquisite detail. This map has such pin marks. More important, the marks include *two* of the routes for a diversionary canal, one military (Plate IX, at A) and another economic (at B).

It is to these two routes that, apparently, Guiducci referred in his memorandum of July 24 when saying that the project would be feasible "whether Arno turned there or remained with a channel" while passing Pisa itself. Leonardo thus made some form of public presentation in which he connected the military proposal to his own suggestions for transforming the Arno River valley. This may explain why the Signoria was eventually persuaded by Soderini in the summer of 1504, since the economic benefits of Leonardo's broader project fulfilled a goal that had been discussed by the government of Florence since the early fourteenth century.

Other maps now in the Windsor Collection and in Madrid demonstrate that Leonardo prepared a public presentation of his project for the economic development of the Arno valley. Among these are a pair of maps showing the proposed changes of the Arno in the city of Florence itself, one a draft and the other a polished version with careful writing from left to right (Plates X and XI).

Several texts in Leonardo's *Notebooks* apparently written at this time refer to the project in a way that suggests he even drafted a document explaining it. In one note, he points out that although the route by way of

Pistoia may seem long, it actually would reduce the distance separating Florence from the sea: "56 miles by the Arno from Florence to Vico; by the Pistoia canal it is 44 miles. Thus it is 12 miles shorter by that canal than by the Arno." Another entry emphasizes economic benefits that will result from the irrigation made possible by the diversion: "By guiding the Arno above and below [Florence] a treasure will be found in each acre of ground by whomsoever will."

The famous bird's-eye view of the entire Arno valley (Plate III) probably was prepared for a presentation of Leonardo's project. On the back of this map are bits of wax, indicating that it was put up on a wall for a viewing of some sort. One can easily imagine members of the Ten of War or the Signoria clustered around this extraordinary map to discuss not only the diversion aimed against Pisa but also the broader plan to develop the Arno valley. As earlier (in the court of Ludovico Sforza) and later (both in Rome for Giuliano de' Medici and in Milan for Charles d'Amboise), Leonardo seriously proposed a major regional plan based on his knowledge of hydraulic engineering.

On July 24, 1503, when reporting from the camp that the projected military diversion of the Arno seemed feasible, Francesco Guiducci informed the Ten of War that on returning to Florence, the experts ("one of your Signoria, Alexandro degli Albizzi, ... Leonardo da Vinci, and some others") would "tell you everything." As secretary of the Ten of War, Niccolò would have been present for this report even if he had not been one of the others to visit the site. Eventually, Niccolò would be in charge of executing the projected diversion, consulting Leonardo and seeking to bring his plans to fruition. In Niccolò's many messages on the subject (there are ninety-three in all), the second chancellor shows just how strongly committed to the scheme he was.

In addition to the short-term military benefits, there was another reason to support the diversion if it could become the first step in Leonardo's dream. By directing the Arno north by way of Pistoia, there would be benefits in flood control, irrigation, waterpower, and commerce. After

1501, it became obvious to a few people that the stakes might be higher than ever.

Ever since the account of Columbus's first voyage had been published in Florence, in 1493, voyages of exploration had attracted the interest of the local merchants. Indeed, two years earlier, Poliziano had written the king of Portugal to congratulate him for sponsoring voyages that made possible "new articles of consumption; new business; new comforts for living" as well as "corroboration of ancient accounts that sometimes seemed incredible." A decade later, it became evident that Florence might itself play a direct role in exploiting these discoveries.

Amerigo Vespucci, whose brother and cousin worked in the Chancery, had gone to Spain as the business agent for his patron, Lorenzo di Pierfrancesco de' Medici. By 1493, he was established in Seville when Columbus astounded the world by returning from his first voyage with the claim of having discovered a short route to India. As a merchant, Amerigo was soon investing in the voyages of discovery, taking charge of outfitting Columbus's third voyage, in 1498.

Amerigo's role soon went beyond commerce. Interested since youth in astronomy and cosmology, in 1499 he himself embarked on a voyage of discovery along with a Spanish admiral and one of Columbus's pilots. Vespucci's goal was to resolve the controversies surrounding Columbus's claims by finding a route to India to the south of the Caribbean.

In late June, Vespucci's ships brought the first Europeans to the coast of what is now Brazil. In August, after his explorations led to a violent encounter with hostile Indians, Vespucci recorded that "since we were grievously wounded and weary, we returned to the ships and went into a harbor to recover, where we stayed twenty days." He apparently used the time to make the first accurate astronomical measurement of the distance across the Atlantic. Amerigo's calculation limited the claims of the Spanish by showing that the papal line demarcating Portuguese territory included lands in what we now call South America. This discovery was of immense political—and potentially commercial—importance.

After recuperating, Amerigo Vespucci and his men engaged in exten-

The Collaboration Begins / 103

sive further exploration before returning to Spain. In July 1500, he wrote a long letter to his Medici patron, Lorenzo di Pierfrancesco, describing the voyage. In addition to outlining the methods used to determine longitude, this letter describes "the character of the land and the nature of the inhabitants," most of whom "go entirely naked."

Convinced that the passage to India was farther to the south than he had been able to go, Amerigo wanted to explore further along the coast. On the basis of his astronomical measurements, however, he realized this required exploration along a southeastern shore that was not Spanish property. Amerigo determined on another voyage, this time in the service of the king of Portugal.

On May 13, 1501, Vespucci sailed from Lisbon to gain scientific information that the Portuguese needed for navigation and geography. He also kept in mind the interests of Florentine commerce and, on July 4, wrote Lorenzo di Pierfrancesco from Cape Verde, reporting on an encounter with a Portuguese fleet returning from a voyage around Africa. After his return the next year, he wrote his Florentine patron again with a brief report of the trip.

At the outset of this letter, he dropped a bombshell. Columbus claimed, in the published account of his first voyage, that he had landed in "the islands beyond the Ganges" and had "reached the mainland of Asia"; to his dying day, Columbus denied that he had found a new continent. In contrast, Vespucci flatly asserted that "we arrived at a new land which, for many reasons that are enumerated in what follows, we observed to be a continent." And Amerigo could back up the assertion with his measurement of longitude. The maps had to be changed. The earth was much larger than supposed on Toscanelli's globe and the map he gave Columbus. What had been discovered was the New World.

In this letter, Amerigo noted that his extensive astronomical observations had apparently been given to the king of Portugal in a "small work" that, when developed, would "win renown after my death." His description of the inhabitants contradicted the beliefs of medieval philosophy and religion alike:

> *Having no laws and no religious faith, they live according to nature. They understand nothing of the immortality of the soul. There is no possession of private property among them . . . they have no king, nor do they obey anyone. Each one is his own master . . . their marriages are not with one woman only, but they mate with whom they desire and without much ceremony . . . they are also a warlike people and very cruel to their own kind. . . . When they fight, they slaughter mercilessly.*

News of Vespucci's discoveries soon spread in Florence. The government decreed a celebration: for three nights, there was a fire of celebration before Vespucci's house. Florentines were proud of their local son. But the businessmen could also imagine the profits that might come if local merchants did not have to go to Lisbon or Cadiz to outfit the voyages of commerce to the New World. If only Florence were a seaport!

Vespucci's discoveries were known to Niccolò, since Amerigo's brother and cousin worked by his side, and Amerigo's patron, Lorenzo di Pierfrancesco, was a leader of those who ousted Savonarola and supported Niccolò's nomination to be second chancellor. By 1503, official documents give the name of Niccolò's assistant as "Augustino Matthei de Vespuccis *de Terrenova*"—adding the honorific title in honor of his cousin's voyages. Leonardo also knew both the Vespucci family and Amerigo's patron, as is proven by his *Notebooks*; according to Vasari, Leonardo did a remarkable sketch of Amerigo's face (though perhaps the portrait was done several years later).

The explorer's patron, Lorenzo di Pierfrancesco, "had treasured Amerigo's letters and had often proudly shown them to his visitors, who in turn started much talk about them throughout Florence." Controversies still swirled around the discoveries of Columbus, Cabot, and the other explorers crossing the Atlantic in the service of Spain and Portugal. Could Florence and her merchants play a part in the exciting race for wealth and power? Although Lorenzo di Pierfrancesco de' Medici died in June 1503, within a year a plagiarized version of Amerigo's letters was published under the title *Mundus Novus*. The fruits of making

Florence a seaport might be a share of the sought-after riches of the newly discovered continent.

Throughout the spring and summer of 1503, Leonardo's principal activity seems to have been the extensive studies of the Arno River and its surrounding hills, including not only the maps reproduced in this chapter, but extensive sketches of the topography of the valley. He was living on his savings, withdrawing fifty ducats about every three months from his accounts at Santa Maria Nuova. In addition, however, Leonardo apparently began work on a portrait—not just any portrait, but perhaps the most famous image of a human face in the history of Western art.

Some historians and biographers have claimed that *La Gioconda* (Figure 6.2) is not a portrait of Mona Lisa, but rather depicts Isabella Gualanda, a mistress of Giuliano de' Medici. Others claim the painting should be called *La Honda* and shows a Spanish courtesan. Recently, however, an extensive study of the painting's history confirms that Vasari was correct, a generation after Leonardo's death, to identify "the beautiful *Gioconda* painted by Leonardo" as Lisa di Anton Maria di Noldo Gherardini, the third wife of Francesco di Bartolomeo di Zanobi del Giocondo.

It is often said that the *Mona Lisa* is mysterious, but much more is known about the subject of the portrait than is usually realized. Lisa Gherardini married Francesco del Giocondo in 1495. He had first married Camilla Rucellai in 1491, but she had died after giving birth to a son; his second wife, Tommasa Villani, likewise died within a year after they were married in 1493. In April of 1503, Francesco Giocondo had two reasons to commission a painting of his third wife, Lisa: she had just given birth to his third son (her second—an infant daughter had died in 1499), and he had just bought a house. Such events were often the occasion for a familial portrait.

La Gioconda probably dates from this time because Raphael copied and imitated it between 1504 and 1506, and the dates are consistent with Leonardo's other activities in Florence. Although no one knows exactly

FIGURE 6.2. Leonardo, *Mona Lisa*, or *La Gioconda* (ca. 1503–7). Despite controversy, the consensus remains that the subject is Lisa Gherardini, the third wife of Francesco del Giocondo. The background shows not only a winding river like the Arno, but a small mountain resembling La Verruca, reflecting Leonardo's concerns when advising the Florentine government. The ethereal quality of this famous image is due not only to Mona Lisa's "smile," but to the aerial perspective on the background, which makes it appear that she is in the sky.

why Leonardo received the commission, Vasari claims he worked on *La Gioconda* for about four years. For some reason, the portrait was never delivered to the merchant who ordered it.

Many stories are told about the way Leonardo painted Mona Lisa. It is said that musicians were brought to the studio to play, thus causing her famous smile. Some claimed the painting was originally larger, and was cut down (a belief that has now been rejected on closer examination of the painting itself). One detail, however, deserves our attention.

The background of *La Gioconda* has been described as a surrealistic landscape, in part because it is seen from a point in the sky, high above the ground. This aerial perspective, which is also visible in the bird's-eye view of Tuscany (Plate III), was invented by Leonardo. He used it repeatedly in his sketches of hills and mountains connected with preparations for the Arno project. As one art historian has noted, the peak in the background of *La Gioconda* resembles the sketch of Monte Verruca in preparation for its fortification. And through the background flows, placidly, a river. Even when painting the wife of one of Florence's solid citizens, Leonardo seems to have had in the back of his mind the projects on which he and Niccolò were collaborating.

Chapter 7

THE ARNO DIVERSION FAILS

(1503–1504)

⚜

During the spring and early summer of 1503, Niccolò was preoccupied by a combination of foreign affairs and domestic politics. Florence, without its own army, relied on France—and the French troops in Naples suffered one defeat after another. Advocates of the use of force against Pisa, lacking sufficient troops for a frontal assault on Pisa itself, determined on an ancient alternative: soldiers were hired to lay waste the countryside around the besieged enemy city. While the upper-class citizens of Pisa might be safe within the walls, the peasants would find their crops ruined, houses destroyed, animals killed, and trees uprooted.

This strategic approach—called the *guasto*—began on May 23. In June, Florentine troops took the towns of Vico and Vernica. But there the advance stalled, while in Florence the governing councils debated the next step. Fears that the Spaniards might completely rout the French and move northward to take Florence and reestablish the Medici outweighed the traditional hatred of Pisa. Troops were given to the French for their battles in the south. And since resistance to taxation remained strong, there was no money for anything else.

Within Florence, the aristocratic alliance that had ousted Savonarola and supported Niccolò's election began to split. A group of wealthy and powerful leaders had imagined that, by electing a *gonfaloniere* for life, their political influence would be protected. Soderini, once elected, seemed to turn his back on reforms that would weaken the popular Great Council and give preeminent power to the aristocrats lead by Alamanno Salviati and his cousin Jacopo.

Although this group did not openly turn against Soderini until 1504, the tensions between Niccolò's original supporters and his current superior placed him in a difficult position. Jacopo Salviati, often vocal in his opinions, refrained from speaking at any public assembly throughout 1503. Things might have been better if the campaign against Pisa had succeeded—but alas, the strategy of laying waste the countryside backfired. Instead of dividing Pisan public opinion along class lines, Florentine military attacks tended to unite diverse social classes. Leonardo's project provided one of the few remaining options for Florentine victory. Compared to a citizen army, which might challenge aristocratic power, the diversion of the Arno was less controversial.

As the Signoria debated how best to levy taxes, provide for defense, and recapture Pisa, events elsewhere in Italy demanded attention. On August 18, 1503, Pope Alexander VI died—supposedly of tertian fever, though some suspected poison. Although only twenty-seven years old, Cesare Borgia fell gravely ill at the same time, which led skeptics to suggest that poison intended for one of the Borgias' enemies (Cardinal Orsini) was accidentally taken by the pope and his son. Niccolò was alerted to go to Rome to report on the election of a successor to Alexander, but there were complications, and before he could leave Florence, a compromise between the French and Spanish cardinals had been reached. A new pope was named on August 28: an aged prelate named Piccolomini, who took office as Pope Pius III.

Twenty-eight days later, the new pope died. This time, Niccolò was able get to Rome before the election of a successor. Niccolò left Florence on October 24, 1503, with instructions to contact cardinals favorable to the city and report on events "until the election of the new Pope." It was his first trip to Rome.

While Niccolò was at the papal court, his wife, Marietta, had their first son. Shortly thereafter, a friend named Luca Ugolini began a letter to Niccolò: "My very dear *compare*. Congratulations! Truly your Madonna Marietta did not deceive you, for he is your spitting image. Leonardo da Vinci would not have done a better portrait." (Ugolini obviously knew Niccolò well, probably as a confraternity member: after complaining that the envoy had failed to do a private favor, Ugolini added: "If you do not do it, I shall say you are a *compare* either of straw or a prick, as you will." In sixteenth-century Florence, as in any other capitol today, men in power were expected to do favors for their friends.)

In Florence, meanwhile, Leonardo finally gained his first major commission for a painting in his native city. Earlier in October, Leonardo had registered again in the painters' guild of Florence. He was now asked to paint a large mural on one wall of the Great Council Hall of the Palazzo Vecchio. To prepare the cartoon for this major project, space in Santa Maria Novella was placed at the disposition of Leonardo and his assistants. On October 24—the very day Niccolò left for Rome—Leonardo received the keys.

Biographers and art historians generally agree that this commission was secured through Niccolò's intervention. Since the newly renovated Great Council Hall served for formal meetings of the republic, its decoration was a matter of public decision. Although many in Florence wanted a work by the painter of the *Last Supper* in their city, Leonardo had a formidable rival for the commission: Michelangelo, younger but of increasing fame, and a protégé of Piero Soderini, the *gonfaloniere*. Ultimately, both were chosen to decorate the Council Hall since, in August 1504, it was decided that Michelangelo would paint a fresco on the wall facing Leonardo's commission.

The scene to be painted by Leonardo was the battle of Anghiari, a skirmish in 1440 in which a Milanese force was defeated by Florence. A description of the event was written in Leonardo's *Notebooks* by Agostino Vespucci, Niccolò's assistant in the Chancery. The text is roughly translated from Bruni's Latin history of Florence, which suggests the scene was assigned by the government.

About this time Leonardo had additional contacts with the administrators in the Palazzo Vecchio. At least one other entry in Leonardo's *Notebooks,* dated around 1504, is in the handwriting of Agostino Vespucci. And in another note, Leonardo reminds himself to ask Niccolò's superior, "Messer Marcello" (Adriani), the first chancellor, to translate a Latin reference to Vetruvius.

During the fall of 1503, Leonardo began to work on the cartoon for the *Battle of Anghiari* (Figure 7.1). Eight meters tall by twenty meters wide, it was to be the largest painting he had ever attempted. His many sketches show a desire to represent what Leonardo elsewhere called the "beastly madness" of warfare. As always, however, he was a perfectionist who would not be hurried. Soderini, concerned about money and anxious to see progress, fumed. There was controversy about payment. Leonardo lost his temper.

On one occasion, the Florentine paymaster gave the great painter his money in small change. Leonardo was furious, asserting "I am not a penny painter." When Soderini complained further about the delays and threatened to insist that Leonardo return the sums advanced to him, Leonardo went to numerous friends, gathered enough money to repay the government, and angrily announced he was giving it all back to the ungrateful *gonfaloniere*. Soderini, embarrassed, relented.

Despite such tensions, Leonardo was obviously respected as an artist. When Michelangelo finished *David,* there was public debate over the best place for this monumental statue. A committee of Florence's leading artists was formed, including Leonardo (as well as Perugino, Botticelli, Filippino Lippi, Il Cronaca, and Andrea Della Robbia). They met on January 25, 1504. Along with some others, Leonardo favored an indoor site to protect the marvelous work. Michelangelo disagreed, insisting—successfully—on its placement in the open air, just outside the Palazzo Vecchio.

Throughout the spring, there were complaints on the slow progress of

The Arno Diversion Fails / 113

FIGURE 7.1. Leonardo, Sketch of the right-hand group of the *Battle of Anghiari* (ca. 1504–5). Leonardo's preparatory sketches reveal the dynamism of his conception for the monumental mural in the Grand Council Hall. For a copy of the central section of the finished painting, see Figure 8.2.

Leonardo's work on the *Battle of Anghiari*. On May 4, 1504, in an attempt to resolve these issues, a formal agreement was reached between Leonardo and the Signoria. This contract was signed by Niccolò, providing the only existing document that explicitly connects the second chancellor to Leonardo. Its terms indicate how much conflict had erupted between the Signoria and the great artist.

> Item dicti Domini simul adunati etc. servatis etc. deliberaverunt etc. infrascriptas deliberationes infra vugari sermone descriptas videlicet: *the Magnificent and Excellent Lordships, the Priors of Liberty and the Gonfaloniere of Justice of the Florentine people, considering that: several months ago Leonardo of Sir Piero da Vinci, Florentine citizen, began to paint the Hall of the Great Council; that Leonardo had already painted a preliminary drawing of it on a cartoon and that he had received 35 large golden florins for this work; that these Lords wish that the work will be completed as soon as possible and that the above mentioned Leonardo will be given at different times a certain amount of money; nonetheless, the Magnificent Lords servatis etc. resolved that Leonardo will have to finish the entire cartoon completely by next February 1504 [1505], no exception or excuse accepted, and that Leonardo shall be paid 15 large golden florins for each month, counting from the 20th of April. And in case Leonardo should not have finished the cartoon within that time, then the Magnificent Lords can compel him in whatever way they consider more opportune, to give back the entire amount of money earned for that work until that day, and to hand over, without compensation, that part of the cartoon which he has managed to finish; in the meanwhile Leonardo has promised to finish the cartoon.*
>
> *It could be the case that Leonardo would consider it proper to begin painting on the wall of the hall the part he had drawn on the cartoon, in which case the Magnificent Lordships will be pleased to give him the wage they will consider as proper for each month of his work and on the day agreed between Leonardo and them. And since Leonardo is engaged in painting the wall, the Magnificent Lords will be pleased to extend the period of time allowed [to him to finish the cartoon], during which*

The Arno Diversion Fails / 115

Leonardo is obliged to finish the cartoon in the way agreed between the Lords and Leonardo. And since it could also happen that Leonardo, during the time he is engaged in finishing the cartoon, should not have the opportunity to paint the wall but went on with the cartoon, according to the agreement subscribed, the Magnificent Lords will not be allowed to have the cartoon painted by anybody without Leonardo's formal permission. On the contrary, they will let Leonardo finish the painting when it is possible for him and let him paint the wall any month they will agree upon, when it will be considered more opportune. Nonetheless, Leonardo will have to declare his acceptance of 35 large golden florins, and all the money he will receive in the future, as the advance on the money that the Magnificent Lords will declare as total reward for his work. Mandantes . . . . . . Actum in palatio dictorum Dominorum presentibus Nicolao Domini Bernardi de Machiavellis Cancellario dictorum Dominorum, et Marco ser Ioannis de Romena cive fiorentino, testibus, etc. [Enacted in the palace of the aforementioned Lords, in the presence of Niccolò son of Bernardo Machiavelli, Chancellor of the aforementioned Lords, and Marco, of ser Giovanni Romena, citizen of Florence, as witnesses . . .]

Clearly, this was no ordinary contract. Leonardo needed the money, but also insisted on his perfectionist standards. Soderini and the Signoria wanted a finished painting—but were insistent on having the work done on time. Niccolò seems to have been the man in the middle.

During the winter and spring of 1504, the second chancellor was a man in the middle in other ways as well. In January, the Great Council finally voted to raise taxes after months of deadlock, but only after Soderini packed the hall with supporters. Thereafter, Soderini's policies increasingly alienated the aristocratic faction, led by Alamanno Salviati and others favorable to the Medici. These circumstances put Niccolò in the middle of a bitter controversy between the faction that originally supported his election and his superior, Piero Soderini—and he needed both sides to support his annual reappointment as second chancellor.

When he signed the agreement between the Signoria and Leonardo, Niccolò had just returned to Florence from another mission. In April 1504, when Cesare Borgia's power evaporated after the election of Pope Julius II, power relations throughout central Italy were again transformed. Jacopo d'Appiani returned as ruler of Piombino on the Ligurian coast. Since Appiani was married to Lorenzo di Pierfrancesco de' Medici's daughter but had been ignored in earlier efforts to keep Cesare Borgia at bay, the Florentines had to placate him. Niccolò went to Piombino on April 2, 1504. The mission was brief, but it led to a six-week-long visit by Leonardo in the fall of the year. Prepared by Niccolò, Leonardo's role would be to provide technical assistance in the design of the fortifications and port installations of Piombino.

Within Florence, there was opposition to additional taxes for the war against Pisa. In April, the Great Council twice defeated a tax proposed for the purpose of laying waste the countryside around the besieged city. Finally, a plan was adopted to finance the war with added loans from wealthy creditors. In the field, for the moment the military campaign against Pisa seemed to be progressing well, and in May 1504, Librafatta—blocking a main road between Pisa and Lucca—was retaken by Florentine troops. Later that month, Cardinal Francesco Soderini wrote Niccolò that there was a general expectation of a military victory over Pisa: "Although many things are being said and threatened, nevertheless they are believed to be rather a diversion than anything else, and it is believed you are not going to have such obstacles that, if you are willing to do quickly what is required, you cannot take Pisa by force."

In Pisa itself, the siege had effectively isolated the city. In one of the few private letters from the city that has survived from this period, a Pisan informed a friend in Palermo on August 4, 1504, that "it is not possible for a man to leave Pisa without running great danger." In Florence, the hope was that conflicts within the besieged city would lead to its collapse. Because poor citizens and rural farmers were given a substantial role in Pisa's government, however, such internal divisions never materialized.

Soderini urgently pushed for a direct assault on the walls of Pisa. Consistent with this goal, Leonardo analyzed in great detail the military technology involved in breaching the walls of Pisa and taking the city. Earlier attacks had shown that it was not sufficient to destroy an entire portion of the wall, especially because attackers would then be vulnerable to fire from the massed defenders of the city. Leonardo therefore designed a comprehensive tactical plan that involved destroying the upper twenty feet of thirty-two-foot-high walls along a length of four hundred feet (Figure 7.2), using the debris to make four bastions from which artillery could fire, while troops entered the city through four portals made in the partially destroyed wall.

If the Florentine attackers were able to control the exterior of the walls, this technique would allow them to make a horizontal cut partway up in the wall but prop it up until artillery had been advanced to the foot of the walls. Then, Leonardo advises, "let the charges at once be ignited that have been placed in each prop . . . causing the wall that rests on them to collapse." Using mortars, Leonardo imagined raining stones on the defenders while the attackers entered the city (Figure 7.3). "And if you do not want the mortars let us fill the ditches [inside the wall] with water, and as they overflow the water will fill up the other ditches that are not connected to the former ones. . . . Water, being released, will prevent the fire that the enemy might have planned to blast off in the mines [that is, defensive artillery hidden in covered bunkers]." Although Leonardo's scheme was obviously intended for consideration by the government, we have no record whether Niccolò (or the committee of the Ten of War that he served) showed a serious interest in it.

Whatever the methods to be used, additional funds were needed for a direct assault on Pisa but were opposed in the assemblies. Soderini finally got an added tax, but the generals decided not to attack when they learned from captured Pisans that there were foreign troops as well as a large force of Pisans armed and eager for battle. "The prisoners said that the defenders feared only one thing, that the Florentines would divert the Arno and so dry up its outlet to the sea, depriving Pisa of the help they had been receiving from ships paid for by Lucca, Siena and Genoa."

Opponents of the diversion apparently conjured up another excuse to defer action: fears of an attack on Florence by a Spanish army. On June 1,

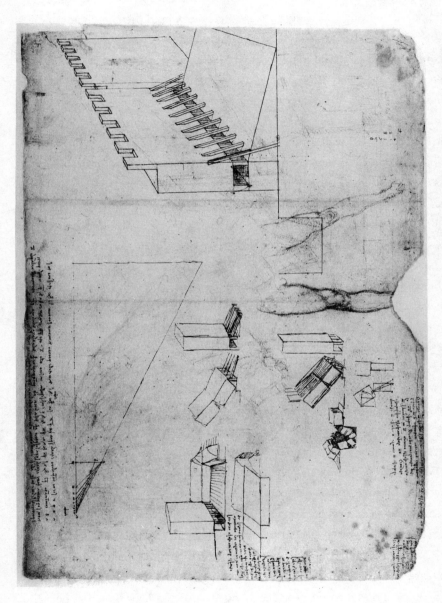

FIGURE 7.2. Leonardo, Fortification studies (ca. 1504). These drawings offer a plan for destroying a stretch of the walls of Pisa with reduced risk to the forces besieging the city; wooden beams would support the walls until exploding mines caused them to fall inward. The legs of a male nude, standing on his right foot, were probably one of the preparatory sketches for the *Battle of Anghiari*.

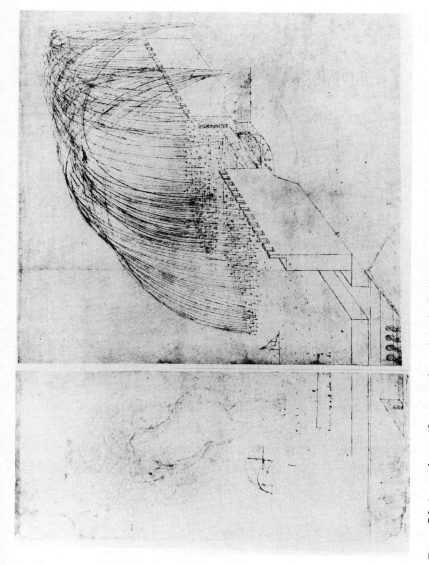

FIGURE 7.3. Leonardo, Fortification studies and sketch of a horse for the *Battle of Anghiari* (ca. 1504). After destroying a section of the Pisan walls (as in Figure 7.2), Leonardo envisioned a mortar attack to facilitate the invasion by Florentine troops. The sketch to the left, belonging to work on Leonardo's mural for the Palazzo Vecchio, confirms that this use of mortars was planned during the campaign against Pisa in 1504.

1504, Niccolò wrote a private letter to the Florentine commissioner in the Romagna, Giovanni Ridolfi, informing him that a force of "two hundred fifty men at arms and three thousand infantrymen" had left Naples for Rome "in order to move on Tuscany and to attack Florence . . . so as to overthrow our government and to bring Tuscany under Spain's control." While Niccolò himself dismissed the widespread fear ("these are not troops that can do harm"), he commented that the rumor "keeps the city on edge, and the Pisan campaign is not being discussed as it would were there not this hesitation."

Around this time, what purported to be Amerigo Vespucci's correspondence with his patron, Lorenzo di Pierfrancesco de' Medici, was published. Although the first edition apparently appeared in Florence, the only surviving copies are a Latin translation, dated August 1504 and published in Vienna. *Mundus Novus* is important as the first printed work claiming that Columbus and other explorers had actually discovered a new continent (and not merely part of Asia).

Although Amerigo Vespucci's reports of his voyages of 1499 and 1501 had been read by his patron's friends, none had been made public. With the death of Lorenzo di Pierfrancesco de' Medici, there was no way to prove the story that there was an entire continent between Europe and Asia. Such a discovery had immense consequences for commerce and political rivalries. If Columbus was right, westward explorers would soon encounter established societies. Vespucci's claim meant that there was an entire continent over which there would be competition for territorial control, wealth, and power. Perhaps Italians could play a role in this New World on their own account.

Using language not found in Amerigo's original letters to his Medici patron, *Mundus Novus* was intended to encourage its readers to think about the possibilities created by the discovery of a massive continent.

> *On a former occasion I wrote to you at some length concerning my return from those new regions which we found and explored with the fleet, at the*

> cost and by the command of this Most Serene King of Portugal. And these we may rightly call a new world. Because our ancestors had no knowledge, and it will be a matter wholly new to all those who hear about them. For this transcends the view held by our ancients, inasmuch as most of them hold that there is no continent to the south beyond the equator, but only the sea which they named the Atlantis; and if some of them did aver that a continent there was, they denied with abundant argument that it was a habitable land. But that this their opinion is false and utterly opposed to the truth, this my last voyage has made manifest; for in those southern parts I have found a continent more densely peopled and abounding in animals than our Europe or Asia or Africa, and, in addition, a climate milder and more delightful than in any other region known to us.

After describing the route in terms that are inaccurate and inconsistent, the published letter depicts the natives of the New World. Then *Mundus Novus* adds an invented story:

> they have another custom, very shameful and beyond all human belief. For their women, being very lustful, cause the private parts of their husbands to swell up to such a huge size that they appear deformed and disgusting; and this is accomplished by a certain device of theirs, the biting of certain poisonous animals. As the consequence of this many lose their organs which break through lack of attention, and they remain eunuchs.

These sexual exaggerations, combined with details about the natives actually found in Vespucci's letters, suggest that the inhabitants of this New World "live according to nature, and may be called Epicureans rather than Stoics." Further challenging the traditional philosophic views of the time, *Mundus Novus* describes the different constellations seen in the southern sky, implying that observation of the stars proves that the earth is a globe.

At this time, Niccolò suddenly showed an interest in astronomy in an exchange of letters with Amerigo's nephew Bartolomeo Vespucci, professor of astronomy in Padua. Bartolomeo's reply of June 4, 1504, in Latin, indicates that Niccolò had written "praises of astronomy, and what utility it has for humankind," and had reflected on the extent to which humans can control their fates even though "of the stars' influences themselves no change can happen through eternity." Bartolomeo also acknowledges Niccolò's "request" for some sort of computation and apologizes for his inability to be of "service" until the end of his lectures on August 18. Was Niccolò checking Amerigo's calculations of longitude?

Leonardo was also probably aware of the discovery of a new continent. He knew the Vespucci family well, as is shown by his *Notebook* entries written in Agostino's handwriting and the remark that "Vespuccio will give me a book of Geometry." Leonardo also refers to some "boxes of Lorenzo di Pierfrancesco de' Medici" in a list of items emphasizing problems of astronomy and cosmography. More important, at just this time Leonardo seems to have devoted attention to the problem of measuring longitude, including both devices for a ship's log to measure actual distances traveled and clocks that would enable an accurate astronomical verification of a ship's location.

While not actually written by Amerigo Vespucci, *Mundus Novus* had propaganda value as an added reason for pursuing Leonardo's scheme of making Florence into a seaport. The authority of traditional science and philosophy was challenged by Vespucci's purported report that "I saw things incompatible with the opinions of philosophers." Why listen, then, to critics of Leonardo's scheme? And the evidence that a Florentine had played a crucial role in maritime exploration could only fuel interest in improved access to the sea.

Unable to launch a direct military assault on Pisa, and tempted to make Florence a seaport, critics relented and the Signoria finally voted to proceed with the enormous task of diverting the Arno. On August 20, 1504, Niccolò wrote the commissioner in the field, announcing the decision as well as the designation of a commissioner, Giuliano Lapi, and a hydraulic engineer, Colombino, to direct the work. In a report on the project written a few months later, Niccolò's assistant Biagio Buonaccorsi described the work in detail.

At this time it was considered taking the Arno River away from the Pisans in order to conduct it into the Stagno [di Livorno], for it was shown with good reasons that besides depriving the Pisans of their source of life, those who were undertaking this project were to benefit our town immensely; therefore the decision to undertake the project being taken, the camp was set at Riglione after having cut the forage, and a Maestro d'Acque, Colombino, was summoned, who was asked to state what was necessary to complete the undertaking. He asked for two thousand laborers a day equipped with the wood necessary to construct a weir in order to retain the river and divert it into two big ditches through which the Arno was to flow, planned to go all the way to the Stagno; and he promised that the undertaking could be carried out with thirty or forty thousand works [that is, laborers' days], and so provided with such a hope, the project was undertaken on 20 August, with two thousand works, which were to be paid each a carlino a day, and according to the design which will be shown at the bottom of the page [Figure 7.4].

The projected diversion was intended to be the first phase of Leonardo's broader project, and not merely a military stratagem to defeat Pisa. Only such a double purpose can explain Buonaccorsi's reasoning that "besides depriving the Pisans of their source of life, those who were undertaking this project *were to benefit our town immensely.*"

The original plan for diverting the river at Pisa (Plate VIII) called for digging two ditches, starting at the Stagno di Livorno (a large pond long since drained, and now marked only by the town of Stagno). These ditches were to have been joined into a single wide opening where the diversion joined the Arno (which would be hard for the Pisans to fill in once the diversion began to work). In one of his *Notebooks,* Leonardo worked out in detail the dimensions and labor involved for a ditch corresponding to this plan. Upon completion, it would be eighty feet wide at its mouth, sixty-four feet wide at its end, thirty feet deep, and one mile long. Leonardo estimated that about 1 million tons of earth would have to be dug out.

To achieve this massive task, Leonardo had engaged in what are now called time-and-motion studies of how much could be moved by an individ-

FIGURE 7.4. Biagio Buonaccorsi, *Sunmario,* Plan of the diversion of the Arno (1504). This sketch of the actual path of diversion, as attempted under the direction of Colombino, was included in the official report of the failure by Niccolò's assistant and friend, Buonaccorsi. The dual canals actually dug under the supervision of Colombino do not correspond to Leonardo's sketches, confirming the difference between two plans mentioned in Machiavelli's correspondence with the Florentine camp at Pisa.

ual worker. He realized that to lift the earth from so deep a trench, workers at the bottom would have to fill buckets that were passed up steps to the rim of the canal; he estimated that each bucket of earth from the bottom of the ditch would have to be hauled by fourteen workers to reach the top. While working in Piombino, Leonardo had sketched such a system (Figure 7.5).

Leonardo was aware, of course, that a large workforce would be re-

FIGURE 7.5. Leonardo, Men digging a ditch (ca. 1504). Leonardo's *Notebooks* include a detailed time-motion analysis for organizing the laborers digging the canal to divert the Arno, as well as this image of the physical disposition needed to move large volumes of earth by human labor. The resulting estimate of the manpower needed was substantially greater than that calculated by Colombino in the attempted diversion.

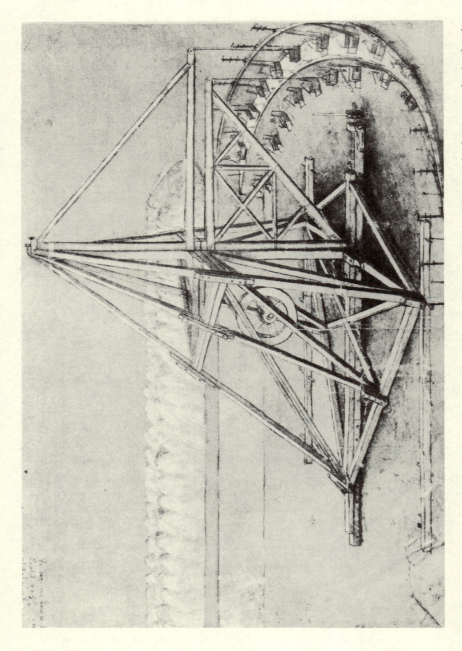

FIGURE 7.6. Leonardo, Machine (ca. 1504). Leonardo's conception of a mechanized device to dig a canal. The notes on the sketch indicate that the width of the ditch corresponds with Leonardo's measurement of his suggested dimensions for the diversion of the Arno.

The Arno Diversion Fails / 127

quired to move so much earth. He calculated that it would take two days for a single worker to move the equivalent of a cube of earth that was sixty-four braccia (128 feet) on a side—called a cube of one canna. At that rate, since he estimated twenty-seven thousand cubic canna, at least fifty-four thousand worker days would have been needed. Should manpower be a problem, Leonardo wrote, "numerous machines" could be used to facilitate the work (as is evident from his a sketch of a mechanized canal-digging system in Figure 7.6).

To dig the diversionary canal, it was necessary first to build a temporary weir, or barrier, along the existing bank of the Arno. Behind the weir, a ditch had to be dug that was deeper than the Arno so that, on its completion, water would naturally flow into the new ditch, allowing construction of a permanent weir damming the normal flow of the river.

In executing Leonardo's plans, the choice of Colombino as hydraulic engineer in charge of the project proved disastrous. To begin with, Colombino changed the design, digging two entirely separate ditches between the bed of the Arno and the Stagno, instead of making a single broad opening leading to two separate ditches as Leonardo wanted (compare Plate VIII and Figure 7.4).

In addition, Colombino underestimated the number of workers required. With two thousand workers on the site, his prediction of thirty to forty thousand worker days implied that in the best case, the project would be completed in approximately two to three weeks. These calculations were significantly below those of Leonardo, who had carefully calculated the difficulty of moving so much earth. Since no attempt was made to build the digging machine Leonardo had designed, work advanced more slowly than promised.

Once work began on August 20, messages between Florence and the headquarters besieging Pisa expressed mounting concern with Colombino. On September 3, Niccolò wrote to Antonio Giacomini, military commissioner of the Florentine camp: "With regard to Colombino, you will urge him to make the work proceed and come to an end, if he does not want to lose an opportune compensation, intended both as reward and as praise to his honor." Giuliano Lapi, the commissioner responsible for the construction of the diversion, replied to the committee of Ten on September 10, defending the hydraulic engineer:

Colombino cannot be held responsible for everything, and I know how much time we would have saved if we had four of them, because we are in urgent need of such men. But since your Lordships do not want to send any more of them, we will do as much as we can. I will send the men we have where I believe it is needed, because even if they did not do anything more than place the workers where it is more necessary, this would already be an achievement.

The next day, Niccolò, accustomed to such complaints, replied to Commissioner Giacomini:

Colombino is an excellent expert on this hydraulic engineering, but as a person he is so reserved that he does not stand out among such a multitude of men and preparations; anyway, after knowing his qualities, it is necessary to support him. We are telling you all this so that, by knowing him as well as we do, you can understand his natural inclination and encourage him when it is needed.

Soon, however, Niccolò was aware of more acute technical mistakes as well. On September 20 he wrote Giuliano Lapi, expressing concern not only about the slow pace of the work but even more concerning a change in plans.

Your letter of yesterday informed us about the ditch; if today, after so many promises, its mouth will be widened, this will please us; if not, without hoping any longer, we will nevertheless believe that you have done or are doing everything possible. As for what you are saying about the plan of widening the mouth of a second ditch in the same way as the first, and afterwards creating an island of that part of the land between the two mouths of the ditch which was to be emptied according to the plan made when Giovanni Berardi was there, our opinion concerning this is that we preferred the first plan to this last one; in fact, if the Arno flows through two ways, neither of them very wide, we believe that it would not flow with the same force as it would have if you were to make a little inlet as in the first plan. Moreover, if for any reason the weir thus created should be ruined, it would be much easier for the Pisans to direct the Arno back to its own course when they had to fill up only two small mouths, than if they had to fill up the space between the opening of the one and the other ditch; anyway, if the difficulties of the work or other unforeseen circumstances should force you to undertake this last project you wrote me about, we will trust your decision, and we will be content with having let you know our opinion.

Niccolò apparently realized that Colombino, having found Leonardo's design too difficult, decided to dig two separate ditches, each only fourteen feet deep, all the way from the Stagno to the Arno. Since it was known that water flows faster through a narrowed channel, presumably Colombino expected that once the flow of water from the Arno began, it would deepen the ditches and by its flow erode the land remaining between them (Figure 7.4). Hence, the change in design was apparently intended to use the force of the river to do some of the work Leonardo thought would be done by human labor, if not by his machine.

These changes are obvious in Buonaccorsi's report, which specified the exact dimensions of the work actually done under Colombino's direction: "The greater of the two ditches was thirty braccia [sixty feet] wide and 7 [fourteen feet] deep, the second twenty braccia [forty feet] wide and as deep as the other." Niccolò was right when he expressed reservations about the change, but as a practical administrator, in his message of September 20, Niccolò deferred to the expertise of those wrestling with the actual problems in the field. Or rather, he deferred for twenty-four hours, and then changed his mind.

On September 21, Niccolò again wrote, but this time raising a technical question of hydraulic engineering. Based on the slowness of the progress, Niccolò made an assumption about the depth of the diversionary canal (ditch) and drew a consequence for the flow of the river:

Your delay makes us fear that the bed of the ditch is shallower than the bed of the Arno; this would have negative effects and in our opinion it would not direct the project to the end we wish. In this case it would be good to widen it with a flood, since we think that low waters would not have the same effect. Anyway we would like to know if the bed of the Arno is shallower or deeper than that of the ditch, and in case the bed of the ditch is shallower, we would think it proper to make up for it.

As there is no evidence that Niccolò or the others at the Chancery had the expertise to infer, from slow progress, that the depth of the ditch would cause a problem, Niccolò probably recognized the danger by talking about the situation with Leonardo after writing on September 20.

Niccolò turned out to be right. The river, which started to flow into the newly dug ditches, returned to the old course of the Arno. Part of the works collapsed. Soderini refused to admit the project was doomed. He turned immediately to the Signoria, then pushed a decree through the assembly, or Council of Eighty, that work be continued. On September 28 and 29, the Florentine commissioners at Pisa were informed that "they ought to go forward and not abandon the project."

Soderini and Niccolò were sufficiently optimistic that a further effort could succeed that in this message, the field commanders were encouraged to go forward with only five hundred workers if they were of high quality rather than pay one thousand workers of whom five hundred were not effective. The message of September 28 emphasized that the weir along the Arno should be protected by soldiers so that the Pisans could not destroy it. Specific instructions were transmitted to the commissioner, Giuliano Lapi, with an urgent demand that the workers enlarge the opening of the "second ditch" at the Arno. A specialist, Marcantonio Colonna—apparently designated by Leonardo—was to be sent to the camp to explain the details.

On September 29, Niccolò wrote another message from the Ten of War to the field that reinforced these instructions, emphasizing the need for soldiers to protect the works in progress "and above all other things, you remember to make the mouth of the second ditch as large as possible."

In the field, the effects of insufficient resources and lack of leadership were increasingly evident. Commissioner Tosinghi wrote the committee of Ten on September 28:

> *And since the workers do not seem to believe that this work can be carried out as carefully as your Lordships wish, they are working with a bad disposition. It seems to Giuliano and me that Master Colombino is beginning to doubt that he can carry out this project, laying the blame on the unfavorable circumstances that accompanied the work.*

On October 3, Niccolò wrote again for the Ten of War, indicating exactly how the situation could be remedied with "seven or eight days" of careful work. But at this moment a violent storm struck. Several boats, which were guarding the mouth of the Arno, were wrecked and eighty lives lost. The walls of the ditches collapsed. One of the military commanders, Tosinghi, asked to be relieved of command. In a matter of days, the Pisans began to destroy the weir on the Arno and to fill the ditches.

The Florentines were forced to abandon further work on the diversionary canals. In an attempt to profit from the investment of time and money, the Signoria issued a proclamation pardoning Pisans who would leave the city to become subjects of Florence. The proposal backfired, as the besieged Pisans used it to solve their food shortage by sending unnecessary people across the lines under safe-conduct. By October 12, the government decided to leave the decision on continuation of the siege to Commissioner Tosinghi in the field. Soon thereafter, operations ceased and the Florentine army was disbanded. The Pisans hastily filled up the diversionary canals. The war was to go on for five more years. The dream of Leonardo and Niccolò went unfulfilled.

Why did the diversion fail? Buonaccorsi's report explains the technical problem:

> *And the undertaking was not completed because it required too much time and money, and if Maestro Colombino had promised to finish the whole*

undertaking with thirty or thirty-five thousand works, eighty thousand works were not even enough to bring it halfway, nor was the expected fall for waters achieved, because with the river in flood the waters entered strongly through the ditch but as the Arno went back to its regular flow the flood-waters began to subside.

As Buonaccorsi adds, if the ditches had been wider and deeper where they joined the Arno, the river would have flowed into the diversion even at low water. Then a permanent weir, blocking the original channel of the Arno, could easily be made. As the river's sediment accumulated against the weir, the newly diverted channel would have become fixed.

When the river flooded unexpectedly, the Arno's water was only partially diverted into the ditches because Colombino did not dig deeply enough. Worse yet, the floodwaters did not last long enough to allow Colombino's workers to complete the weir across the Arno. As soon as the flood subsided, water returned to the river's original channel. And as that channel had been narrowed by the partially constructed weir, the water flowed through it with greater speed. That dug the river's old channel even deeper, making it impossible to get the water to flow through the diversion.

New experts were "called in from Lombardy," where Leonardo had worked extensively on water projects. These experts confirmed "that the river had a fifteen braccia [thirty foot] slope"—in other words, at the point of the diversion, the Arno was approximately thirty feet above sea level. Their report confirmed that Colombino's ditches were not dug deeply enough. The Milanese experts added that "the reason" for the failure "was understood through experience"—namely, the effect we now call Bernouilli's principle (after the scientist who worked it out in 1738). When water is channeled through a narrower pipe or canal, the rate of flow is increased. Although in 1504 hydraulic engineers could only explain this effect "through experience," ironically, Leonardo's *Notebooks* show that he anticipated Bernouilli's analysis of the theoretical reasons for what happened.

The failure of the Arno project was a disaster for Niccolò and Leonardo as well as for Soderini and the government of Florence. As Buonaccorsi concluded sadly, "This undertaking came to cost seven thousand ducats, or more, because in addition to the salary for the workers and other things, it was necessary to keep a thousand soldiers in that place to protect the workers from the attacks of the Pisans." To understand the implications, imagine that the atomic bombs dropped on Hiroshima and Nagasaki both failed to explode, leading to a costly and prolonged invasion of Japan by American troops and the abandonment of nuclear technology.

Although the diversion of the Arno failed, Leonardo and Niccolò continued to embark on innovative projects. Often, these also turned out to be failures. Four centuries before the Wright brothers, Leonardo tried to fly, without success. In painting the *Battle of Anghiari* on the walls of the Palazzo Vecchio, his experimental technique with oils ran badly, ultimately requiring the destruction of one of his most extraordinary works of art. Three centuries before the French revolutionaries and Napoleon changed Europe by raising mass armies, Niccolò tried to develop a citizen militia. Although at first successful, Niccolò's troops were routed in 1512, leading to the return of the Medici, the end of republican self-rule, and Niccolò's loss of power.

More than any of these disappointments, however, the Arno diversion could be called a magnificent failure. Niccolò and Leonardo tried to control both the flow of history and the flow of the river by combining science, technology, and political power. The ambition to use this means to conquer nature, commonplace today, had never been attempted in quite this way on such a scale. In the twentieth century, the Army Corps of Engineers built the Boulder Dam, the Tennessee Valley Authority, and the other dams and river projects that transformed America, uniting engineering and technology with pure science and public policy. It is worth wondering if history would have changed had Leonardo and Niccolò succeeded in transforming Florence into a seaport and irrigating the Arno valley.

Chapter 8

THE AFTERMATH
(1504–1506)

After the Arno diversion was abandoned, Leonardo and Niccolò did what truly great artists, scientists, and leaders often do in the face of disaster. They went back to work.

In response to the collapse of the Arno project, Cardinal Francesco Soderini, Niccolò's friend and brother of the *gonfaloniere*, wrote a letter of commiseration to Niccolò:

> Notable man and very dear compare. *It gave us great pain that so great an error should have been made in those waters that it seems impossible to us that it should not have been through the fault of those engineers [sc. Colombino], who went so far wrong. Perhaps it also pleases God thus, for some better end unknown to us.*

Francesco often spoke for his brother in correspondence with Niccolò, and it seems that the *gonfaloniere* himself also attributed the failure to lapses of execution in the field rather than to Leonardo's plan.

Francesco Guicciardini, who served in high office and knew Niccolò well, presents a similar assessment in his *History of Florence:*

> *this undertaking, begun with the greatest of expectations and pursued with even greater expenses, turned out to be in vain because, as so frequently happens in such ventures,* even though the surveys are based on virtually manifest proof, *experience will prove them to be failures (the truest of examples of the distance that exists between plan and action).*

While Niccolò's friends thus put the disaster in the most positive light, critics were obviously furious. Piero Soderini, who had supported the plan so vigorously, had many enemies who blamed him for the failure. Niccolò, now widely viewed as the *gonfaloniere*'s lackey, or *mannino,* by critics, was even more exposed. This may explain why, immediately after the failure of the diversion, Niccolò was suddenly "allowed" the "leisure" to write, in verse, the history of the last ten years of Florentine foreign policy.

Called the *First Decennale,* the poem was dedicated to Soderini's leading critic and Niccolò's former supporter, Alamanno Salviati. In the Dedication, Niccolò says that the work's brevity should be "excused" because of "the short time allowed for me for such avocation." Did Niccolò volunteer to get out of the Palazzo Vecchio for several weeks until things cooled down, or did Soderini ask him to do so? Or, since Salviati and his aristocratic friends were opposed to Niccolò's citizen army, a plan supported by Soderini, was the poem written to placate a powerful critic?

In the poem, which borrows many stylistic devices from Dante, Machiavelli recounts briefly the historical events of his lifetime as if he is singing them to Florence. Throughout the poem, he praises his native city, which is addressed as "you." Near the end, he brings the story up to the time of his composition:

> Nor did you desist from assailing the Pisans; instead, you took their third harvest away and attacked them by sea and by land. And because they did not fear your swords, with various schemes you tried to turn Arno aside through different courses.

In apparently the only explicit reference to the diversion in Machiavelli's published works, Niccolò justified the failed project by referring to the equally unsuccessful attempts to take the city by armed force. In referring to the diversion, moreover, he speaks of "various schemes" and "different courses" in the plural, confirming that the channel to deprive Pisa of water was not the only change proposed for the Arno River.

At the end of his poem, Niccolò encourages Florence to use armed force. This literary exercise had a political objective. If technology would not defeat Pisa, Niccolò was determined to pursue the strategy of raising an army composed of Florentine citizens. Whether or not writing the *First Decennale* was an excuse to get the second chancellor out of the Palazzo Vecchio for several weeks, Niccolò was ambitious to get back to work.

While escaping from the limelight to write this poem, Niccolò also saw to it that Leonardo left town. Despite the contract to finish the *Battle of Anghiari* as quickly as possible, the artist was suddenly dispatched on a technical-assistance mission to Piombino at the end of October 1504. Niccolò, as a witness to the contract with the Signoria, knew that the cartoon for the painting had to be completed by February 1505, "no exception or excuse accepted" (to quote Leonardo's contract with the Signoria). Even so, Leonardo was to be in Piombino on the Ligurian Sea well into December.

Leonardo's mission to Piombino for the Florentine republic confirms that he was not held responsible for the failure of the diversion (at least in the eyes of Niccolò and his superior, Soderini). In April 1504, Niccolò had been sent to placate the ruler of Piombino, Jacopo d'Appiano; now, to confirm the good intentions of the Florentine government, Niccolò arranged for technical assistance to him.

Leonardo was in Florence on October 31, when he drew money for his trip. He arrived in Piombino the next day (November 1) and immediately presented sketches to the newly restored ruler, indicating how the break- water of the port could be redesigned and the fortifications strengthened (Figure 8.1). Although he stayed in Piombino for six or seven weeks, out-

FIGURE 8.1. Leonardo, Fortifications at Piombino (1504). One of the sketches from Leonardo's military assistance mission to Piombino, showing improvements of the fortifications at the fortress.

lines for Leonardo's proposed renovations for the fortifications and breakwater were already in his possession before he left Florence. In fact, in his free moments while in Piombino, Leonardo sketched the shape and flow of waves on the seashore, exploring them as an issue in theoretical physics.

In sending a technical expert to Jacopo d'Appiano, therefore, Niccolò must have known that Leonardo had already inspected and planned repairs at Piombino while serving as Cesare Borgia's architect and general engineer. In all likelihood, this is something else Niccolò learned from discussions with Leonardo by the fire on cold November days in Cesare's court in Imola.

By the end of 1504, Leonardo was back in Florence and working on the *Battle of Anghiari*. He seems to have worked with a vengeance, because the long-delayed cartoon was finished on time in February 1505. The Great Council Hall was made ready for Leonardo's work on March 14. On April 30, the painter received another payment. After preparing and smoothing the wall with several assistants, in June he started to paint. Leonardo recorded the moment in his *Notebooks:*

On 6 June 1505, a Friday, at the thirteenth hour [9:30 A.M.], I began to paint in the palace. I was just picking up my brush when the weather took a turn for the worse and the churchbells rang the alarm, calling people together. And the cartoon [made of pieces of paper stuck together] began to come apart, water went everywhere, for the vessel in which it was being carried broke. Suddenly the weather grew worse still, and it poured with rain until evening; the day had been transformed into night.

Leonardo was not given to astrology. Had he believed in such things, he might well have seen this as an evil omen.

As a copy by Rubens shows (Figure 8.2), the painting had an extraordinary vitality and power. To increase the effectiveness of the colors and the precision of his artistry, Leonardo used a technique based on methods described by Pliny. Normally, a fresco was painted in with egg-and-water-based colors that dry very rapidly. Leonardo, who was one of the first Italian artists to use oils for painting, sought a method that would allow him to retouch and modify his work repeatedly.

The solution involved paints mixed with linseed oil, which were then heated after being applied to the wall. A test panel worked perfectly. Apparently, however, when the paints were applied to the wall in full scale, the heating from the brazier was uneven and the paint began to run. Some have thought the brazier too far from the wall or too small to heat the upper portion of the painting. Others have said the problem was faulty linseed oil. Leonardo's purchases of materials continued until the winter of 1506, then stopped. Discouraged, he apparently abandoned the project.

The surviving parts of Leonardo's work and Michelangelo's parallel

FIGURE 8.2. Peter Paul Rubens, Copy of the battle around the standard from Leonardo's *Battle of Anghiari* (ca. 1604). Rubens' drawing—actually a copy of a copy—was only one of many reproductions of Leonardo's destroyed mural.

cartoon of the battle of Cascina, intended for the facing wall (never painted because the pope invited Michelangelo to Rome), were put on display. Artists flocked to see them. As Benvenuto Cellini put it, these two cartoons were "the school of the world." According to Vasari, Raphael studied Leonardo's style and sought to forget everything he had learned in order to copy it. As late as 1549, part of Leonardo's painting—a group of horses—was recommended in an artistic guide to Florence as "a marvelous thing." But the paint continued to deteriorate rapidly and, in 1560, was covered with plaster for a new fresco, by Vasari.

Undaunted by another failure, Leonardo continued to work on everything that interested him. The science and technology of controlling water was still on his mind. Leonardo's extensive *Notebook* on hydraulic engineering (the Codex Leicester), although started as early as 1503–4, was written in good part from 1508 to 1510. In addition to continued studies of hydraulics and plans for improved canals, Leonardo further explored means of improving global navigation through better cosmology and the design of effective clocks. In coming years, he was to apply his knowledge of hydraulics to projects for channeling rivers and developing canals in Milan (1506 onward), in the papal territories (1513–14), and in France (1516–19).

Leonardo's interest in linking science, technology, and power can be seen in other domains. In the spring of 1503, immediately after his return to Florence from Cesare's court, he resumed his studies of the mechanics of bird flight—an issue that had attracted his attention in Milan during the 1490s. As a military engineer, Leonardo had worked on submarines and tanks, so perhaps this interest was a means of providing Florence with a weapons system even more terrifying than cannon.

Leonardo was convinced that he could become the first human to realize the dream of Daedalus. In a *Notebook* entry, he wrote enigmatically: "The great bird will take its first flight from the back of the great swan, dumbfounding the universe, overwhelming with its renown all writings, and bringing eternal glory to its birthplace." Scholars explain that this doubtless refers to "a high hill outside Florence that in the sixteenth century was called Monte Ceceri [Mount Swan]" and suggest that if Leonardo actually attempted to fly, it probably was in 1505 or early 1506. One tradition has it that peasants long recalled the brief appearance of a huge bird in those hills. Not surprisingly, of course, Leonardo's designs for aircraft lacked the motor power to stay aloft: another failure, again four centuries ahead of its time.

While Leonardo painted and then abandoned the ill-fated *Battle of Anghiari*, explored varied scientific questions, and perhaps tried to fly, Niccolò was intensively raising a citizen army for Florence and seeking a competent general to command it. In March 1505, Pisan troops defeated a Florentine force and retook some of the countryside around the besieged city. Enabled to cut off the shipment of wheat from the seacoast to Florence, the Pisans caused a sharp increase in the price of food. Famine threatened. After the failure to divert the Arno, pressure for a military victory over Pisa increased.

A coalition subsidized by Venice, led by Bartolomeo d'Alviano, threatened Florence. Aligned with the powerful Orsini family in Rome, this force, it was assumed, sought to restore Piero de' Medici. Niccolò was sent to negotiate with Giampaolo Baglioni, the notorious parricide and ruler of Perugia, who had refused to continue to provide military forces for Florence. He then went to the court of the marquis of Mantua (who was offered thirty-three thousand ducats—over four times the cost of the ill-fated diversion—for a year of service along with three hundred men-at-arms). Then Niccolò was sent to Pandolfo Petrucci, ruler of Siena and another of the condottieri potentially hostile to Florence. Niccolò did not return to Florence from the last of these missions until the end of July 1505.

The choice of condottiere was a matter of domestic as well as foreign policy. Alamanno Salviati and his allies had strongly favored the selection of Baglioni, and when Baglioni defected as part of a secret plot to restore the Medici, favored the marquis of Mantua. Soderini favored a Spanish general. Niccolò was again the man in the middle, serving his superior but aware of the hostile intentions of the clique that had originally supported his nomination as second chancellor. These complications were aggravated when the powerful Lanfredino Lanfredini—an old ally of the Machiavelli family and a leading figure in tax policy—openly opposed Soderini's choice of military captain.

In July, while Niccolò was in Siena, his assistant and friend Buonaccorsi wrote to reassure him that "we here find ourselves at present with such forces and so much money that we should not suffer much, if nothing else turns up." In August, Florentine forces fought and defeated d'Alviano. This event gives a striking example of Niccolò's devious methods. The soldier who led the troops for Florence, Ercole Bentivoglio, wanted to be named military captain and took credit for the victory. Niccolò, aware that other soldiers also played a role, wrote the commissioner at Pisa a revealing letter:

> *Keep what I am writing you a secret. The consultative meeting this morning decided upon conferring the [marshal's] baton to Messer Ercole [Bentivoglio], but they want to put off announcing it for a day or two in order to see what they have to do to placate Marco Antonio [Colonna, another condottiere], fearing that he may raise the devil. It would be a good idea to do two things: first . . . send someone here to let people know that the glory for the rout is not all Ercole's because he sent word several days ago seeking to have his prowess proclaimed; two, for you to write to some authoritative friend here. . . . In short, the honesty of [two other captains] has made this third man too insolent and has given him too much prestige. You can remedy the situation. Tear up this letter.*

To follow up the victory, Pisa was once again attacked. Niccolò was dispatched to the camp. Once again, although the artillery breached the besieged city's walls, the infantry failed to attack successfully. And so, again, Florence had failed to recapture Pisa. Niccolò, who had been actively lobbying for a citizen army for several years, finally convinced

Piero Soderini to ignore the fears of the Florentine elite and recruit and arm local peasants.

The project of a citizen militia, which was to occupy Niccolò extensively in the fall of 1505 and first months of 1506, was intensely political. The old Florentine political families, accustomed to wealth and power, distrusted Soderini and saw Niccolò as his lackey. They feared that Soderini would use a citizen army to become a tyrant and "remove the citizens who were his enemies," as one notable later put it. Though the Signoria acquiesced, their fears were compounded by Niccolò's choice of a general to lead his new troops: Don Michele, formerly Cesare Borgia's lieutenant and executioner, feared for his brutality.

Once recruitment was approved, Niccolò personally toured the hill villages around Florence to enroll peasants for the militia. By February 15, 1506, during Carnival celebrations, the first troops were paraded through the Piazza della Signoria. Dressed in "a white doublet, a pair of trousers half white, half red, a white cap, and shoes, an iron breastplate and lance, and some with guns," and drilled in "the Swiss manner," the local troops were praised by the crowd—and condemned by the wealthy. Niccolò set off again to recruit more troops. He was not to return to Florence until the end of March 1506.

A few weeks later, Leonardo—discouraged by the failures of the diversion of the Arno, the *Battle of Anghiari*, and his "great bird"—left Florence for Milan at the invitation of the French governor, Charles d'Amboise, count of Chaumont. An entry in his notebook used in 1506 records, for "the 15th day of April," the receipt of "25 florins from the chancellor of Santa Maria Nuova," where Leonardo kept his money. On April 27, 1506, the Confraternity of the Immaculate Conception in Milan agreed to pay him two hundred lire to retouch the *Virgin of the Rocks*, which Leonardo had painted years before when working in Milan with Ambrogio de Predis. By late April, therefore, he was probably back in Milan, now under French control.

The Aftermath / 145

After the spring of 1506, the careers of Leonardo and Niccolò diverge. Leonardo was to return to Florence to fight for the inheritance of his uncle Francesco's property in 1507–8. It is possible they met then or during Leonardo's later visits, associated with the Medici, but there is little evidence that they ever worked closely again.

Both Leonardo and Niccolò had learned greatly from their failures, but the lessons differed. For Leonardo, it had been intolerable to be without money and without influence. The king of France and his governor in Milan, Charles d'Amboise, had ample resources and, unlike the *gonfaloniere* of the Florentine republic, could spend money without begging governmental committees and assemblies for permission. What is more, the French obviously respected Leonardo and wanted his advice on technical matters.

The Arno project had failed in part because neither Niccolò nor Piero Soderini could enforce their will on reticent field commanders and suspicious civic leaders. The choice of Colombino as engineer had been a mistake, but it could have been rectified if the commissioners in the camp at Pisa had insisted he follow Niccolò's suggestions. Redirecting a river required daring engineering and a willingness to persist in the face of a temporary setback. Leonardo learned that to combine science and technology with public policy, he would need to work with stronger leaders than Piero Soderini. His choice of patrons from 1506 until his death in 1519—Charles d'Amboise, French governor of Milan; Giuliano de' Medici, brother of Pope Leo X; King Francis I of France—shows he learned the lesson well.

Niccolò came to share the opinion that Piero Soderini was too weak and indecisive a leader. Given their long association, he was discreet in expressing such views. In 1513, after Giovanni de' Medici was elected pope, he pardoned the Soderini family, and Cardinal Francesco took on important functions at the Vatican; there is little sign that Niccolò relied on their earlier familiarity to gain favor. In fact, although the exiled *gonfaloniere* was to offer Niccolò a well-paid job in 1521, there is no evidence that Niccolò was seriously tempted. A year later, when Piero Soderini died, Niccolò wrote a poetic epitaph that is a biting characterization of his superior:

That night when Piero Soderini died, his spirit went to the mouth of Hell. Pluto roared: "Why to Hell? Silly spirit, go up into Limbo with all the rest of the babies."

Elsewhere, Niccolò indicates his respect for Soderini's basic decency, but also his frustration for his indecision and unwillingness to undertake bold initiatives.

As Niccolò reflected on Florence's failures during these years, however, he realized that no one individual was responsible. He never wrote a public document analyzing the diversion of the Arno, but he did analyze the failure of the siege of Pisa in 1505–6. His reasoning in Book I, chapter 53 of the *Discourses on Titus Livy* applies to the events of 1504 as well:

there is no easier way to make a republic where the people has authority come to ruin than to put it into mighty enterprises, for where the people is of any moment, they are always accepted; nor will there be any remedy for whoever is of another opinion. But if the ruin of the city arises from this, there arises also, and more often, the particular ruin of citizens who are posted to such enterprises, for since the people had presupposed victory, when loss comes it accuses neither fortune nor the impotence of whoever has governed but his malevolence and ignorance; and most often it kills or imprisons or confines him, as happened to infinite Carthaginian captains and to many Athenians. Nor does any victory that they have had in the past help them, because the present loss cancels everything, as happened to our Antonio Giacomini: not having captured Pisa as the people had presupposed for itself and he had promised, he came to such popular disgrace that notwithstanding his infinite past good works, he survived more by the humanity of those who had authority over him than by any other cause that would defend him among the people.

In a republic, in other words, popular opinion is fickle, easily swayed by "mighty promises" about "mighty enterprises," and—"when loss comes"—the public is just as easily turned against those who are identified with failed hopes. What Niccolò says here of others can, of course, apply to himself.

Niccolò's skepticism about "mighty enterprises" and "mighty promises" is given an interesting twist in the *Art of War*. There, Machiavelli discusses the potential of technological and scientific inventions, concluding they are likely to be used to "deceive" the enemy with "false" appearances rather than to have lasting effects. Though gunpowder and cannon may transform warfare, the essential factor for Machiavelli is and remains the morale and civic virtue of the soldiers.

Leonardo drew a different lesson from failure, concluding that, to succeed, he should work for kings or rulers with the power and resources to act independently. While Niccolò also sought to gain a position of influence, he argued that strong and intelligent leadership is best channeled into the creation and maintenance of republican governments. After 1506, therefore, Leonardo and Niccolò went their separate ways. Leonardo kept trying to use science and technology to solve human problems. Niccolò turned to politics.

For Niccolò, the failure of the Arno project was a combination of "fortune" and "the impotence of whoever has governed." As he would put it in *The Prince*, the solution is to conquer fortune through "virtue" and "one's own arms." What is needed for political success are "good arms" and "good laws," not a reliance on science and technology. Such "mighty enterprises" as moving the Arno to make Florence a seaport, providing quick and easy solutions to complex problems, were best forgotten. The experience of working with Leonardo was like a dream—a bad dream.

Chapter 9

LEONARDO IN THE COURTS OF POWER

(1506–1519)

Leonardo was fifty-four when he returned to Milan in 1506. Despite pressure from Soderini and the government, he had lacked the heart to go back to work on the *Battle of Anghiari*—and with payments for the damaged painting stopped since the previous winter, Leonardo had no income and few prospects in Florence. At the height of his intellectual powers, he sought not only status and respect, but economic independence.

When the French governor of Milan, Charles d'Amboise, invited Leonardo to his court, the Florentine government had little choice but to grant him a three-month leave of absence. France was, after all, a key ally in the war against Pisa. But Soderini's reluctance was evident in the condition that Leonardo pay a penalty of 150 florins should he delay his return.

In Milan, the French governor wanted Leonardo to design a palace and improvements to the locks and dams of the city's canals. Using his knowledge of hydraulics, Leonardo also invented a machine to measure the amounts taken from public water supplies by each user. In return, he was to be granted the income from the tax on "twelve ounces of water" from one of the canals on which he had worked. And the vineyard he had been given by Sforza years before was restituted. Leonardo seemed assured of a solid income for the first time in years.

Leonardo had little reason to return to Florence, and in August, Charles d'Amboise asked for an extension of his term in Milan. The request was met with hostility. Soderini wrote to the French governor that Leonardo had

> *received a large sum of money and has only made a small beginning of the great work he was commissioned to carry out. We do not wish further delays to be asked for on his behalf, for his work is supposed to satisfy the citizens of this city. We cannot release him from his obligations—having committed ourselves in this matter—without exposing ourselves to serious damage.*

The French governor wrote back, praising Leonardo in terms that suggest the Florentines did not properly appreciate his genius.

> *The excellent works accomplished in Italy and especially in Milan by Master Leonardo da Vinci, your fellow citizen, have made all those who see them singularly love their author, even if they have never met him. . . . If it is fitting to recommend a man of such rich talent to his fellow citizens, we recommend him to you to the best of our ability, assuring you that everything you can do to increase either his fortune and well-being or the honors to which he is entitled would give us as well as himself the greatest pleasure, and we should be much obliged to you.*

Soderini's government lacked either the money or the will to match the benefits Leonardo enjoyed in Milan. The vice chancellor of Milan, followed by King Louis XII in person, intervened, urging that Leonardo be allowed to stay. Leonardo did just that, though Soderini asked that the city be repaid for the money spent on the *Battle of Anghiari*. Niccolò was unlikely to have been involved in this correspondence, since he was on mission to the papal court from late August through October 1506.

Just as it appeared Leonardo had left Florence for good, his uncle Francesco died (probably in May 1506) and a legal battle erupted over his will. Leonardo's half brothers, who previously had excluded him from a share in his father's estate, now contested Francesco's will, hoping to block Leonardo's inheritance of a property in Vinci. Leonardo was furious. He determined to fight for his legal rights.

When King Louis XII visited Milan in May 1507, Leonardo organized and designed the festivities, including "arches of greenery" with the royal arms and "a triumphal chariot [that] bore the cardinal virtues and the god Mars, holding in one hand an arrow and in the other a palm, symbol of victory." Profiting from the occasion, Leonardo had the king write the Signoria of Florence on behalf of his suit: "We singularly desire that this lawsuit be brought to a conclusion in the best and swiftest rendering of justice possible; we have willingly written in support of this cause." Despite the importance of the French alliance—and another supporting letter from the governor of Milan—nothing happened.

In June 1507, Leonardo cleared his bank account in Florence. It is probable that he repaid the government for its expenses associated with the *Battle of Anghiari*, hoping thereby to overcome the negative feelings created by his departure a year earlier. A decision was still not forthcoming.

Leonardo decided to prosecute his claim in person. On August 15, 1507, Governor Charles d'Amboise wrote the Signoria that Leonardo had been given leave to return to Florence to settle the case. Leonardo set up a temporary residence in Florence as the guest of Piero di Braccio Martelli (whose father had been one of Lorenzo de' Medici's best friends). In the same house lived the sculptor Rustici, a former apprentice of Verrocchio who was working on magnificent bronze statues for the Baptistry at the Duomo. Rustici and his friends in the local artistic community—Andrea del Sarto, Aristotele Sangallo, and Piero di Cosimo—formed a humorous confraternity called the Company of the Caldron. Leonardo joined this fun-loving group, which shared parties, jokes, and shoptalk.

Leonardo spent free time reorganizing his *Notebooks*. He helped Rustici with his statues. In September, seeking additional pressure for a favorable decision, he sent a letter to Cardinal Ippolito d'Este, asking his intervention with the judge in the case. Leonardo had apparently first met the cardinal in the 1490s, while at Ludovico Sforza's court.

This text is the only surviving letter signed personally by Leonardo and actually sent (it was found in the cardinal's archives in Modena). Dated September 28, 1507, the body of the letter is in the handwriting of Niccolò's deputy, Agostino Vespucci.

> *I arrived from Milan but a few days since and finding that my elder brother refuses to carry into effect a will, made three years ago when my father died—as also, and no less, because I would not fail in a matter I esteem most important—I cannot forbear to crave of your most Reverend Highness a letter of recommendation and favor to Ser Raphaello Hieronymo, at present one of the illustrious members of the Signoria before whom my cause is being argued; and more particularly it has been laid by his Excellency the Gonfalonier into the hands of the said Ser Raphaello, that his Worship may have to decide and end it before the festival of All Saints. And therefore, my Lord, I entreat you, as urgently as I know how and am able, that your Highness will write a letter to the said Ser Raphaello in that admirable and pressing manner which your Highness can use, recommending to him Leonardo Vincio, your most humble servant as I am, and shall always be; requesting him and pressing him not only to do me justice but to do so with despatch; and I have not the least doubt, from the many things that I hear, that Ser Raphaello, being most affectionately devoted to your Highness, the matter will issue ad votum. And this I shall attribute to your most Reverend Highness' letter, to whom I once more humbly comment myself.* Et bene valeat.

To settle a lawsuit in Florence, why did Leonardo write to a cardinal in Ferrara? And why was the letter dictated to or written by Niccolò's deputy? The answers are suggested by the text, which shows that Leonardo was well informed: the judge, Rafaello Girolami, had twice been nominated for office by Piero Soderini. Soderini himself, critical of Leonardo, was not likely to have suggested this letter be written. In contrast, Niccolò, back in Florence at the time, was in a position to know

Girolami's connections and see to it that his assistant Agostino gave Leonardo assistance in writing Cardinal Ippolito.

Around the same time, the marquis de Mantua, whose wife, Isabella d'Este, had befriended Leonardo years before, apparently offered to negotiate a settlement between Leonardo and his stepbrothers. Ser Giuliano da Vinci, spokesman for those contesting the will, proposed an arrangement acceptable to Leonardo, but it seems the other brothers resisted. Leonardo wrote the marquis, asking for his help in persuading the recalcitrant stepbrothers.

When the decision was not made by All Saints' Day (November 1), Leonardo prolonged his stay. Because he had settled his debt with the Florentine government and no longer feared suit for failure to complete the *Battle of Anghiari*, his presence in Florence did not generate a public controversy. As time went on, Leonardo's negotiations with his stepbrothers finally bore fruit, leading to a reconciliation with his stepbrother Ser Giuliano.

By the late winter or early spring of 1508, a letter Leonardo drafted to the French governor of Milan shows he was planning his return to Lombardy and was seeking to ensure his income and status.

> *I am afraid lest the small return I have made for the great benefits I have received from your Excellency, have not made you somewhat angry with me, and that this is why to so many letters which I have written to your Lordship I have never had an answer. I now send Salai to explain to your Lordship that I am almost at an end of the litigation I had with my brother; that I hope to find myself with you this Easter, and to carry with me two pictures of two Madonnas of different sizes. These were done for our most Christian King, or for whomsoever your Lordship may please. I should be very glad to know on my return thence where I may have to reside, for I would not give any more trouble to your Lordship. Also, as I have worked for the most Christian King, whether my salary is to continue or not. I wrote to the President as to that water which the king granted me, and which I was not put in possession of because at that time there was a dearth in the canal by reason of the great droughts and because its out-*

lets were not regulated; but he certainly promised me that when this was done I should be put in possession. Thus I pray your Lordship that you will take so much trouble, now that these outlets are regulated, as to remind the President of the matter; that is, to give me possession of this water, because on my return I hope to make there instruments and other things which will greatly please our most Christian King. Nothing else occurs to me. I am always yours to command.

This issue was extremely important to Leonardo, for his *Notebooks* contain another draft of this letter, a draft of a similar text addressed directly to the president of the canals, and a letter to his protégé Francesco Melzi, asking for help in securing the promised income from the water tax.

After the suit with his stepbrothers was finally decided in Leonardo's favor and an agreement reached on the contested property, Leonardo returned to Milan in the summer of 1508. During Leonardo's stay in Florence, Niccolò was on several diplomatic travels, including a prolonged mission to the court of Emperor Maximilian from December 1507 through June 1508. As a result, Niccolò could not have seen Leonardo during much of his stay in Martelli's house, although they could have met whenever they were in Florence together. Although Leonardo's *Notebooks* contain the draft of a letter to "Messer Niccolò" that some have dated at this time, it was probably written to someone else almost a decade later.

In any event, Niccolò's main concerns during this period were diplomatic and military rather than hydraulic. There is no indication of renewed interest in plans for the Arno. As Leonardo's letter to the governor of Milan indicates, his mind was on other waters.

Back in Milan, Leonardo happily rejoined the life of the French governor's court. He continued to design improvements to the city's canals and hydraulics, worked on several famous paintings (including probably the *Virgin with St. Anne* and *Leda*), engaged in extensive studies of human anatomy, devised numerous inventions, and explored mathematical problems (notably squaring the circle).

In 1510, he was consulted as one of the city's engineers on interior construction in the cathedral of Milan. Among his projects was an ambitious canal to join Milan with Lake Como. And he reflected deeply on astronomy, hydrology, and geology, to name but a few of the domains he sought to master. While engaged in this dazzling variety of activities, Leonardo continued to meet with leading scholars and to record his thoughts and conclusions in his *Notebooks*.

The unstable politics of Italy and the vicissitudes of human life threatened this fruitful activity. French control in Lombardy was contested by the pope and his Spanish, Swiss, and German allies. In 1511, Leonardo's patron, Charles d'Amboise died, probably of malaria. His successor was Marshal Trivulzio, for whom Leonardo had designed a life-sized equestrian tomb several years earlier.

Leonardo's relationship with Trivulzio doubtless continued after the marshal became governor of Milan. From his first stay there, in the early 1480s, Leonardo had been concerned with military technology and the mobility of armed forces. Among his designs were movable bridges, tanks, and other wheeled vehicles. It is not impossible that these ideas contributed to Trivulzio's brilliant success several years later in the battle of Marignano.

In 1512, the pope and his allies restored Massimiliano Sforza, Ludovico's legitimate son, to power in Milan. Leonardo prudently left the city, staying with his aristocratic apprentice Francesco Melzi and his family in Vaprio. From the summer of 1512 through mid-1513, during the events following the expulsion of the French from Milan and the overthrow of the republic in Florence, Leonardo remained in the country. With these events, once again Leonardo had lost his patronage and his income. It is not clear how he chose his next patron, but as his *Notebooks* record, "I left Milan for Rome on the 24th day of September, 1513, with Giovanni, Francesco Melzi, Salai, Lorenzo [a pupil], and Il Fanfoia [probably a servant]."

Leonardo traveled to Florence, where he deposited three hundred florins of his savings in Santa Maria Nuova in October and met his new patron,

Giuliano de' Medici. A year earlier, after the fall of the Florentine republic in September 1512, Giuliano had become the effective ruler of Florence. Then, in March 1513, his brother Giovanni de' Medici had been elected Pope Leo X. As a consequence, Giuliano had just been called to Rome, where he was to become the commander of the papal armies.

In October 1513, Leonardo and Giuliano traveled together from Florence to Rome. Once there, Leonardo was established in the Belvedere, a villa within the Vatican near the pope's residence; it was extensively renovated for his needs. Giuliano de' Medici, interested in the natural sciences, is said to have treated Leonardo "like a brother."

In Rome, Leonardo worked extensively on scientific research as well as numerous inventions. He does not seem to have competed with Michelangelo, Raphael, and the younger generation of artists who vied for the favors of Pope Leo X. Instead, he devoted himself to the study of physics, anatomy, mathematics, and botany as well as practical devices and projects directly useful to his patron, Giuliano.

The pope decided that the marshes on either side of the Appian Way should be drained, and entrusted the task to Giuliano. Working with another hydraulic engineer, Leonardo designed drainage canals. His map of the project (Figure 9.1) shows his continued interest in environmental development through controlling the flow of water. Work was begun—but, like the planned modification of the Arno in Florence and the Adda in Milan, the project was not completed. Not until the nineteenth century would the Pontine Marshes outside Rome be drained.

Embarking on a new challenge, Leonardo made "carefully disguised" notes on how to make a curved mirror. Some of these computations and notes concern a device for looking at the sky so that "the image of the planet . . . will show the surface of the planet much enlarged." Although this might seem to be little more than a lucky anticipation of the idea of Sir Isaac Newton's reflecting telescope, Leonardo was also doing something practical for Giuliano de' Medici. As his notes show, Leonardo had in mind an invention that would combine the ancient genius of Archimedes, who used "burning mirrors" to defend the city of Syracuse, with a com-

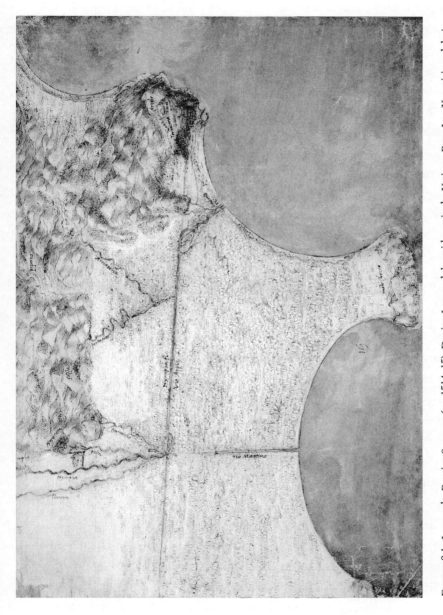

FIGURE 9.1. Leonardo, Pontine Swamps (ca. 1514–15). During Leonardo's residence in the Vatican, Pope Leo X envisioned draining the swamps outside Rome, and delegated its supervision to Leonardo's patron, Guiliano de' Medici. Realization of such a project did not occur until the nineteenth century.

mercial project of his patron. The Medici were in the cloth business. For the purpose of dyeing, large vats of hot water were needed. Leonardo was designing a kind of mirror that could be used not only for telescopes, but for harnessing solar energy in industrial processing: "with this one can supply heat for any boiler in a dyeing factory. And with this a pool can be warmed up, because there will be always boiling water."

In December 1514, Leonardo's half-brother Ser Giuliano da Vinci visited him while in Rome, confirming the reconciliation with his half-brothers. While in the Vatican, Leonardo occasionally amused himself by playing practical jokes on the papal entourage. Vasari describes one such trick. Leonardo cleaned a bull's intestines and attached them through tubes to a blacksmith's bellows hidden in the next room. Once a group had come into the "very big room" where the apparatus was set up, the intestines were inflated to become "transparent objects full of air" that pushed the unsuspecting victims into the corners.

Despite his efforts, Leonardo was not at ease in the Vatican. And soon his patron, Giuliano de' Medici, was gone. Although Giuliano was ill and apparently more interested in business and science than politics, the Medici had other plans for him. Pope Leo X projected the creation of a state in the Romagna, and expected Giuliano to be its head. Part of the scheme involved a royal marriage with Philiberta of Savoy.

Giuliano's departure for the wedding left Leonardo without support within the Vatican. As with other events that were important to him, Leonardo noted the date: "The Magnifico Giuliano de' Medici left Rome on the 9th of January 1515, just at daybreak, to take a wife in Savoy, and on the same day fell the death of the king of France." At a stroke, his previous patron Louis XII was dead and his current patron gone.

Giuliano de' Medici's departure was followed by a crisis in the project of the great curved mirror. To assist Leonardo, Giuliano had hired a German glassmaker named Master Giovanni of the Mirrors and a smith named Master Giorgio to work with Leonardo in its construction. Master Giovanni and his assistant apparently preferred drinking beer to working.

Leonardo was convinced that Master Giovanni sought to steal his inventions. Instead of carrying out instructions, moreover, Giovanni set up a salesroom in his studio, selling his own productions for private profit.

Leonardo wrote several drafts of a bitter letter to his absent patron, complaining that the German Giovanni of the Mirrors and his assistant were preventing work on Giuliano's project:

> *I was so greatly rejoiced, most Illustrious Lord, by the wished for recovery of your health, that my own ills have almost left me; and I say God be praised for it. But it vexes me greatly that I have not been able completely to satisfy your Excellency's wishes by reason of that German deceiver.*

Master Giorgio retaliated, denouncing Leonardo for performing autopsies and charging him with black magic or worse. The pope was forced to forbid Leonardo from continuing his anatomical studies. Ill, angry, and frustrated, Leonardo felt isolated and vulnerable in the Vatican's maze of intrigue. The fate of Leonardo's parabolic mirror, intended to combine scientific research and practical technology, symbolizes much in his career.

In 1515, the newly crowned Francis I was determined to reestablish French power in the Italian peninsula. The resulting campaign, led by Marshal Trivulzio, was a brilliant success. The Venetians, allied with the Swiss, had assumed that the French army would take one of the main passes over the Alps. Trivulzio fooled them. Using complex techniques of block and tackle, he brought the powerful French artillery across a rough peasant track through the mountains, surprised the Swiss, and routed them at Marignano in 1515.

At the time, the victory was attributed to the young Francis I. It established the newly crowned king on the European diplomatic and military stage. The idea and technology for the success have all the earmarks of Leonardo's inventive mind and might explain why, almost immediately after the victory of Marignano, Leonardo responded to his frustrations in

Rome by joining with the pope as he went to Bologna to meet the victorious Francis. As soon as he could, Leonardo met the young king, secured his patronage, and accepted an invitation to move to France. It was as well, for within a year Giuliano de' Medici would be dead of tuberculosis.

Sometime in 1516, Leonardo left Rome. Traveling by stages, the aging genius arrived at Francis I's castle of Amboise on the south shore of the Loire. The king installed Leonardo in the Clos Lucet, a small but elegant house nearby.

The castle was joined to Leonardo's house by an underground passage, allowing the king to visit him at any time without arousing the suspicions of courtiers. No longer able to paint due to a stroke that affected his right arm, Leonardo pursued scientific research, architectural plans for a new royal castle at Romoranton, and technical innovations. Construction was even begun at Romoranton, only to be abandoned when an epidemic hit the workers.

For the young Francis, Leonardo was a "philosopher" as well as an artist and engineer. But he was also an ornament in the life of the court. In April and May 1518, Leonardo helped organize the festivities for the marriage of Madeleine de la Tour d'Auvergne with Lorenzo di Piero de' Medici, governor of Florence and Giuliano's nephew. For the event, on May 18 Leonardo even re-created the Masque of the Planets first performed for Ludovico Sforza some twenty years earlier.

As his energies dwindled, Leonardo spent more time in geometrical pastimes and conversation. Unable to paint himself, he relied on his protégé Melzi, who seems to have completed some copies of the maestro's paintings as well as works of his own. On April 23, 1519, Leonardo drafted his last will:

> *Be it known to all persons, present and to come that at the court of our Lord the King at Amboise before ourselves in person, Messer Leonardo da Vinci painter to the King, at present staying at the place known as Cloux near Amboise, duly considering the certainty of death and the uncertain-*

ty of its time, has acknowledged and declared in said court and before us that he has made, according to the tenor of these presents, his testament and the declaration of his last will, as follows . . .

After specifying the burial, funeral services, and masses befitting one of the king's household, Leonardo left Francesco Melzi "each and all of the books the Testator is at present possessed of, and the instruments and portraits appertaining to his art and calling as a painter" and named him "sole and only executor." His servant Battista de Vilanis and his former ward, Salai, each received one half of the vineyard in Milan that Sforza had given Leonardo years before. His bank account at Santa Maria Nuova in Florence, worth four hundred scudi, went to his brothers.

Less than a month later, on May 2, 1519, Leonardo was dead. Leonardo was not only visited frequently by Francis I during his final illness but—according to the story reported by Vasari but contested by many historians—died in the king's arms. At the very end, after a priest had given him Extreme Unction, Leonardo is supposed to have admitted to the king "how much he had offended God by not working on his art as much as he should have." Historians have challenged the story, noting that a royal decree was signed at St.-Germain-en-Laye on May 3. But since the king himself did not sign the document, one cannot be sure.

Leonardo left behind staggering collections of *Notebooks*, some—he thought—in condition to be edited and published. He left these manuscripts to his student and friend Francesco Melzi. The task of editing them, however, proved too great. The exception was the *Treatise on Painting*, which Melzi—himself a painter—left in good enough condition that it circulated within years of Leonardo's death and was published in the seventeenth century. For the rest, the pages of Leonardo's *Notebooks* came to be valued as collectibles, to be bought for the honor and pleasure of owning sheets with the sketches and writing of the universal genius. Progressively dismantled, Leonardo's *Notebooks* were distributed to the winds. Only in the last 125 years have they begun to be reconstituted.

Leonardo's aim was universal knowledge placed in the service of human life. He turned his back on scholastic learning, dogmatic religious belief, and traditional ways of doing and making things. In science, he insisted no theory was valid unless it could be based on mathematical precision and tested by observation and experiment. At the same time, he constantly sought practical applications of abstract principles, moving on a single page of notes from the purest scientific theory to a useful device to settle a problem of the moment.

Putting Leonardo back into context does more than reveal the complexities and ambition of his character. It also shows his political goal: a society based on science and technology, in which individuals can compete economically for wealth without challenging the laws of the land. We take it for granted that a foreign-born physicist like Einstein could link purely scientific theories to the technology of nuclear fission, which won a major war for the United States and revolutionized twentieth-century society. Leonardo made the integration of science, industry, and politics his conscious goal.

The irony is that, contrary to Leonardo's intention, so much of his foresight was so long unknown. He always assumed that the ideas contained in his *Notebooks* would be published. Given his commitment to developing a science that would be a guide to practice, he had little patience for the view that knowledge should be pursued for its own sake: "Avoid studies of which the result dies with the worker." Whatever their differences, on this principle Leonardo and Niccolò saw eye to eye. By this standard, however, it was Leonardo—not Niccolò—who failed.

Chapter 10

NICCOLÒ'S STRUGGLE, VICTORY, AND DEFEAT

(1506–1527)

❦

When Leonardo went to Milan in 1506, Niccolò was thirty-seven. After eight years as second chancellor, Niccolò was trusted by Piero Soderini, the head of the republic, and his brother Francesco, cardinal of Volterra. Although the clique of Soderini's enemies, led by Niccolò's former patron Alamanno Salviati, now disliked him, many in Florence had confidence in Niccolò's political judgment and recognized his subtle negotiating skills.

Over the next six years, Niccolò would overcome numerous obstacles, create a citizen's militia that finally captured Pisa, play a central role in Florentine foreign policy—and then lose office in 1512, when Spanish armies defeated the republic, Soderini was expelled, and the Medici returned to power. Tortured as a potential conspirator not long after this, Niccolò stubbornly sought employment from the Medici, finally succeeded, and began to play a political role again—only to lose it all when, in 1527, the Medici were replaced by a short-lived republican regime. Depressed, Niccolò died only days after this last disappointment.

These repeated misfortunes had an ironic result. Deprived of political power, Niccolò was forced to rely on his training as a poet and man of letters. He became, as he signed a letter near the end of his life, "Niccolò Machiavelli, historian, comic author, and tragic author." The works that came from his pen changed the shape of Western history.

After the failure of the Arno diversion, Niccolò turned his attention to the project of raising a militia through conscription. The project was violently opposed by wealthy aristocrats, who saw it as a challenge to their influence. In February 1506, however, the first chancellor, Marcello Adriani, wrote a warm note—using the personal address *tu*—reporting that "here the idea [of the militia] is being considered more favorably every day." A month later, Cardinal Francesco Soderini wrote from Rome that he was pleased that "your new military idea, which corresponds to our hope for the welfare and dignity of our country, is progressing. . . . You must get no small satisfaction from the fact that such a worthy thing should have been given its beginnings by your hands. Please persevere and bring it to the desired end."

Raising the militia meant traveling the countryside, actively enrolling troops. Every household was expected to provide one draft-age recruit. As in most countries, some people did not want to serve in the military draft. Sometimes powerful people intervened to gain exemptions for needy clients.

When Niccolò wasn't raising the militia in the towns and villages controlled by Florence, he was often on a diplomatic mission. Members of the Signoria, many relatively unfamiliar with foreign affairs due to their short terms in office, badgered him for reports. Niccolò was not above ignoring such requests or writing an insulting reply.

There were also suggestions that Niccolò was enjoying himself too much when recruiting in the countryside or traveling on diplomatic missions. Soderini's nephew Giovan Batista, after wondering whether letters "went astray" since they hadn't been answered, suggests "it might perhaps not be a good idea to fool around too much." Sometimes, Niccolò's sin was

Niccolò's Struggle, Victory, and Defeat / 165

lust. One instance became a joke that Niccolò told on himself when writing a friend, Luigi Guicciardini.

> *Hell's Bells, Luigi, see how Fortune hands out to mankind different results under similar circumstances. Why, you had hardly finished fucking your woman before you wanted another fuck, and you want to take another turn at it. But as for me, why I had been here three days, losing my discrimination because of conjugal famine, when I came upon an old woman who launders my shirts.... One day, I was passing by when she recognized me and greeted me profusely; she asked me to be so kind as to enter her house for a moment, she wanted to show me some fine shirts that I might want to buy. So, naive prick that I am, I believed her and went in; once inside, I made out in the gloom a woman cowering in a corner affecting modesty with a towel half over her head and face. The old slut took me by the hand and led me over to her saying, "This is the shirt I wanted to sell you, but I'd like you to try it on first and pay for it afterwards." I, shy fellow that I am, was absolutely terrified, still, to make a long story short, alone there with her in the dark (because the old bawd promptly left the room and shut the door), I fucked her one. Although I found her thighs flabby and her cunt damp—and her breath stank a bit—nevertheless, hopelessly horny, I went to her with it. Once I had done it, and feeling like taking a look at the merchandise, I took a piece of burning wood from the hearth in the room and lit a lamp that was above it, but the light was hardly lit before it almost fell out of my hands. Ugh! I nearly dropped dead on the spot, that woman was so ugly.*

After describing in gruesome detail the woman's disgusting appearance and the "stench on her breath," Niccolò reported that he "threw up all over her" and left.

Niccolò's correspondence tells us even more about his character. Lust as well as candor, wit, and self-deprecation: Niccolò was no angel, but he was honest. He was also often helpful, responding to numerous requests, entreaties, and favors. Not all of Niccolò's mail involved helping others.

His most frequent correspondents were his colleagues and friends in the Chancery.

Biagio Buonaccorsi, perhaps his closest friend, wrote witty, frank, newsy—and sometimes imploring—letters, often expressing fears that Niccolò is unwisely offending those with power: "I shall be happy for you to be well-served; if not, go scratch your ass." Sometimes the target is someone they both dislike: "tell that asshole Ser Battaglione to go easy." Sometimes, Biagio criticizes Niccolò: "I am so sick and tired of making excuses for you that if you were my father, more than once I would have said: Go and retch." Most of the time, however, Biagio's letters combine personal concerns and expressions of devotion with matters of great importance.

Agostino Vespucci, who had the official post of coadjutor (or assistant) to the second chancellor, also wrote informative letters and did favors for Niccolò. In 1506, Agostino arranged—for his own profit as well as his superior's benefit—to publish Niccolò's *Decennale*. Lacking copyright protection, Niccolò's poetic account of Florentine foreign affairs was promptly republished in a pirated edition; Agostino intervened, seeing to it that the guilty party was fined and the pirated copies seized. Agostino also reported that, as Niccolò had requested, copies of his own edition were presented to a number of officials, adding that "I have just come back from your house, and I took care of everything.... They are all well, very well. Marietta [Niccolò's wife] was anxious for me to give you her and the children's regards . . . only Bernardo is a little cranky."

Throughout the late spring of 1506, after Leonardo went to Milan, Niccolò was energetically recruiting the new militia. Pope Julius II was desirous of recapturing the towns and lands in the Romagna, which the church lost at the fall of Cesare Borgia. To this end, the pope raised an army and set out to eject the tyrant of Bologna. In August, Niccolò was sent to the papal court as it moved by stages to Perugia and then farther north. Niccolò had to ensure the pope's favorable disposition to Florence without openly antagonizing the French, who were supposedly protecting Bologna against Julius. While Niccolò was with the papal court (among other things seeing to its provisions while in territory controlled by Florence), a reference in his correspondence suggests he may have written to Leonardo in Milan. But later, when Leonardo returned from Milan to Florence to contest his uncle's will between 1507 and 1508, there is no record of contact between Niccolò and Leonardo (although Agostino Vespucci's assistance in the legal case suggests no bitter conflict between them). In the meantime, however, another old friendship had turned to enmity toward Niccolò—and it was to have immense consequences.

The web of personalities was a big part of the way things worked in Renaissance Florence. Niccolò became severely depressed, apparently due to the hostility of his former patron Alamanno Salviati. This personal crisis arose from the principal new element in Florentine politics: the threat that Maximilian, the Holy Roman Emperor (that is, the elected ruler of the patchwork of German principalities), would invade Italy, defeat the French, and ultimately overturn Soderini's regime. An observer was sent to the imperial court, but reports were not always accurate. Soderini's critics, led by the two Salviati cousins, pressed for the appointment of ambassadors to the emperor authorized to establish an alliance that would replace dependence on the French. For Soderini, the French alliance was the cornerstone of policy.

In June 1507, it was decided to send a more reliable observer to the imperial court. Niccolò was nominated. Then the appointment was cancelled when powerful citizens insisted that "there were many decent young men well-suited for going to Germany, and it would be good that they might become experienced." Even granted a tradition of sending young aristocrats on diplomatic missions, the decision was a direct insult to Niccolò. In his place, Francesco Vettori was sent (though in sending him, the Salviati clique could hardly know they would begin one of Niccolò's deepest friendships).

The rejection clearly had a great effect on Niccolò, even though only months before, as the Signoria formally embarked on Niccolò's projected militia, he had been named secretary of a new committee to direct the citizen army. In late July, after he had a month to get over his disappointment and anger, a friend wrote him: "My good, and *not* unfortunate Machiavelli, now that you are completely over it . . . I am glad that you have shat out the imperial commission, since you are entirely purged, I believe it is a very good thing, particularly for you, to be in Florence rather than in Germany."

Why was Niccolò so angry and depressed over the rejection of his nomination to go to the imperial court in June 1507? Niccolò's emotional reaction was doubtless triggered by domestic politics, not by an overwhelming insistence on being in Germany. His nomination had been vetoed by Alamanno Salviati, whose description of the second chancellor as a "rogue" had been reported by Buonaccorsi. This hurt because Niccolò had long benefited from close ties to the wealthy Salviati family: both Alamanno and his cousin Jacopo had helped Niccolò with money while he was in Cesare Borgia's court in 1502, at which time Alamanno had written to Niccolò, "I am your devoted friend." Later, Alamanno Salviati was one of the few whom Niccolò ever addressed as "Honored Patron." But when a former ally and friend turns against you, it rankles. And in a patron-client system like Renaissance Florence, it is dangerous—especially when your job depends on annual reelection.

It was the old story of Niccolò caught in a cross fire between Soderini and the clique led by Salviati. There were conflicts over the sending of formal ambassadors to Emperor Maximilian, the naming of a new archbishop for Florence, and the marriage of Clarice de' Medici to Filippo Strozzi, a wealthy Florentine. In these issues, Soderini's critics blamed Niccolò as well as the *gonfaloniere* for the policies they opposed, even though Niccolò was often not responsible.

Ironically, not long after the election of Francesco Vettori as official representative at the imperial court, Niccolò was sent to join him. Soderini needed to send instructions with a trusted agent. Once in Germany, Niccolò found himself working with Vettori, first as an assistant but ultimately as a colleague. In a twist of fate, the end of Niccolò's close relationship with Alamanno Salviati became the occasion for his deep and historically important friendship with Francesco Vettori.

In June 1508, Niccolò returned from his mission to the imperial court.

Niccolò's Struggle, Victory, and Defeat

Prosecution of the campaign against Pisa was intensified. Niccolò, having been responsible for recruiting the militia, was sent to the camp in August as commissioner. As the campaign dragged on, diplomatic negotiations between the principal European powers came to a head. In December, the French reached an agreement with Emperor Maximilian, later joined by the Spanish and Pope Julius II, to combine against Venice. The Pisans were the real losers, since they no longer could play one major power off the others.

In secret negotiations with France, Florence now offered to pay fifty thousand ducats for the recapture of Pisa, with half of the sum as a down payment and the remainder due when the city was retaken. For once Soderini was on the same side as Alamanno Salviati, who was chosen commissioner for what hopefully would be the final campaign. Niccolò himself went to the field as the troops of his militia were stationed around Pisa, cutting off all possible access.

Personal relations were not always easy. One day, in the camp before Pisa, Salviati—angered by the deference shown Niccolò—described him in insulting terms when speaking to a subordinate. Niccolò wrote a protest. Salviati replied that he had not intended to insult the secretary, justifying his behavior on the grounds that although the troops "wish to recognize your authority, you are not always present everywhere."

Isolated, the Pisans sent representatives to Piombino to discuss possible capitulation. Niccolò, sent in March to meet with them, thought the lower-class Pisan negotiators—chosen from the inhabitants of the countryside—were little better than animals. In May, negotiations for surrender began in earnest, with Niccolò playing a central role. The final surrender, signed for Florence by both Marcello Virgilio Adriani as first chancellor and Niccolò as second chancellor, took effect June 8, 1509.

The Florentines were jubilant at the news that Pisa had fallen, achieving a goal sought since Piero de' Medici had given up the city in 1494. On June 8, when the news reached Florence, Agostino Vespucci wrote his superior that "in some measure every man has gone mad with exultation, there are bonfires all over the city, although it is not yet three in the afternoon, just think what they will do this evening after nightfall."

It was a great moment for Niccolò. His friends congratulated him as a principal architect of the victory. Filippo Casavecchia, serving as Florentine commissioner in Barga, wrote:

> *I wish you a thousand benefits from the outstanding acquisition of that noble city for truly it can be said that your person was cause of it to a very great extent, although I do not thereby blame any of those very noble commissioners concerning either their wisdom or indeed their efforts. . . . Every day I discover you to be a greater prophet than the Hebrews or any other nation ever had.*

At the same time, however Casavecchia admits he is "extremely anxious" and suggests it is a propitious occasion for Niccolò to mend fences with Alamanno Salviati.

In effect, the moment was propitious. Salviati had agreed with Soderini on the final strategy to retake Pisa, and had worked with Niccolò in the field and in the negotiations leading up to the success. An occasion arose to seek a rapprochement. Niccolò di Alessandro Machiavelli—a member of the family whose election to governmental offices was supported by Salviati and his friends—promptly asked his cousin to help a friend, adding that "if a word should need to be said about him to Alamanno [Salviati] on my behalf, do so."

Niccolò took the hint. Writing Salviati in his capacity of commissioner to Pisa on September 28, Niccolò addressed him as "Honored Patron." The letter is a detailed analysis of the reasons Florence had nothing to fear from Emperor Maximilian's invasion of Italy. While obviously intended to mollify Salviati, the argument was not exactly felicitous since it challenged the principal theme of Salviati's pro-imperial policies in recent years. A week later, Salviati answered—"My dearest Niccolò"—politely thanking him, but concluding that

> *I believe that our duty is rather to look to God and pray Him to let whatever is best befall rather than to hope to form some other judgment; although I do not know whether this conclusion is one that will satisfy you*

much, not because I believe that you are lacking in faith but I am sure that you do not have much left.

Niccolò's attempted reconciliation failed. Perhaps his reputation for licentious behavior and religious laxity was still offensive to Salviati, whose family was known for its piety and strait-laced behavior. Within a short time, ironically, Salviati died of malaria contracted in the swamps outside Pisa. One wonders what would have happened if the diversion of the Arno had been successful and this area had been drained as part of Leonardo's grand project.

Nothing stands still in politics. Emperor Maximilian finally brought troops to Italy. Niccolò was dispatched to Mantua with a consignment of ten thousand ducats of gold as a payment to the emperor, then went to Verona. He was barely back in Florence before he was on further missions to various towns under Florentine control. Then, for the third time in his career, he was sent on a diplomatic mission to King Louis XII of France.

The goal was to encourage good relations between the French and the pope. With Pope Julius II gathering an army and advancing in the Romagna, Louis XII and his advisors felt impelled to block further advances. By treaty, Florence was bound to support them. But the second chancellor had instructions to avoid embroiling the city in war with the papacy if at all possible. Pope Julius made neutrality difficult—and began to speak of overturning the Florentine republic as well as siding with Spain to expel the French from Italy. With little accomplished, Niccolò returned home at the end of October 1510.

Within weeks, Niccolò was off again to recruit for the militia, this time raising cavalry. A war between France and the pope would put Florence in the middle, in desperate need of troops. The French, confident of victory, insisted that a council of cardinals packed against the pope be held in Pisa. Niccolò was sent on a mission to Count Grimaldi of Monaco, returned, and was dispatched to France for a fourth time. He failed to convince the French cardinals to do more than delay their planned consistory in Pisa, leaving Florence exposed as an accomplice in a plan to chastise or remove the pope.

Suddenly Julius II lost Bologna, and the papacy seemed in disarray. Despite hesitations, the Florentines officially accepted a schismatic consistory to be held on their territory in Pisa. Pope Julius II recovered and placed an interdict on Florence, forbidding the administration of the sacraments. Spain sided with the pope, and war was imminent. Through these bewildering twists and turns, Niccolò had a flurry of missions, raising troops and inspecting fortifications.

Soderini and the Signoria issued confusing commands. The pope and the Spanish forces, at the instigation of Cardinal Giovanni de' Medici, decided their goal was the removal of Soderini. Although he had an opportunity to negotiate a settlement, the *gonfaloniere* refused—even though the Spanish would probably have allowed him to stay in power. Niccolò's militia had been a match for Pisa, but would it be ready for a Spanish infantry, one of the most feared military forces in Europe?

Ultimately, much of the Florentine militia was stationed in Prato, about ten miles north of Florence, where it was attacked by the better trained and larger Spanish infantry. A first attack was repulsed. Niccolò advised Soderini to negotiate a peace, even if it involved leaving office; the *gonfaloniere* hesitated, playing for time. On August 29, 1512, a second attack of the Spaniards caused a crushing defeat and the sack of Prato.

Earlier in August, within Florence a group of young men began plotting for the return of the Medici. Some were later to be associated with Niccolò, including Paolo Vettori, one of the plot's leaders. Just before the Spanish attack on Prato, several of those involved in this plot, along with others seen as a threat to Soderini, were arrested. Among those who had been imprisoned as threats to Soderini were Tommaso del Bene and Donato del Corno (two of Niccolò's good friends), Filippo Strozzi (who would become one of Niccolò's circle), and Piero Guicciardini (whose son Luigi had been a close friend for years, even before Niccolò's famous correspondence with Luigi's younger brother Francesco).

On August 31, immediately after the defeat at Prato, a band of young men stormed the Palazzo Vecchio, led by Antonfrancesco degli Albizzi.

Niccolò's Struggle, Victory, and Defeat / 173

To the astonishment of the Signoria, they demanded the release of the prisoners and the reinstatement of all those who had been "reprimanded for sodomy," including a young relative of the Medici (Giovanni di Pierfrancesco de' Medici, later known as Giovanni delle Bande Nere), as well as the departure of Soderini. Overcoming the *gonfaloniere*'s resistance, Niccolò and Francesco Vettori engineered his resignation and flight to exile.

In the events that led to the return of the Medici, it is impossible to figure out which side Niccolò really supported. His description of the coup, in a letter to an unnamed "noblewoman," provides a firsthand account of the fall of Soderini.

> *[After the defeat at Prato] everyone's fear intensified so much that the palace and its customary guard provided by the government's men were abandoned and left totally defenseless; the Signoria was compelled to release many citizens who, since they were thought to be suspect and friendly to the Medici, had been detained for several days in the Palazzo under a heavy guard. These people, together with many other of the city's most noble citizens, who sought to recoup their prestige, took heart. Consequently, on Tuesday morning they came armed to the Palazzo, and after they seized every site in order to force the gonfalonier to depart, several citizens persuaded them to do no violence but to let him leave as agreed. And so, accompanied by these same citizens, the gonfalonier returned home; with the Signoria's consent and with a large escort, he went off to Siena when night fell.*

The resulting situation in Florence was confused. During the first days of September 1512, the youthful supporters of the Medici demanded a change of regime, in which the Great Council would be abolished and a system of government like that under Lorenzo the Magnificent reinstated. Leading the opposition to the demand for constitutional changes were men of wealth and family who feared the Medici and sought the retention of the Great Council as a means to securing their own power. In short, Niccolò's enemies were trying to keep the Great Council and its republican tradition, whereas Niccolò's friends and acquaintances were on the side of a restoration of Medici leadership.

On September 7, the youthful supporters of Giuliano de' Medici, and his family were temporarily defeated by the wealthy aristocrats. Cardinal Giovanni de' Medici, leader of the family's negotiations, remained in Prato. Then, on September 16, his nephew Giuliano and his young activists took matters into their own hands. Entering the Palazzo Vecchio with hidden weapons, they packed the square outside with mercenary soldiers—and suddenly engineered a coup d'état that returned the Medici to power. Among this group was a young man who was to become one of Machiavelli's friends and disciples, Cosimo di Cosimo Rucellai.

Niccolò described the events in his letter to the unnamed noblewoman:

> *On the sixteenth of this month [September], the Signoria assembled many citizens at the Palazzo [Vecchio], and with them was the Magnificent Giuliano [de' Medici], and they were discussing governmental reform when there chanced to be an uproar heard in the Piazza, so that [the condottiere] Romazzotti with his soldiers and some other men seized the Palazzo shouting, "Palle, palle" [the Medici cry]. The entire city was suddenly up in arms, and that name was echoing everywhere throughout the city, so that the Signoria were compelled to summon the populace to an assembly which we call a parliament, where a law was proclaimed that reinstated the Magnificent Medici in all the honors and dignities of their ancestors.*

For Niccolò himself, the situation was surely complex. Republican institutions were replaced with the system used by Lorenzo the Magnificent. Niccolò's militia was disbanded. He had long been frustrated by the indecision and weakness of Soderini, and had no love lost for the wealthy aristocrats who were unable to block the Medici return. On the other hand, young Giuliano de' Medici—presumed to be the leader in Florentine politics—was inexperienced, and the family's goals were unclear.

Niccolò made it clear he was willing to work with the Medici by immediately drafting a memorandum advising them how to increase their power in Florence. In his letter to the noblewoman, Niccolò concludes that "the city is quite peaceful and hopes, with the help of these Medici, to live no less honored than it did in times past, when their father Lorenzo the Magnificent, of most happy memory, governed." Finally, on September 29, Niccolò wrote a letter to Cardinal Giovanni de' Medici, of which only a fragment survives.

> *I therefore believe that it is necessary for your house to win friends over to your side and not to turn them away—and this is not the way. I should like to give you an example of it derived from your house. . . . Hence I repeat that I should like to make friends for your house, not enemies. And so I should see to it that there would be a discussion in the Balìa in which it would be decided that you should have from the Commune of Florence for a certain period four or five thousand ducats per year to give an imbursement to your house.*

During this period of upheaval, Niccolò did not express concern over losing his own position. Just as his father's friend Bartolomeo Scala continued as first chancellor when Savonarola replaced the Medici regime, Niccolò had every reason to expect that, along with First Chancellor Marcello Adriani, he would continue his work in the chancery.

Whatever Niccolò's hopes, fate ruled otherwise. Whether as a result of his earlier enmity with Alamanno Salviati or of his reputation as a tool of Soderini, on November 7, 1512, the Signoria "dismissed, deprived and totally removed" Niccolò Machiavelli from the posts of second chancellor and secretary to the Ten of War. His friend and assistant Biagio Buonaccorsi was removed at the same time.

The action was not merely motivated by a desire to fill the position of second chancellor with an agent personally responsible to the Medici, though his replacement—Niccolò Michelozzi—was a notary with a long career of personal service to the Medici family. Aristocrats appointed to the Medici counsels took punitive action to exclude Niccolò from all forms of political activity. Three days later, on November 10, Niccolò was restricted to Florentine territory and required to post a bond of one thousand florins.

Clearly, there were those in the Signoria who feared that Niccolò would plot to restore Soderini. A week later, another decision of the Signoria forbade Niccolò from setting foot in the Palazzo Vecchio for a year.

No one knows who put up the money for Niccolò's bond. But as the year 1512 came to an end, he found himself out of a job. To add insult to injury, with special permission he was allowed back into the Palazzo Vecchio, but only to verify the account books of his disbursements when recruiting the militia.

Niccolò was forty-three years old when he lost office. His entire career had been devoted to politics. As he wrote Francesco Vettori, "Fortune has seen to it that since I do not know how to talk about either the silk or the wool trade, or profits or losses, I have to talk about politics." Now he was not only out of office, but prevented from engaging in political action. And lacking wealth, his loss of job also meant the loss of income.

Worse was to come. Early in the new year, two young men, Pietropaolo Boscoli and Agostino Capponi, plotted to assassinate Giuliano de' Medici and restore the republic. Captured, they were discovered to have a list of names. In all probability, the list merely indicated those who had been treated with suspicion by the Medici and hence were likely to join the conspiracy. Niccolò's name was on the list. On February 8, 1513, he was arrested.

Imprisoned, Niccolò was tortured with the method known as the *strappado:* with the prisoner's hands tied together behind his back and attached to the ceiling, his body is dropped from a platform. At worst, the arms forced unnaturally upwards can be torn from their sockets. At best, the pain is severe. Niccolò continued to claim his innocence and was surprised by his strength under torture.

Languishing in prison after this ordeal, Niccolò did something quite in character (though it has puzzled several biographers). He wrote two sonnets to the newly powerful Giuliano de' Medici. The opening lines of the first sonnet are readily comprehensible in the light of the discovery that, around 1493, Niccolò had dedicated a court poem to the youthful Giuliano:

Niccolò's Struggle, Victory, and Defeat

Giuliano, I have a pair of shackles on my legs and six drops of the strappado on my back; my other misfortunes I shall not tell, since that is the way they treat poets.

After reporting his emotions as he heard the conspirators taken to their execution, Niccolò concludes with an appeal to be released in the name of the Medici's reputation: "Now let them go, I pray, if only your mercy may turn towards me, and surpass the fame of your father and your grandfather."

Since this poem did not secure his release, Niccolò wrote a second sonnet from prison, imagining that a muse came to him and said: "You are not Niccolò, but Dazzo, for you have your legs and heels tied together, and are chained up like a lunatic." Andrea Dazzo was, like Niccolò, a former student of First Chancellor Marcello Adriani. This second sonnet seems intended to remind the young Medici ruler that Niccolò was not merely a poet, but also a former second chancellor: "Give her [the muse] proof, Magnifico Giuliano, in the name of high God, that I am not Dazzo, but am myself."

The first of these sonnets was written on or after February 23, 1513, the morning of the execution of plotters Boscoli and Capponi. Two days before, Pope Julius II had died. On March 11, Cardinal Giovanni de' Medici was elected his successor, as Leo X. A son of Florence had become the pontiff. Amid the general rejoicing in the city, prisoners were pardoned. Niccolò was released.

Niccolò's first act was to write his friend Francesco Vettori, serving as Florence's ambassador to the pope, thanking him and his brother Paolo. After asking for help in getting his brother Totto a position in the pope's household, Niccolò adds a request in his own name: "If it is possible, remind Our Lordship about me in order that, if it should be possible, either he or his family might start engaging my services in some way or other."

Francesco Vettori replied, expressing his concern for Niccolò and exhorting him to "take heart against this persecution." The former secretary answered, gaving thanks "because I can say that all that is left to me of my life I owe to the Magnificent Giuliano and your Paolo" and predicting that while he would be "happy" if he received a job from "these new masters of ours," he would "get on" if nothing were forthcoming.

In the exchange of letters between Niccolò and his friend that followed, one constant theme is Niccolò's desire to work for the Medici. On April 9, he writes: "I hear that Cardinal [Francesco] Soderini is busying himself a lot with the pontiff. I should like you to advise me whether or not you think it would be appropriate for me to write him a lètter requesting a recommendation to His Holiness." Vettori advised against contacting Cardinal Soderini "because, although he is very busy and is in good credit with the pope as far as what can be seen outwardly, he still has many Florentines opposed to him, and if he put you forward, I do not think it would be suitable."

When it became clear that Vettori's embassy to Rome would be prolonged, Niccolò expressed optimism about his chances for employment. Yet no job offer came.

Part of the problem was Niccolò's reputation as a man without moral rectitude and religious faith. When a friar predicted a coming catastrophe, for example, Niccolò admitted that "I myself did not hear the sermon, for I do not observe such practices." Stories of playful jokes and sexual promiscuity abound in Niccolò's letters. In 1510, there had been an anonymous accusation that he "committed an unnatural sexual act with a certain Lucretia, known as *La Riccia*, a courtesan." While the accusation had been dismissed, Niccolò's letters to Vettori frequently refer to his continued sexual relations with her.

Such behavior occasionally gave rise to bitter comments by others. As a friend was to write later in his life, "the fame of your revelries has spread and continues to spread, not only throughout all Tuscany but also throughout Lombardy." His personal reputation and political enemies combined to leave Niccolò without a job.

Feeling bored, useless, and poor, Niccolò often wrote to his friend Vettori in Rome. In these letters, Niccolò described "the gang" of mutual friends who would meet to fool around, eat, and discuss sex or politics; Francesco replied with gossip from Rome. On occasion, Niccolò sought favors for others. His friend Donato del Corno had lent five hundred

Niccolò's Struggle, Victory, and Defeat / 179

ducats to Giuliano de' Medici. Niccolò asked the Florentine ambassador to arrange for Donato's name to be "put in the bag" so he could be elected to office, and to ask Giuliano to repay the debt.

Often the correspondents wrote of their own pleasures. Vettori described his infatuation with Costanza, the twenty-year-old daughter of a "Roman widow lady of good family" living next door: "you never set eyes on a more beautiful woman, nor a more seductive one." Niccolò advised against resisting the passion: "take off the saddlepacks, remove the bridle, close your eyes, and say, 'Go ahead, Love, be my guide, my leader.'"

Politics soon intruded and became the focus of most of the correspondence between the Florentine ambassador to Rome and the former secretary. When Vettori realized he would have to stay in Rome, he asked Niccolò for his analysis of the tangled relationships between France, Spain, Germany, Switzerland, and the Italian cities: "I shall agree with your judgment because, to tell you the truth without flattery, I have found it more sound in these matters than that of any other man that I have spoken with."

Bittersweet words for Niccolò. Welcome recognition of his abilities, it was also a reminder that despite his experience and understanding, no one in power would trust him. As it became apparent that Giuliano would not take the initiative and that Vettori was not likely to be successful with the pope, Niccolò tried another sonnet:

> *I send you, Giuliano, some thrushes, not because this gift is good or fine,*
> *but that for a bit Your Magnificence may recollect your poor Machiavelli.*

A reminder of Niccolò's persistent desire for a job, this poem had no more effect than Niccolò's earlier sonnets and letters to Vettori.

Niccolò was depressed, admitting to one correspondent that "Physically I feel well, but ill in every other respect." He turned to writing what at first may have been an extended policy memorandum for Giuliano. As it expanded, Niccolò realized that it was becoming a small book. Perhaps the world was lucky that he could not get a job after all.

Originally entitled *On Principalities*, the book we know as *The Prince* (Figure 10.1) began as advice on how to combine power over several different cities or territories, focusing on a form of government, not a kind of ruler. When Vettori first refers to the manuscript, he calls it "a certain work about states."

At first the work was dedicated to Giuliano de' Medici (not, as at present, to his nephew Lorenzo). In context, this is hardly surprising. Niccolò had directed three sonnets to Giuliano since his imprisonment in February, and made extensive efforts to contact him through such intermediaries as Francesco Vettori. He apparently had known Giuliano as a boy, and was convinced that "His Magnificence Giuliano" was "naturally disposed to please me" (as he wrote Vettori in April).

Most interpreters have assumed that *The Prince* is a manual for deceptive and ambitious rulers, cynically written to get Niccolò a job. The changes between what Niccolò wrote in 1513 and what was published after his death show that the traditional reputation is somewhat misleading. Niccolò set out to write a practical guide to Medici policy. Critics have often written as if Niccolò was inventing the brutality and deception of the rulers he praised. In fact, many of the passages that have contributed to this interpretation were descriptions of the ordinary practices in Renaissance politics. Throughout the sixteenth and seventeenth centuries, it was not at all rare for dissidents to be tortured and put to death. Often rulers, and even popes, violated treaties as soon as the ink was dry, and, especially before the Reformation, their religious practice was frequently little more than a façade.

In the book, Niccolò presents himself as commenting on the realities he observed, writing as a practicing statesman rather than a moral theorist. As he told Vettori, "through this study of mine, were it to be read, it would be evident that during the fifteen years I have been studying the art of the state I have neither slept nor fooled around."

Niccolò continued to work on his manuscript. By June 1514, he wrote Vettori in despair of living "amid my lice, unable to find any man who recalls my service or believes I might be good for anything." He expressed the fear that, out of poverty, "I shall be forced to leave home and to place myself as tutor or secretary to a governor, if I cannot do otherwise, or to

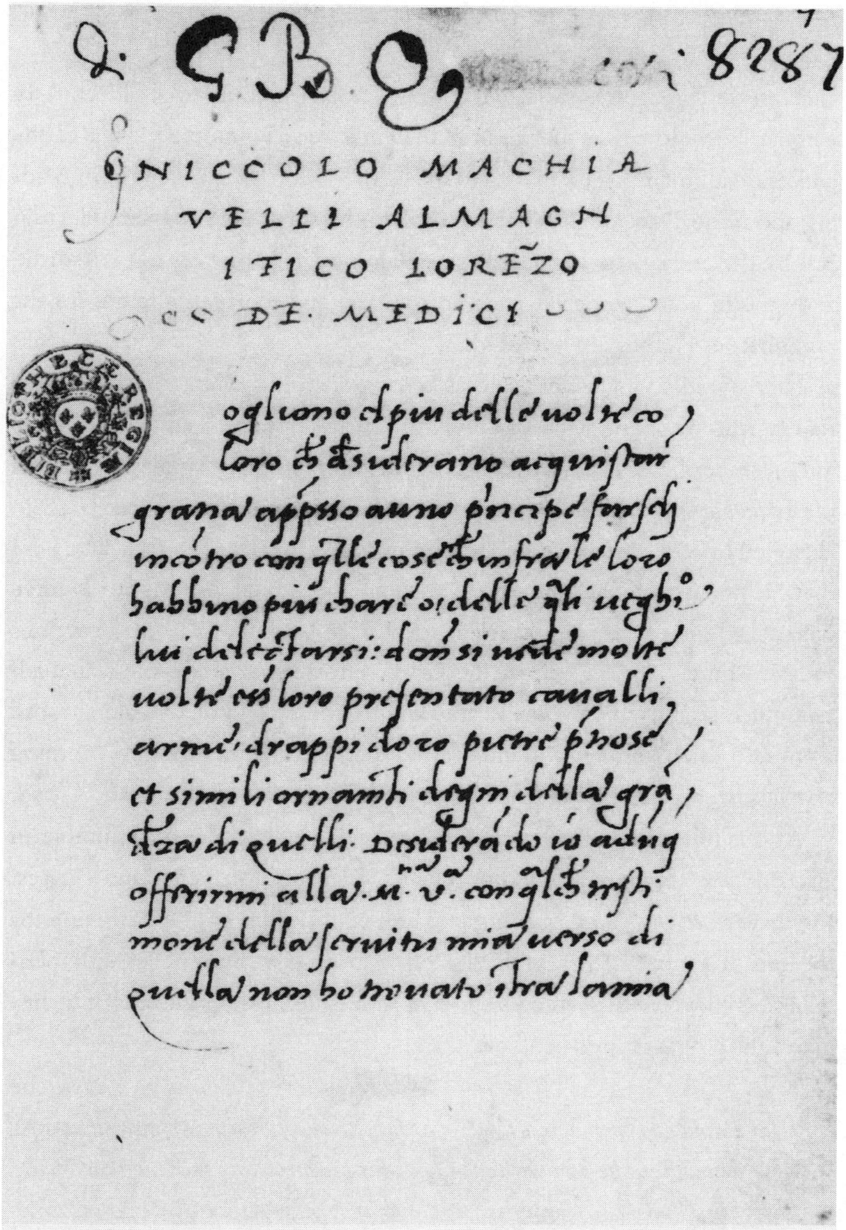

FIGURE 10.1. Machiavelli, *De Principatibus*, opening page from a manuscript copy by Biagio Buonaccorsi (ca. 1518–20). Of the extant manuscripts of Machiavelli's work, now known as *The Prince*, this copy is the only one to include the title and chapter headings in Italian. It was probably destined for a friend (Francesco di Bernardo Quaratesi) who was, like Niccolò, a godfather to one of Buonaccorsi's children; the initials "G.B.Q." are apparently those of a later member of this family. The seal records the manuscript's entry into the French royal collection (NM, *De Principatibus*, ed. Inglese, pp. 50–51).

stick myself in some deserted spot to teach reading to children." In August, Niccolò writes that he has fallen in love so completely that "I have laid aside all memory of my sorrows" and "no longer . . . delight in reading about the deeds of the ancients or in discussing those of the moderns." But by the end of the year, he is complaining again that his life is "sordid and ignominious," especially "amid so many and so great felicities for the Magnificent Family" of the Medici.

Niccolò still viewed himself as a long-standing client of the Medici family who was being treated unfairly. Vettori admitted as much, for early in December he wrote Niccolò, asking his opinion on the question of how the pope should respond to the political ambitions of the French. Niccolò hastened to reply at length on December 10. Vettori replied five days later that "I have not yet shown it to Monsignor [Cardinal Giulio] de' Medici, who asked me to have you write it for him"—adding, "I think he will be satisfied by it." By the end of the year, Vettori reports Niccolò's analysis "has been seen by the pope and Cardinal Bibbiena and de' Medici, and all were astonished at their wit and praised their judgment," though "nothing else has been gotten from them but words."

At this time, Pope Leo made Giuliano de' Medici ruler of a number of cities in the Romagna, including Parma, Piacenza, Modena, and Reggio. Paolo Vettori was to be in charge of one of the cities of the new state. At the end of January 1515, with *The Prince* probably more or less completed, Niccolò wrote Francesco Vettori in Rome, describing the advice he had given the ambassador's brother:

> *Your Paolo has been here with His Magnificence [Giuliano] and, among other discussions he had with me about his prospects, he told me that His Lordship [Pope Leo] promised to appoint him governor of one of those cities. . . . If these new states, taken over by a new ruler, are to be preserved, they present countless problems. And if problems exist in preserving those states accustomed to being unified as if they were one body—for example, the dukedom of Ferrara—many more problems exist in preserving those that are recently formed from diverse elements—as this*

state of Lord Giuliano's would be because one section of it is part of Milan and another of Ferrara.

Readers of *The Prince* will not only recognize the problem that Machiavelli posed in chapter 3 ("Of Mixed Principalities") but will be familiar with most of Niccolò's personal advice to Giuliano:

> *whoever becomes prince over such states must concentrate on unifying them into a single body and training them to think of themselves as one unified body as soon as possible. This can be accomplished in two ways: either by dwelling there in person or by appointing one of his lieutenants to rule them all.*

In Giuliano's case, since Rome is so attractive to the Medici, a governor should be empowered to rule the entire area. Niccolò proposes Paolo Vettori for such a post, and advises him to imitate the way Cesare Borgia "appointed Messer Remirro president in Romagna."

In the projected new state, Paolo Vettori had offered Niccolò a position. Niccolò's hopes of a job were therefore high at the end of January 1515, only to be immediately shattered. When word of Niccolò's proposals reached the pope, his secretary Piero Ardinghelli wrote Giuliano:

> *Cardinal de' Medici questioned me yesterday very closely if I knew whether Your Excellency had taken into his service Niccolò Machiavelli, and as I replied that I knew nothing of it nor believed it, His Lordship said to me these words: "I do not believe it either, but as there has been word of it from Florence, I would remind him that it is not to his profit or to ours. This must be an invention of Paolo Vettori: . . . write to him on my behalf that I advise him not to have anything to do with Niccolò."*

And so—having persuaded Paolo Vettori with his dreams of helping Giuliano create a new state in the Romagna—Niccolò's projects were vetoed in Rome.

In 1515, Francis I became king of France, beginning a year of monumental events in European politics. After the French victory at Marignano, Niccolò's hopes were renewed. Francesco Vettori, named Florentine ambassador to France along with Lorenzo de' Medici, was in a position of power in Florentine affairs. Moreover, his principal task now became the negotiation of a French marriage for Lorenzo.

Niccolò, long a partisan of the French alliance and experienced in negotiations at the French court, saw yet another chance. At some time between September 1515 and August 1516, he changed the dedication of *On Principalities*, to "the Magnificent Lorenzo." The change must have been before August 18, 1516, when the pope—having ousted the ruler of Urbino and taken over the city—invested Lorenzo with the title of duke of Urbino; "the Magnificent" would have been an insufficient honor for a duke.

There is a story that, around the time the dedication was changed, Niccolò personally offered a copy of *On Principalities* to Lorenzo de' Medici. The presentation occurred "at a moment when he [Lorenzo] was being offered a pair of coursing dogs, and he spoke and looked more kindly on the man who gave him the dogs than on him (Machiavelli)." Not surprisingly, Niccolò "departed in anger." Despite his relationship with Francesco Vettori, Niccolò was as unable to get a job from Lorenzo de' Medici as he had been from his uncle Giuliano.

With hopes of a position once again dashed, Niccolò had little choice but to continue writing. All he had was his training as a poet and writer. Niccolò would use his pen to become the "unarmed prophet" of a future political life, better than that he had known. He also began meeting regularly with a group of young thinkers hosted by Cosimo Rucellai at the Rucellai gardens.

The few letters from this period, mainly to his favorite nephew, who was a merchant in Turkey, express deep depression and fatalism: "I have become useless to myself, to my family, and to my friends." Niccolò did begin to receive a few small business commissions, traveling to Leghorn in 1516 for Paolo Vettori and to Genoa to untangle a bankruptcy in 1518. But mostly he was so hard at work that, as he wrote his nephew, "the times . . . have made me forget even myself."

Niccolò's literary output in these years was prodigious. In addition to major works in political theory (the *Discourses on Titus Livy*) and military strategy (the *Art of War*), he worked on poems *(The Ass)*, fables *(Belfagor)*, and plays, including what has been called the greatest comedy in Italian *(La Mandragola)*. All challenge conventional opinions and seek a lasting change in Western civilization. Having failed in political practice, Niccolò sought to "open a new route, as yet untrodden" in the way his contemporaries thought and acted.

To influence public opinion through poetry, Niccolò turned to theater. *La Mandragola* extols the benefits of replacing traditional piety with the enjoyment of natural pleasure. The play was probably written and first published in 1518, and after readings in the Rucellai gardens and a performance in Florence, Pope Leo was to have it performed in Rome early in 1520.

In 1519, Niccolò's young friend Cosimo Rucellai died. Soon thereafter, Niccolò dedicated the *Discourses* to Cosimo and his friend, Zanobi Buondelmonte, both of whom had been active in the circle at the Rucellai gardens. The *Art of War*, which presents itself as a dialogue on military strategy in the form of a conversation among that same group in the Rucellai gardens, was completed about this time; copies circulated in 1520, and it was published the next year with a dedication to Lorenzo di Filippo Strozzi and some introductory remarks praising Cosimo.

Meanwhile, Lorenzo de' Medici had died in 1519, leaving a power vacuum in Florence. The pope sent Cardinal Giulio de' Medici to the city to reestablish the family's control. In 1520, Lorenzo Strozzi introduced Niccolò to the cardinal in the Rucellai gardens. Always alert to opportunity, Niccolò wrote his policy recommendations for the Medici ("Commentary on Florentine Affairs after the Death of Lorenzo de' Medici the Younger").

At this point, prospects for employment by the Medici finally brightened, though as a writer rather than a political advisor. In April 1520, a member of the Rucellai gardens "gang" wrote from Rome that the pope "was very well disposed toward you" and "will be very pleased" if his "good will . . . toward your desires should henceforth be put into effect. . . . This concerns commissioning you to do some writing or something else." Since communication of this message to Cardinal Giulio in Florence was "authorized" by Pope Leo himself, Niccolò took it seriously.

Another commercial mission, again to settle a bankruptcy case, sent Niccolò to Lucca, where he wrote an essay on the political situation of the city ("A Summary of Matters in the City of Lucca") and the *Life of Castruccio Castracani*. The latter was intended as a "model of a history" he could write as a commission for the Medici.

By the end of the year, Cardinal Giulio formally gave him the desired commission. Niccolò himself drafted a contract to write "the history of the things done by the state and city of Florence, from whatever time may seem to him most appropriate, and in whatever language—either Latin or Tuscan—may seem best to him." Technically, Niccolò became an employee of the university, or Florentine Studio; symbolically, he was to follow in the footsteps of several famous humanist first chancellors, who had in the past often been commissioned as historians of the city.

Niccolò's fortunes slowly began to recover. Early in 1521, Niccolò was appointed on an official mission from Florence to the Chapter General of the Minorite Friars at Carpi. By September 1521, the first printed copies of the *Art of War* had been delivered to Cardinal Giovanni Salviati—son of Jacopo Salviati—in Rome, who praised Niccolò for publishing "this book for the common welfare of all Italians" and exhorted him "to continue thinking and writing things, and to adorn our country with your talents."

During the next three years, Niccolò was hard at work on his *Florentine Histories*. By March 1525, the history had been completed up to the death of Lorenzo the Magnificent, and Niccolò was asking Francesco Vettori if he should present it to the pope.

As Niccolò was writing in his country house, his fate was influenced by events in European and Italian politics. In May 1521, Pope Leo X, after hesitating whether to commit himself to France or to Spain, came down on the side of the Spanish king, Charles V. By the end of the year, the Spaniards had driven the French from Milan, and Pope Leo X was dead. Two Florentine cardinals, Giuliano de' Medici and Francesco Soderini, sought the papacy, reopening the violent conflict between their families. In January, the new pope was elected: a Fleming named Adrian VI.

Cardinal Giulio de' Medici returned to govern Florence, while Cardinal Francesco Soderini began plotting against the regime. Giulio asked Niccolò for a project of governmental reform, which he duly submitted, suggesting continued Medici rule during the cardinal's lifetime to be followed by a return to republican government. Then, in early June, a plot to assassinate Cardinal Giulio was discovered. The leaders were Niccolò's friends from the Rucellai gardens, led by Zanobi Buondelmonti (to whom the *Discourses on Livy* were dedicated) and the poet Luigi Alamanni. They fled along with most of the plotters, though two unlucky participants were caught, tortured, and beheaded. Niccolò, fortunately, was not directly involved.

On September 14, 1523, Pope Adrian died. This time, Cardinal Giulio de' Medici was successful in the election. Under the name Clement VII, once again there was a Medici pope. Niccolò now had all the more reason to finish the *Florentine Histories* in a manner pleasing to his patron. As time passed, however, he also was having more fun.

As Niccolò began to be accepted politically, his social activities expanded. In the next year, probably during the fall, Niccolò's *La Mandragola* was performed in Monteloro, a town outside of Florence. In his *Lives of the Artists,* Vasari notes that the scenery for this performance was painted by Andrea del Sarto and Aristotele de Sangallo. With the Rucellai gardens closed as a result of the abortive plot, around this time Niccolò began to frequent the house and banquets of Jacopo Fornaciaio. A wealthy man who had been banished to his estate outside the walls of Florence, Fornaciaio's gatherings were focused on good food, good wine, and good fun. There Niccolò, now fifty-five years old, met and fell in love with Barbera Salutati, a beautiful young singer and actress.

Niccolò, enamored, resorted to poetry. A poem to his beloved admits to the difference in age that separates them:

I cannot complain of you
but rather of myself
because I see and confess
that such beauty
must love more tender years.

Barbera clearly was not deterred. She offered to perform in *La Mandragola* at a party Fornaciaio planned in January 1525 to celebrate the end of his exile. Instead, Niccolò—always the poet—wrote a new play for her. Based on an ancient Roman play, Plautus's *Casina*, Niccolò's *Clizia* was an instant hit for some—and a scandal for others. The plot concerns a seventy-year-old father and his son who both fall madly in love with the same young beauty—and, as Niccolò admits in the Prologue, it contains "immodest" material (such as the father, Nicomaco, in bed with a male servant who is impersonating the object of his desire).

Fornaciaio invited "all the leading citizens" of Florence, including Ippolito de' Medici, who was acting as the pope's agent as head of the government. According to Vasari, Aristotele Sangallo again did the scenery, which "pleased everyone very much." According to one historian, who criticized the behavior of the younger members of the audience, there was widespread "desire to see" Niccolò's play.

One of Niccolò's friends, serving as Florence's governor in Modena, wrote asking him to "send me this comedy . . . as soon as you can," because

Fornaciaio and you, you and Fornaciaio have managed things so that the fame of your revelries has spread and continues to spread not only throughout all Tuscany but also throughout Lombardy. . . . I know about the garden leveled off to make it into a stage for your comedy. I know about the invitations not only to the first and noble patricians of the city but also to the middle class and after them to the plebeians. These are things that are usually done only for princes.

The same friend wrote Niccolò's brother-in-law complaining about the scandalous "gossip" surrounding "a paterfamilias of such character" who is "galloping off" (with Barbera) and writing "a comedy that, according to what I have heard, has some fine things in it."

While some were complaining about Niccolò's reputation, fate had more tricks in store. Just as the former secretary painstakingly edged his way back into power, big-power rivalries changed the scene yet again. Francis I, seeking to establish French power definitively in northern Italy, boldly led his army into battle with the Spanish. In February 1525, the French were decisively defeated at Pavia and their king taken to Madrid as a prisoner.

The pope decided to send, as his personal legate, Cardinal Salviati. The cardinal's father, Jacopo—a patron of Niccolò since his years as second chancellor—wrote his son: "As a secretary, and as a man with whom you might take counsel, Niccolò Machiavelli would please me better than anyone. I have spoken about it to His Holiness, and he is undecided; I shall see if I cannot get him to make up his mind." Pope Clement decided against the idea.

At the end of May, Niccolò went to Rome anyway in order to present his *Florentine Histories* to the pope. At the same time, Niccolò proposed to Clement the creating of a citizen army in the papal states. This project, like the ill-fated militia in Florence, struck Guicciardini as "useful and praiseworthy" but unlikely to produce immediate benefits. The pope, known for his vacillation, could not decide what to do.

Niccolò visited Guicciardini, who as president of the Romagna was living with great comfort in Faenza. They discussed politics, military affairs—and a production of *La Mandragola*. Back in Florence later in the summer, Niccolò's eligibility for governmental office was finally restored in August. Although the pope did not adopt his proposals for a popular militia, Niccolò's salary at the university was doubled. He was asked to go to Venice to deal with a charge that merchants from Florence had been defrauded there. Things were looking up.

During the 1526 Carnival season in Venice, the Florentine community mounted a production of *La Mandragola*, which had already been performed there four years earlier. This time, Niccolò's play was in competition with Plautus's *Menaechmi*, and the Roman classic was completely "dead" by comparison. Guicciardini's production, however, had to be cancelled because of the political situation.

With the French king a prisoner of Charles V, now Holy Roman Emperor as well as king of Spain, the pope was terrified that the Spanish would conquer Italy and began to seek a French alliance. Niccolò was convinced that Charles would hold Francis I more or less permanently, pretending to negotiate with both France and the papacy as a cover for gaining control of Italy. Unexpectedly, Charles V signed a treaty with France: if the French would abandon claims in Italy and cede control of Burgundy, the Spanish would release the French king.

Niccolò was astounded by what seemed a foolish blunder. He predicted that Francis would break his word and wrote an epigrammatic poem, imagining Pope Clement gloating that "brainless Charles King of the Romans and the Viceroy [Lannoy], because they cannot see, have released the King." As predicted, Francis I immediately broke his agreement with Charles V, renewing French claims in Italy. The pope summoned Guicciardini to Rome to become deputy commander of the papal troops. War was inevitable.

Niccolò, seeing the war clouds gather and despairing of the lack of preparation, proposed a popular militia again and suggested the construction of new walls around Florence. The author of the *Art of War* was called to Rome in April, then received the new post of Florence's curator of the walls. No sooner had he begun to organize improvement of the city's defenses than Guicciardini summoned him to the papal armies outside Milan to benefit from his services and advice.

In the last months of 1526 Niccolò was once again traveling constantly on government business, in the midst of military preparations and crises. In September, Pope Clement foolishly allowed his pro-Spanish rivals to stage a coup in the Vatican itself, forcing him to sign a truce for four months. The following spring, Spanish forces advanced on Florence, then turned and attacked Rome instead. Both cities had been virtually undefended. An army of Spanish Catholics and German Lutherans sacked Rome in May. The pope was taken prisoner.

In Florence, popular disgust with Medici rule led to another coup. Republican institutions were restored and the young Medici who ruled the city forced into exile. Niccolò, on a mission to the front with Guicciardini, returned to find that he was again on the wrong side of a revolution. But this time, he was associated with the Medici against a popular republican government.

Niccolò made a last effort to regain his position as secretary, but his association with the pope and the Medici made him unacceptable. On May 20, 1527, old and discouraged, he fell ill. A month later, on June 21, he was dead.

In his final illness, surrounded by his family and in pain, Niccolò described a dream. Seeing a group of poor and ragged people, he asked who they were and was told they were the blessed in Paradise. He then saw another group, well dressed, including such ancients as Plato, Plutarch, and Tacitus—and was told they were condemned to hell. When asked which he preferred to join, it is said Niccolò "replied that he would rather go to Hell with noble minds to discuss politics than to be in Paradise with that first beggarly contingent."

What manner of man was Niccolò—"Machia" to those very close to him? To the end, he was first and foremost a poet and storyteller. Like Dante, his political career had ended in failure—but through a combination of genius and skill as a writer, that failure became the ground for works of lasting success. Like Plutarch and Shakespeare, Niccolò was to portray individual political leaders and the problem of leadership in a way that profoundly influenced generations to come.

Niccolò, for us, is a great political theorist. For his contemporaries, he was an astute commentator on the ever-changing kaleidoscope of politics, an effective civil servant, an outrageous libertine, an important military strategist, and a maddeningly annoying gadfly. He was also, to his friends and family, impossibly funny and—whatever his amorous adventures—profoundly devoted.

Above all, however, is one trait that stands out sharply against the times. In an era when Christian faith was still dominant, Niccolò was primarily concerned with the affairs of this world and ways of improving them. And while most men he knew had parochial horizons, Niccolò was an Italian patriot, even more intent on preserving Italy than on serving his native Florence.

On April 16, 1527, writing in despair to his old friend Francesco Vettori, Niccolò declared, "I do not believe there were ever more difficult problems than these, where peace is necessary and war cannot be renounced." In such times, priorities become clear. Niccolò put his own priorities on the line, with friendship and patriotism trumping religious faith and otherworldly piety: "I love Messer Francesco Guicciardini," the friend with whom he was serving, and "I love my native country [*mia patria*], more than my own soul."

Chapter 11

THE LEGACY

❖

Niccolò started his career in a position of power and prestige, and died in poverty and disgrace. Leonardo started life as a lowly apprentice and ended as a valued advisor to a powerful foreign king. Although both men ultimately contributed deeply to the flow of Western civilization, when they died nothing would have seemed less likely to their Florentine contemporaries.

As the years passed, the project of making Florence a seaport was a fading memory. Many of those who remembered Niccolò's efforts to divert the Arno at Pisa doubtless associated it with his dangerous enthusiasms and unprincipled character. If anyone recalled Leonardo's more ambitious plans for the river, it would probably have been with amused regret. Even Leonardo's specific drawings for improving the river's flow through Florence were no longer associated with his name. When a flash flood inundated Florence on August 28, 1520, a local coppersmith noted in his diary that work had begun to deepen the Arno and build embankments, describing the project merely as something planned years before.

We usually think of Leonardo da Vinci as an artist and inventor. In fact, from his arrival in Milan in 1483 to his death in 1519, Leonardo continually sought to integrate science and technology while serving as a consultant to rulers. Yet even his successful public projects, like the water distribution system in Milan, get little attention compared to paintings like the *Mona Lisa* and the *Last Supper.*

Leonardo's artistic legacy is quite literally visible. Tourists by the thousands wait in line to see the originals of his famous works; reproductions and imitations are everywhere. For art historians, he marks a sharp break with tradition, ushering in a new age. As one survey of Renaissance painting concludes, "With Leonardo modern art and modern life were knocking at the door."

Within years of his death, Leonardo's achievements in other spheres became legendary. In the first edition of the *Lives of the Artists* (1550), Vasari proclaimed: "Heaven sometimes sends us beings who represent not humanity alone but divinity itself, so that taking them as our models and imitating them, our minds and the best of our intelligence may approach the highest celestial spheres."

Leonardo clearly intended to publish his discoveries. In 1517, the secretary of a Spanish cardinal recorded a visit "to see Messer Lionardo Vinci, the Florentine." Describing Leonardo as an "old man" and "excellent painter," the secretary adds:

> *This gentleman has written an extraordinary treatise on anatomy, with the demonstration in pictures of the limbs, as well as the muscles, nerves, veins, joints, intestines, and whatever one may wish to see of the bodies of both men and women, in a manner never before achieved by any other person. All this we saw with our own eyes, and he says that he has dissected more than thirty bodies, male and female, of every age. He has written concerning the nature of water, of divers machines and other things—according to what he says, an infinity of volumes, and all in the vulgar tongue, which when they are published will be most useful and interesting.*

Although Leonardo did not publish these scientific discoveries during his lifetime, many of his ideas and inventions were circulated by word of mouth. Because his influence depended on oral communication rather than printed works, Leonardo's influence on specific disciplines is often hard to prove. Even so, innumerable ideas that he sketched in vain were realized long after his death.

Spread throughout Leonardo's *Notebooks* were the unparalleled fruits of his attempt to understand the many facets of nature and of human nature. In seeking to rival and surpass such ancients as Plato and Aristotle, Leonardo outlined the way of thinking that became modern science. In place of scholarly citations of classical writers, he insisted that "Wisdom is the daughter of experience." Prevailing beliefs and customs often lead us astray: "The greatest deception men suffer is from their own opinions." A science of nature is important for daily life because "we ought not to desire the impossible." Since "necessity is the theme and the inventress, the eternal curb and law [rule] of nature," science can help us avoid painful errors by discovering regularities that cannot be violated with impunity.

To learn about nature, one needs to begin with careful observation: "All our knowledge has its origin in our perception." Passive records of the world are not sufficient, however: "Nature is full of causes that have never occurred in experience." To discover these hidden principles of nature, the scientist needs to formulate "rules" in objective, mathematical terms: "There is no certainty in sciences where one of the mathematical sciences cannot be applied, or which are not in relation with these mathematics."

Science is not, however, merely a question of idle curiosity or philosophic disputation. "Instrumental or mechanical science is of all the noblest and the most useful, seeing that by means of this all animated bodies that have movement perform all their actions." While philosophers need to be aware of the practical applications of their theories, technicians and workers need to understand pure science: "Those who fall in love with practice without science are like a sailor who enters a ship without a helm or a compass, and who never can be certain whither he is going."

Time is always fleeting: "The water you touch in a river is the last of that which has passed and the first of that which is coming. Thus it is with the present." The soul is merely the animating life of the body, not an immortal, immaterial being. In place of the otherworldly goals of medieval Christianity, Leonardo focuses emphatically on human life. "As a day well spent procures a happy sleep, so a life well employed procures a happy death."

While revealing of Leonardo's temperament, such a summary gives little idea of the scope and power of Leonardo's scientific work. There is hardly an area in which his theories and inventions did not foreshadow—and sometimes directly influence—future developments. In pure science, he points the way to such crucial modern concepts as Galileo's view of inertia, Harvey's theory of the circulation of blood, and Newton's mathematics of motion (based on a point of no dimension). In practical matters, it was often centuries before such inventions as the airplane, the armored tank, the bicycle, the machine gun, and the submarine were implemented.

Leonardo also had a well-developed approach to human social and political theory. His view of human nature was hardly naive: many people are selfish and narrow-minded. Or as he put it in a particularly blunt remark,

> *Some there are who are nothing else than a passage for food and augmentors of excrement and fillers of privies, because through them no other things in the world, nor any good effects are produced, since nothing but full privies results from them.*

The quest for material wealth is dangerous: "virtue is our true good and the true reward of its possessor. That cannot be lost; that never deserts us, but when life leaves us. As to property and external riches, hold them with trembling."

To avoid vice requires self-control and intelligence. "The man who does not restrain wantonness, allies himself with beasts. You can have no dominion greater than over yourself. He who thinks little, errs much." While resembling much traditional morality, Leonardo's conclusions were anything but traditional.

To establish a decent community, Leonardo concluded that strong leaders are necessary. "Justice requires power, insight, and will; and it resembles the queen bee. He who does not punish evil commands it to be done." Leonardo was not a democrat who thought universal voting would lead to just laws and fair societies.

Human communities need to be designed, using a scientific approach to city planning and architecture. One of the principal needs would be defense, since foreigners can be expected to have evil intentions. Only an alliance between powerful rulers (like the French kings) and skilled experts (like Leonardo himself) can achieve the combination of internal prosperity and external defense:

> *To preserve nature's chiefest boon, that is freedom, I can find means of offense and defence, when it is assailed by ambitious tyrants, and first I will speak of the situation of the walls, and also I shall show how communities can maintain their good and just Lords.*

Both the leaders and citizens of such communities will benefit: "There will be eternal fame also for the inhabitants of that town, constructed and enlarged by him."

Leonardo's basic principle in all things was best summarized by the aphorism "Science is the captain, and practice the soldiers." Knowledge of nature, society, and human life is essential if humans are to take control of their own lives—but that science must become practical and useful. For the last two centuries, natural scientists and engineers have put these ideas into practice.

By the early seventeenth century, the possibility of a scientific conquest of nature had begun to be considered openly by a few serious thinkers like Galileo and Bacon. Unlike these contemporaries, Shakespeare apparently had doubts that such a goal could be achieved. As the bard put it in *The Winter's Tale*,

> *Yet nature is made better by no mean*
> *But nature makes that mean; so, over that art*
> *Which you say adds to nature, is an art*
> *That nature makes.*

How did Shakespeare know about "an art" that "shares with nature" the possibility of making things to satisfy all human desires? In his last plays, why did he find it important to question whether a rational, scientific worldview could produce a peaceful and prosperous society in total control of nature?

Something like Leonardo's design of a scientific and technological society was still far from common in Shakespeare's own time. Most intellectuals and philosophers, not to mention most common people, believed in astrology, not in astronomy. Yet Shakespeare didn't rely on religion or common belief to question what one of his characters baptized a "brave new world." Instead, he conjured up the image of a scientifically constituted universe, presented it onstage, and then suggested it could not last because of human nature itself.

The Tempest is one of Shakespeare's most difficult but also most thought-provoking works. In it, Shakespeare created the ultimate philosopher-king. Prospero is a scientist and technologist with total power, who understands all natural things, controls the natural environment, and can create material objects at will. The result of this "so potent art" is an island of unlimited comfort—Prospero's prosperity. But in the end, Prospero must give up his godlike powers in order that his daughter may fall in love.

Is Leonardo the model for Prospero? Shakespeare tells us that his magical ruler was, before arriving on the island, duke of Milan—and Leonardo's tombstone in Amboise called him "Milanese." The lack of further evidence is, however, typical of Leonardo's legacy. To trace his influence, we have to rely on hunches. The more Leonardo's ideas were implemented, the less credit he got for them.

The Legacy

Niccolò died in poverty, surrounded only by a few friends and family, accepting the services of a local priest (whether from newfound piety or to calm his family). At his death, like other "unarmed prophets" described in his *Prince,* Niccolò seemed a failure.

Niccolò, trained as a poet and experienced as a writer, left the manuscripts of two important books to be published at his death. One, which we know as *The Prince,* soon earned him evil repute, yet is still read by millions of students each year. The other, the *Discourses on Titus Livy,* initiated a stream of modern political thought that influenced Sir Francis Bacon, John Locke, and the framers of the United States Constitution. Although Niccolò died in relative obscurity, his legacy is anything but obscure.

Key elements in Niccolò's thought can be stated in nine basic principles.

• First, *enjoy yourself—and don't worry about frying in hell.* The lesson was put most succinctly in the song he wrote at Guicciardini's request for the performance of *La Mandragola* they planned in 1525:

> *Because life is brief*
> *and many are the pains*
> *which, living and struggling, everyone sustains,*
> *let us follow our desires,*
> *passing and consuming the years,*
> *because whoever deprives himself of pleasure,*
> *to live with anguish and with worries,*
> *doesn't know the tricks*
> *of the world, or by what ills*
> *and by what strange happenings*
> *all mortals are almost overwhelmed.*

Political doctrines or religious beliefs that lead humans to substitute "how one should live" for "how one lives" do more harm than good to human freedom and excellence.

- Second, *people can't be trusted*. "For one can say this generally of men: that they are ungrateful, fickle, pretenders and dissemblers, evaders of danger, eager for gain." Men are "wicked and do not observe faith."
- Third, *politicians and leaders can't be trusted either*. "Many times underneath a merciful work a beginning of tyranny is concealed." "The sins of peoples arise from princes . . . not from the wicked nature of men."
- Fourth, *history is written by the winners*. In life generally—but especially in politics—moral judgments are inevitably based on the outcome. As Niccolò put it in *The Prince,* "in the actions of all men, and especially of princes, where there is no court to appeal to, one looks to the end." People are usually selfish and shortsighted. To counter "ills" and "strange happenings," sometimes leaders need to do brutal things. Piero Soderini, for example, was a failure because he failed to see that "his works and his intention had to be judged by the end," or outcome. Sometimes a leader like Moses or Romulus has to kill people to establish a free and just society; "when the deed accuses him, the effect excuses him; and when the effect is good . . . it will always excuse the deed."
- Fifth, *luck is being at the right place and the right time*—and *taking advantage of it*. Unless leaders take bold action to impose order on society, fortune (or chance) controls human events. "He is prosperous who adapts his mode of proceeding to the qualities of the times; and similarly, he is unprosperous whose procedure is in disaccord with the times." Fortune "lets herself be won more by the impetuous than by those who proceed coldly."
- Sixth, *republics are better than hereditary monarchies—you can at least throw the bastards out*. Given "respect for the laws," Niccolò asserts, "a people is more prudent, more stable, and of better judgment than a prince." For example, "in the election of magistrates people judge according to the trust marks that they can have of men; and when they can be counseled like princes, they err less than princes." Republics are therefore more likely to conquer rivals and "acquire the world" with lasting victories, whereas monarchies cannot do so without the accident of effective kings succeeding each other. The greatest freedom is achieved when humans can compete openly for power and status in a government of laws capable of defending itself and expanding as the need arises.

- Seventh, *at times, civilized society depends on individual leadership.*

> *This should be taken as a general rule: that it never or rarely happens that any republic or kingdom is ordered well from the beginning or reformed altogether anew outside its old orders unless it is ordered by one individual. . . . So a prudent orderer of a republic, who has the intent to wish to help not himself but the common good, not only for his own succession but for the common fatherland, should contrive to have authority alone; nor will a wise understanding ever reprove anyone for any extraordinary action that he uses to order a kingdom or constitute a republic.*

Even in a republic under law, the need for virtuous individual leadership provides a role for a prince.

- Eighth, *grow your own soldiers and don't cut the defense budget.* Armies are essential to defend freedom: "there cannot be good laws where there are not good arms, and where there are good arms there must be good laws." In addition to protection from foreign conquest, a citizen army protects domestic freedom: "a republic with its own arms is brought to obey one of its citizens with more difficulty than is a republic armed with foreign arms."
- Ninth, *the times require national unity.* Italy, a national community of language, culture, and manners large enough to defend its inhabitants, is the proper focus of love and devotion. "The Fatherland ought to be defended, whether with ignominy or with glory, and it is well defended in any mode whatever." Such changes as artillery and printing make it impossible to defend smaller provinces and cities, and knowledge of this fact needs to be put into practice. "In Italy at present the times have been tending to the honor of a new prince" who could unite her "and free her from the barbarians."

To sum up Niccolò's tough-minded principles, a realistic view of human nature and politics shows that selfishness and conflict are inevitable. The people's goal of lasting freedom can become consistent with its leaders' desire for lasting fame. Ambitious leaders need to seek glory by furthering the common good in the creation of expansionist nation-states based on both good laws and good armies. In short, understanding the necessities of politics makes it possible to control some—but not all—of the unanticipated events we call "fortune."

Niccolò's support of the Medici arose from his belief that their family's desire for glory might provide a leader to unite Italy, and not merely from a desire for employment. "Thus, one should not let this opportunity pass, for Italy, after so much time, to see her redeemer. I cannot express with what love he would be received in all those provinces that have suffered from these floods from outside."

Unlike Leonardo, Niccolò did not leave his unpublished manuscripts to be compiled and edited by a student. The two major works he left for posthumous publication were circulated in final form long before he died. Under its original title of *On Principalities,* numerous copies were made of *The Prince,* which shows how Machiavelli's ideas started to spread even during his lifetime.

Niccolò's blunt teachings obviously made a strong impression. In 1524, a plagiarized Latin version appeared in Naples. After Niccolò's death, approval for publication of his works was given by Pope Clement VII. This achieved, *Discourses on Titus Livy* were published in Rome by Antonio Blado on October 18, 1531. *On Principalities*—now entitled *The Prince*—followed on January 4, 1532. Four months later, an edition appeared in Florence. Perhaps the most famous book in the history of political theory was launched on its public career.

Throughout the sixteenth century, statesmen and political theorists became more aware of *The Prince.* Machiavelli's advice to rulers was increasingly read—sometimes for its forthright advice, more often to be criticized as unnecessarily immoral. Even before its first printing, *The Prince* may have changed the course of English history.

In 1538, Cardinal Reginald Pole—a kinsman and enemy of King Henry

VIII—dedicated an essay in defense of the unity of the church to Emperor Charles V. In this work, Pole claimed that as early as 1529, Thomas Cromwell had acquired a copy of Machiavelli's *Prince* and shown it to Henry VIII. Pole asserted, moreover, that in the same year Cromwell had recommended the book to him as a necessary corrective to the imaginary teachings of theorists like Plato.

According to Pole's account, it was Cromwell—armed with what Pole called the satanic ideas in Machiavelli's book—who convinced the king to dissolve monasteries and claim the status of head of the English church. These steps, which paved the way for Henry's divorce from Catherine of Aragon, led to the execution of Sir Thomas More, the brutal suppression of the Pilgrimage of Grace, and eventually to the establishment of the Anglican Church. If Pole's account is to be believed, Machiavelli's ideas animated Cromwell's career and triggered Henry VIII's abandonment of policies aimed at a papal annulment of his first marriage.

As time passed, the *Discourses* and *Florentine Histories* were also becoming better known. In 1550, the first edition of Machiavelli's *Collected Works* appeared. Three years later, the first French translation of *The Prince* came out. Much of the reaction to Machiavelli was negative. In 1559, the pope put all of Machiavelli's writings on the *Index of Prohibited Books*.

Soon "Machiavellian" entered the vocabulary as a description of deceit and wickedness. The first use recorded in the *Oxford English Dictionary* dates from a satirical poem in 1568 ("This false Machivilian"). The next year, we find record of the word "Machiavel" for a follower of his teachings or anyone "practicing duplicity in statecraft or in general conduct."

In the last third of the sixteenth century, overt hostility to Machiavelli's political thought continued to grow. After the French Catholics, under the leadership of Catherine de' Medici, killed some fifty thousand Protestants in 1572 (the Saint Bartholomew's Day Massacre), many European Protestants came to associate Machiavelli with treachery, violence, and absolute rule. By the end of the century, both Catholics and Protestants had reason to vilify *The Prince* and its author.

⚜

In 1590, the negative image of Niccolò and his writing was put in new light by Christopher Marlowe. His *Jew of Malta* begins with Machiavelli himself onstage, reciting a powerful Prologue in which he says:

> *I am Machevill,*
> *And weigh not men, and therefore not men's words.*
> *Admired I am of those that hate me most;*
> *Though some speak openly against my books,*
> *Yet will they read me, and thereby attain*
> *To Peter's chair; and when they cast me off,*
> *Are poisoned by my climbing followers.*
> *I count religion but a childish toy,*
> *And hold there is no sin but ignorance.*

Without challenging Niccolò's reputation as a teacher of evil, Marlowe thus began the process of openly citing Machiavelli as a realistic and prudent political theorist.

In the decade after Marlowe's work, Shakespeare published three plays in which a character refers to Machiavelli. Of these, the most memorable is the soliloquy of the duke of Gloucester, the humpback who becomes King Richard III. In act III, scene ii of *Henry VI, Part 3*, Gloucester outlines his strategy for gaining the crown:

> *Why, I can smile, and murder whiles I smile,*
> *And cry "Content" to that which grieves my heart,*
> *And wet my cheeks with artificial tears,*
> *And frame my face to all occasions.*
> *I'll drown more sailors than the mermaid shall;*
> *I'll slay more gazers than the basilisk;*
> *I'll play the orator as well as Nestor,*
> *Deceive more slily than Ulysses could,*
> *And, like a Sinon, take another Troy.*
> *I can add colours to the chameleon,*

Change shapes with Proteus for advantages,
And set the murderous Machiavel to school.

Although at first this seems like a conventional assessment of Machiavelli, Richard III was hardly the founder of a lasting regime; according to some Shakespearean scholars, the Bard had a more nuanced view of Machiavelli.

After decades of attacks on Niccolò as an exponent of brutality and tyrannical ambition, as the seventeenth century advanced, authors began to discuss openly his theories as realistic, intelligent, and useful. Sir Francis Bacon was among the first to begin this transformation, with numerous passing references to the truths contained in Machiavelli's works. By the middle of the century, as the wars of religion raged, many were willing to abandon pretensions of religious purity in order to regain law and order, not to mention political and economic freedom.

James Harrington's *Oceana* (1656) and Algernon Sidney's *Discourses Concerning Government* (written 1683, published 1698) broke openly with the traditional hostility to Machiavelli. Early in the eighteenth century, *Cato's Letters* by John Trenchard and Thomas Gordan are outspoken in their reliance on Machiavellian arguments in support of republican principles. For these authors, Machiavelli's central works were the *Discourses on Titus Livy* and the *Florentine Histories,* rather than *The Prince*. Of particular importance in their eyes was Machiavelli's view that, because humans are more likely to be selfish than virtuous, all societies tend to become corrupted over time, making it necessary to "return to first principles"—that is, to restore constitutional law, if need be by violent revolution.

On the continent, a similar shift began. Montaigne, reflecting on his travels to Europe, had mentioned Machiavelli's works without formally endorsing his republican principles. Spinoza, writing in the middle of the seventeenth century, openly challenged the prevailing condemnation of *The Prince,* asserting that the work was a covert argument for the return to republics that provide the modern equivalent of ancient Roman glory and power. While some continued to decry Machiavellianism as the embodiment of evil, others (often quietly) endorsed his realism, his view of human nature, and his emphasis on the independence of secular power from papal control.

In addition, the early sixteenth century saw another major shift in the history of ideas. Francis Bacon, who was one of the first to praise Machiavellian realism openly, proposed a transformation in science akin to that envisaged by Leonardo. For Bacon, the "last or furthest end of knowledge" was "the benefit and use of men" and "the relief of man's estate"—that is, the typically modern integration of scientific research, technical innovation, and public policy.

In *The New Organon* (1620), one of Bacon's most famous aphorisms proclaims that "Nature to be commanded must be obeyed." Perhaps more important was his admonition that "natural philosophy be carried on and applied to particular sciences, and particular sciences be carried back again to natural philosophy." And, like Leonardo, Bacon constantly sought to introduce into both natural science and politics the progress observed in "the mechanical arts which are founded on nature and the light of experience."

Whether by independent discovery, by research into other things, or by some chance encounter with the vestiges of Leonardo's genius, Bacon proposed an attitude toward science and technology that brought together the legacy of both Leonardo da Vinci and Niccolò Machiavelli. One passage suggested as much when illustrating this unification of natural science and politics:

> *"Things are preserved from destruction by bringing them back to their first principles" is a rule in Physics; the same holds good in Politics (as Machiavelli rightly observed), for there is scarcely anything which preserves states from destruction more than the reformation and reduction of them to their ancient manners.*

Bacon's project of a "conquest" of nature "for the relief of man's estate" was to be developed by his onetime secretary and amanuensis, Thomas Hobbes, as well as by Descartes, Locke, and other modern thinkers. By the end of the seventeenth century, therefore, the notion of using human knowledge to control both natural necessity and political events began to transform both science and politics. Although both Leonardo da Vinci and Niccolò Machiavelli had contributed to the emergence of what came to be modern society, further developments took on a life of their own. Tracing their exact influence is like trying to isolate a cup of water thrown into the headwaters of the Arno as it flows all the way to the Ligurian Sea.

By the eighteenth century, Leonardo was remembered primarily as an artist, whereas Machiavelli had achieved the status of a famous—albeit controversial—political theorist. Philosophers and political theorists often took Leonardo's scientific worldview and Niccolò's tough-minded realism for granted without mentioning either of them. Bernard Mandeville set the tone in *The Fable of the Bees,* whose subtitle—*Private Vices, Public Virtues*—marks the explicit rejection of traditional Christian values as a guide in politics. It was a short step to Adam Smith and David Hume, who emphasize the market economy and private self-interest as the only feasible basis of political stability and wealth. While America's founding fathers obviously differed in temperament and theoretical principles, some—notably Hamilton, Madison, and John Adams—were directly inspired by Niccolò's realistic assessment of human selfishness and the means of controlling it.

For example, Alexander Hamilton wrote a pamphlet in 1775 to defend the "sacred rights of mankind," quoting a passage from Hume's *Essays:* "Political writers . . . have established it as a maxim, that, in contriving any system of government, and fixing the several checks and controuls of the constitution, *every man* ought to be supposed a *knave;* and to have no other end in all his actions, but *private interest.*" Hume was referring, of course, to Machiavelli.

Like two mountain streams above Arezzo flowing into the Arno, the legacies of Leonardo da Vinci and Niccolò Machiavelli have become inseparable from Western civilization. Their ideas are part of our inheritance even when we are not fully aware of the source. Even their dream of moving the Arno, a failure in 1504, lies quietly under the surface of modern society.

In *The Prince,* Machiavelli wrote that fortune (or, as we would say, history) is like a river that occasionally floods, causing untold damage. Echoing Leonardo's plans to move and tame the Arno, Machiavelli adds: "And although [rivers] are like this, it is not as if men, when times are quiet, could not provide from them with dikes and dams so that when they rise later, either they go by a canal or their impetus is not so wanton nor so damaging."

Whatever they shared, Leonardo and Machiavelli ultimately drew very different lessons from their experiences along the Arno. For Leonardo, the problems of controlling the flow of rivers needed to be taken literally and solved by science and technology. One branch of what C. P. Snow called the "two cultures" has sought to build on that legacy.

The science of hydraulic engineering has played a major role in Western civilization. Some of Leonardo's projects in Milan, Rome, and France were realized. As commerce spread in the seventeenth and eighteenth centuries, canals became the principal means of inland transport until displaced by railroads and highways. Malarial swamps have been drained, flood-control dams erected, and rivers dredged.

Something like Leonardo's dream took material form across the Atlantic Ocean at a critical moment in history. After the British surrendered at Yorktown in 1783, ensuring the independence of the United States, George Washington left his responsibilities as commander in chief to return to Mount Vernon. He did not, however, limit himself to the activities of his farm.

Always concerned for the public good, Washington soon became active in the Potomac Company, organized to dig a canal that would open commercial routes between Virginia, Maryland, and areas to the west. Such an enterprise encountered obstacles due to the conflicting politics of the several states. To overcome such resistance, Washington encouraged calling a convention at Annapolis, which, in turn, gave rise to the Constitutional

Convention in Philadelphia and the document on which the United States government has been based for over two centuries.

In the United States as elsewhere, canals, dams, and river projects have long been a central feature of governmental legislation. From the Erie Canal to the Tennessee Valley Authority and the Fort Peck Dam, when politicians made funds available, engineers built massive projects for transportation and flood control. Complemented by highways (those rivers of automobiles and trucks) and airports (organizing the flow of planes through the sky), such constructions have provided the basic infrastructure of industrial society.

Niccolò Machiavelli drew a very different lesson from his attempt to redirect the Arno. As a poet and a statesman, he came to use the river as a symbol or metaphor for the inundations of foreign armies that can destroy the freedom and happiness of a society. For example, in one letter he explains that he has delayed his analysis because "I wanted to see which way the water was going to flow."

Controlling a river in this sense entails a tough-minded understanding of human behavior in war as well as in peace. For Machiavelli, therefore, the Arno could have lessons to teach that were related to concrete historical events. Unlike Leonardo, who sought the universal and technical understanding of all rivers, Niccolò was to show how the knowledge of specific individuals could lead to military victory and political success.

A powerful example is found in his *Life of Castruccio Castracani*, written in Lucca in 1520 to demonstrate to Pope Clement VII that Niccolò could write a suitable history of Florence. Castruccio was a general from Lucca whose astute strategy used the force of the river as a weapon to defeat a large and powerful Florentine army.

Machiavelli tells the story of the decisive battle when "the Florentines . . . determined to assail Castruccio."

At that time the Arno River was so low that it could be forded, but not, however, to such an extent that infantry would not get wet up to the shoulders and horses up to the saddles. When the morning of June 20 came, then, the Florentines, drawn up for battle, began the crossing with part of their cavalry and a force of ten thousand infantry . . . the Florentine infantry were weighed down by the water and by their equipment, and not all of them had climbed up the bank of the river. The horses, after some of them had crossed, since they had broken up the bottom of the Arno, made passage by the others difficult. As a result, many, getting into the ruined ford, fell on their riders; many were so stuck in the mud that they could not get out.

The generals from Florence tried to cross "higher upstream," but Castruccio was ready for this maneuver.

To them were opposed the infantry that Castruccio had sent up along the bank; these, lightly armed with shields and with gallery-darts in their hands, with loud shouts wounded the horses in the face and in the breast, so that frightened by the wounds and the shouts, not wanting to go ahead, they fell on top of one another . . . the fresh troops coming to blows with the tired ones did not delay long before they drove them into the river.

Moving downstream worked no better for the Florentines; "since the banks were high and their tops were held by [Castruccio's] men, [the Florentines] tried in vain."

The Arno, like any river, can be an ally or an enemy. To make it an ally, however, one has to know about human affairs. Politics, history, culture matter. If Leonardo represents the scientist's side of the two cultures, Machiavelli represents the social scientists and humanists.

Most of us like to believe that modern science and technology assure the control of floods and other natural catastrophes. Like Sir Francis Bacon, we think a "conquest of nature" is possible and, once assured, will provide for the "relief of man's estate." When the floods come, as they did to many American states in the spring of 1997, politicians decree a "disaster area" and provide funds for reconstruction, all the while lamenting the failure of technology.

Is our control over these events more tenuous than is popularly realized? No matter how advanced science and technology could become, Niccolò—unlike Leonardo—thought that only "about half" of the accidents of fortune could be controlled. Of the two men and a river who have been the subject of this story, perhaps the river deserves more attention.

Now, as in the time of Leonardo and Niccolò, the Arno still floods. As recently as 1966, a devastating flood ravaged Florence. Officials still promise a system of flood control that will prevent a recurrence. Italian politicians, hesitant to raise taxes for the immense sums involved, still fail to implement the plans.

Not long after the disastrous failure of the attempt to divert the Arno at Pisa, when Niccolò was on a mission to the papal court, two of his friends wrote him in a humorous vein. After warning Niccolò to avoid excesses in "the delicious enjoyment and pleasant fruits" of his surroundings and expressing fear that the second chancellor would "take priestly vows and become a thoroughly modern curial ecclesiastic," Niccolò's friends concluded: "There is no other news from here, except that the Arno is running downhill as it did before."

Notes

To understand the maps, memoranda, and notes cited in this book careful examination is needed: neither Leonardo nor Machiavelli left a record of his own role in the failed project, let alone admitted working with the other. This need not be surprising: few people go out of their way to attract attention to a costly political disaster for which they can be held responsible. As in many a mystery, material evidence must be pieced together and analyzed in detail.

Although all readers deserve to know how to find the basic evidence, the discursive footnotes underlying my analysis—while important for scholars and the especially curious—are too lengthy to publish here. Technology now makes it possible to resolve this dilemma. Essential citations are included in this section; more extensive scholarly footnotes are available, using the same reference system, on the World Wide Web at:

http://www.Dartmouth.edu/~rmasters

Readers who do not have access to the Internet can receive a hard copy of these additional notes by writing: Prof. Roger D. Masters, c/o Department of Government, Dartmouth College, Hanover, NH 03755. Please enclose $5.00 to cover photocopying and mailing.

The notes that follow are keyed to the text by a page number and italicized phrase. Abbreviated citations refer to works described in "Sources."

CHAPTER 1. A MYSTERIOUS FRIENDSHIP

3. *"a great and continuous malignity"*: NM, *The Prince*, Dedicatory Letter, ed. Mansfield, p. 4.
4. *"for some time now"*: NM to Francesco Guicciardini, May 17, 1521, *Machiavelli and His Friends: Their Personal Correspondence*, ed. Atkinson and Sices, #270, p. 336 (also in NM, *The Prince*, ed. Adams, pp. 133–35.)
5. *"I wish I could write"*: Francesco Vettori to NM, January 16, 1515, *Machiavelli and His Friends*, #246, p. 310.
5. *At different times in their careers:* On the charge against Leonardo for sodomy, see Bramly, *Leonardo*, pp. 117–19; see also Chapter 3, "Leonardo Achieves Fame." For the charge against NM, see Ridolfi, *Machiavelli*, pp. 112–13.
5. *"your adversaries are numerous"*: Biagio Buonaccorsi to NM, December 28, 1509, *Machiavelli and His Friends*, #181, p. 193 (italicized words originally in code).
5. *"I wrote you that idleness"*: Vettori to NM, January 16, 1515, *Machiavelli and His Friends*, # 246, p. 311.

CHAPTER 2. THE ARNO

8. *"Amid all the causes"*: Leonardo, *Notebooks*, ed. I. Richter, pp. 26–27.
9. *"a river which is to be turned"*: Leonardo, *Notebooks*, ed. J. Richter, pp. 351–52.
10. *While in Milan:* For Fancelli's plan, see his letter to Lorenzo the Magnificent, dated August 12, 1487, in Baratta, *Leonardo da Vinci negli Studi per la Navigazione dell' Arno*, pp. 52–53.
10. *"I liken her [that is, Fortune]"*: NM, *The Prince*, chap. 25, ed. Mansfield, p. 98.
11. *"And although they [rivers] are like this"*: NM, *The Prince*, chap. 25, ed. Mansfield, p. 98.
11. *In the* Divine Comedy: Dante, *Inferno* XXXIII, 82–84.
11. *Early in the fifteenth century:* See G. Cavalcanti, *Istorie Fiorentine*, VI, xviii, ed. F. Polidore (Florence, 1838), vol. I, p. 328, in *Brunelleschi in Perspective*, ed. Isabelle Hyman (Englewood Cliffs, N.J.: Prentice Hall, 1974), p. 60; and NM, *Florentine Histories*, IV, 23, ed. Banfield and Mansfield, pp. 169–70.
12. *The centers of early civilizations:* The classic source of this analysis is Karl Wittfogel, *Oriental Despotism* (New Haven: Yale University Press, 1957).
14. *"since the city of Fiesole"*: NM, *Florentine Histories*, II, 2, ed. Banfield and Mansfield, p. 53.
15. *"For already in the time of Tiberius"*: NM, *Florentine Histories*, II, 2, ed. Banfield and Mansfield, p. 54 (citing Tacitus, *Annals*, I, 79).
16. *Around Milan, a network of canals:* Carlo Zammattio, "The Mechanics of Water and Stone," in *The Unknown Leonardo*, ed. Reti, pp. 206–7.
16. *"equilibrium of the Renaissance"*: David Hackett Fischer, *The Great Wave* (New York: Oxford University Press, 1966).
16. *Commerce developed along with banking houses:* Fischer, *The Great Wave*, pp. 60–61.
17. *"equal liberty exists"*: Quoted in Nicolai Rubenstein, "Cradle of the Renaissance," in *The Age of the Renaissance*, ed. Denys Hay, p. 18.

18. *Among these elective officials:* Nicolai Rubenstein, "The Beginnings of Niccolò Machiavelli's Career in the Florentine Chancery," *Italian Studies* 11 (1956): 72–91. See also the sources in the next note.
18. *"a league of Mafia families":* See Richard C. Trexler, *Public Life in Renaissance Florence,* chap. 1; H. C. Butters, *Governors and Governed in Early Sixteenth Century Florence, 1502–1509;* Felix Gilbert, *Machiavelli and Guicciardini,* chap. 1. The phrase "a league of Mafia families" is from Karl Morrison, *Europe's Middle Ages* (Glenview: Free Press, 1970), p. 82, quoted by Trexler, p. 27.
18. *For example, both the Vangelista:* The classic study is Ronald F. E. Weissman, *Ritual Brotherhood in Renaissance Florence.* See also John Henderson, *Piety and Charity in Late Medieval Florence,* especially pp. 437, 439; Richard C. Trexler, *Public Life in Renaissance Florence,* chap. 11.
18. *Although some confraternities stressed:* Henderson, *Piety and Charity;* Christopher F. Black, *Italian Confraternities in the Sixteenth Century.*
19. *"Florence harbours the greatest minds":* Quoted in Rubenstein, "Cradle of the Renaissance," p. 12.
19. *"You may have and possess":* Pico della Mirandola, "Oration on the Dignity of Man," cited in Fischer, *The Great Wave,* p. 62.
20. *Both the Florentine field commander:* F. Villari, *Machiavelli e i suoi tempi,* pp. 213–15.
21. *"Certainly, as far as human judgment":* Ercole Bentivoglio to NM, February 25, 1506, *Machiavelli and His Friends,* #107, p. 119.
21. *Niccolò presented a theory:* NM, *The Prince,* chap. 26, ed. Mansfield, p. 103.

CHAPTER 3. LEONARDO ACHIEVES FAME

23. *In the biographical details throughout this chapter,* I follow primarily Serge Bramly, *Leonardo: Discovering the Life of Leonardo da Vinci.* Of great value are the works of Carlo Pedretti, including *Leonardo: A Study in Chronology and Style* and his invaluable analysis and dating of the *Notebooks* in *Literary Works of Leonardo da Vinci.* For further references, see the listing of Sources.
24. *The architect and art historian:* Giorgio Vasari, *Lives of Seventy Painters, Sculptors, and Architects,* ed. Blashfield, Blashfield, and Hopkins, vol. II, p. 370.
24. *Leonardo was an innovator:* See esp. Letze and Bucksteiner, *Leonardo da Vinci;* Reti, *Unknown Leonardo;* and Galluzi, *Leonardo da Vinci.*
24. *Painters and artisans:* Peter Burke, *Culture and Society in Renaissance Italy.*
25. *"I am fully conscious":* Leonardo, *Notebooks,* ed. J. P. Richter, #10, vol. I, p. 14 (c. 1490: Pedretti, *Literary Works,* vol. I, pp. 109–10). Leonardo's reference does not seem to be exact, since scholars cannot find such a citation of Marius.
26. *When Milan fell to the French:* Maria Grazie Pernis, *Ficino's Platonism and the Court of Urbino,* Ph.D. dissertation, Columbia University (Ann Arbor: University Microfilms, 1990), p. 167; Bramly, *Leonardo,* p. 290.
26. *Leonardo's* Notebooks *contain:* One passage often cited, concerning the dream of a bird, is probably best left to one side. When Freud used this passage in a

famous analysis of Leonardo's sexuality and art, he based the interpretation on an erroneous German translation of the Italian word for a kite (*nibbio*), as if it referred to a vulture. See Bramly, *Leonardo*, p. 49.

27. *"I have seen motions"*: Leonardo, *Notebooks*, ed. J. P. Richter, #1338, vol. II, p. 394 (c. 1508: Pedretti, *Literary Works*, vol. II, pp. 293–94 as well as 170–71).
27. *In the* Florentine Histories: *Florentine Histories*, VI, 34, ed. Banfield and Mansfield, p. 270. On the possibility that Machiavelli's passage reflects conversations with Leonardo, see Pedretti, *Leonardo: A Study in Chronology and Style*, pp. 11–14; Masters, *Machiavelli, Leonardo, and the Science of Power*, p. 24 and notes.
27. *"Unable to resist"*: Leonardo, *Notebooks*, ed. J. P. Richter, # 1339, vol. II, pp. 394–95 (c. 1480: Pedretti, *Literary Works*, vol. II, pp. 293–94; Bramly, *Leonardo*, p. 86).
28. *Together, they formed the nucleus:* Bramly, *Leonardo*, pp. 63–74.
28. *The shield in turn was sold:* Vasari, *Lives*, ed. Blashfield, Blashfield, and Hopkins, vol. II, pp. 377–79; Bramly, *Leonardo*, pp. 97–98. Although Vallentin claims this event occurred while Leonardo was still a child in Vinci, Bramly's account more plausibly places it during his years of apprenticeship in Florence. To get an idea of the values involved, Machiavelli's salary when he was appointed second chancellor of Florence, one of the highest administrative positions in the government, was 192 *fiorini di suggello*, or 128 ducats (or gold florins) a year.
28. *Art historians are generally agreed:* Vasari, *Lives*, ed. Blashfield, Blashfield, and Hopkins, vol. II, p. 376; Bramly, *Leonardo*, pp. 104–6.
29. *"dressing up, taming horses"*: Bramly, *Leonardo*, pp. 96, 115; Antonina Vallentin, *Leonardo da Vinci*, pp. 30–35.
29. *Some have suggested:* Bramly, *Leonardo*, pp. 118–19.
29. *"There is no record"*: Bramly, *Leonardo*, pp. 119–33.
30. *Unlike most artists:* Vallentin, *Leonardo da Vinci*, pp. 22–24; Bramly, *Leonardo*, pp. 109–11.
30. *lectures on Aristotle's natural philosophy:* Bramly, *Leonardo*, p. 158.
30. *to "a globe" and to "my map of the world"*: Leonardo, *Notebooks*, ed. J. P. Richter, #1444, vol. II, p. 433 (c. 1506–7, or perhaps 1504: Pedretti, *Literary Works*, vol. II, 342–43).
30. *While studying with Toscanelli:* Frederick J. Pohl, *Amerigo Vespucci* (New York: Columbia University Press, 1944), pp. 13–25. For a later text that apparently refers to Amerigo Vespucci's reports of his voyages of exploration, see Leonardo's *Notebooks*, ed. J. P. Richter, #844, vol. II, p. 130 and note (c. 1513: Pedretti, *Literary Works*, vol. II, p. 114).
30. *"Vespuccio will give me"*: Leonardo, *Notebooks*, ed. J. P. Richter, #1452, vol. II, p. 436 (c. 1503–5: Pedretti, *Literary Works*, vol. II, p. 346). Pedretti suggests that the note refers to Agostino Vespucci, NM's assistant in the Florentine chancery; see also ibid., vol. II, pp. 381–8.
30. *Amerigo's uncle:* Leonardo, *Notebooks*, ed. J. P. Richter, #1444, vol. II, p. 433; Pohl, *Amerigo Vespucci*, pp. 15–16.

31. *In the years after 1480:* Bern Dibner, "Machines and Weaponry," in *Unknown Leonardo*, ed. Reti, p. 170 (citing especially the design of a machine tool in Codex Atlanticus, 6 recto, c. 1480); Paolo Galluzi, "The Career of a Technologist," in *Leonardo, Engineer and Architect*, ed. Galluzi, pp. 48–63. On work associated with channeling rivers, see esp. Fig. 40, from Codex Atlanticus, 90 recto/33 verso a (c. 1480–82), p. 57.
31. *He imagined a number of technical:* Galluzi, "Career of a Technologist," pp. 60–61.
31. *Although Leonardo doubtless met:* Bramly, *Leonardo*, pp. 72, 89–93, 98, 109–11, 156–60. Because Leonardo rarely recorded personal information in his *Notebooks* before moving to Milan in 1482–83, textual evidence of his early contacts with intellectuals in Florence is relatively limited. See *Notebooks*, ed. J. P. Richter, #1438, vol. II, p. 432 (c. 1480; Pedretti, *Literary Writings*, vol. II, p. 338); #1442, p. 433 (c. 1480; Pedretti, *Literary Writings*, vol. II, p. 340); #1553 (c. 1480; Pedretti, *Literary Writings*, vol. II, p. 384). Later lists of Leonardo's books, such as the catalog he made when storing his library during his trip to Piombino in 1504, show extensive erudition that may be in part traced to his earlier contacts (Pedretti, *Literary Works*, vol. II, p. 355–68). In 1505–7, he reminded himself, "On meeting Lorenzo de' Medici you should ask about the treatise on water of the Bishop of Padua" (Pedretti, *Literary Writings*, vol. II, p. 333). Since the Medici were exiled from Florence long before Leonardo's return in 1503, the occurrence of such a meeting, as well as the specific question, presupposes earlier connections with the Medici.
31. *Leonardo was critical:* Bramly, *Leonardo*, pp. 111, 157–59.
31. *In 1481, a number:* Bramly, *Leonardo*, pp. 155–60.
31. *As always, Leonardo sought perfection:* Pedretti, *Chronology and Style*, pp. 32–34.
33. *Others, however, suggest:* Bramly, *Leonardo*, pp. 160–67. The second interpretation is all the more probable because, a few years later, the *Virgin of the Rocks* was to elicit a negative reaction from the religious order that had commissioned it (Bramly, *Leonardo*, pp. 184–89).
33. *The contract Leonardo signed:* Bramly, *Leonardo*, p. 160.
34. *Leonardo sought the independence:* Evidence of this desire can be found not only in Leonardo's increasing interest in technology, but in a notebook entry apparently referring to Paolo Toscanelli, the famous scientist and physician whose maps were to be used by Columbus and Amerigo Vespucci (Codex Atlanticus, 42 verso/12 verso a, dated c. 1480). Galluzzi, "The Career of a Technologist," p. 63.
34. *Later in life, Leonardo:* Bramly, *Leonardo*, pp. 356–57.
34. *He was to stay there:* Bramly, *Leonardo*, pp. 171–82.
35. *It apparently took some time:* Bramly, *Leonardo*, p. 183.
35. *Sforza, a proud and often devious:* Bramly, *Leonardo*, pp. 183, 211.
36. *Whereas Leonardo's letters:* Leonardo, *Notebooks*, ed. J. P. Richter, #1348, vol. II, p. 402; #1350, p. 404 (1507–8: Pedretti, *Literary Works*, vol. II, pp. 298–303).

36. *Having, my most Illustrious Lord:* Leonardo, *Notebooks*, ed. J. P. Richter, #1340, vol. II, pp. 395–98 (c. 1482; Pedretti, *Literary Writings*, vol. II, p. 295). The word "my" is omitted in Richter's translation. As Pedretti comments, while the letter is not written in Leonardo's hand and does not reflect his characteristic style, he seems to have edited the text.
37. *Often Leonardo was engaged:* Leonardo, *Notebooks*, ed. J. P. Richter, #1265–1335, vol. II, pp. 335–79 (mainly dated 1493–94: Pedretti, *Literary Works*, vol. II, pp. 259–90).
37. *Leonardo was frustrated:* Leonardo, *Notebooks*, ed. J. P. Richter, #1344 and #1345, vol. II, pp. 399–400 (c. 1495: Pedretti, *Literary Works*, vol. II, pp. 196–97).
38. *"a method of letting a flood":* Leonardo, Ms. B, folio 64, cited in Ignazio Calvi, "Military Engineering and Arms," in Istituto Geografico d'Agostino, *Leonardo da Vinci*, p. 290.
39. *Although the diversion of the Arno:* Leonardo, Ms. B, folio 64, cited in Calvi, "Military Engineering and Arms"; Ludwig H. Heydenreich, "The Military Architect," in *The Unknown Leonardo*, ed. Reti, pp. 136–65.
41. *Three years later:* Bramly, *Leonardo*, pp. 204–11. On Leonardo's architectural career, see Carlo Pedretti, *Leonardo, Architect* and *Leonardo da Vinci: The Royal Palace at Romorantin*.
41. *Reflecting on the health risks:* Bramly, *Leonardo*, pp. 193–96.
43. *"tried to survey":* Sigfried Giedion, *Space, Time and Architecture* (Cambridge: Harvard University Press, 1959), p. 74.
44. *Although these projects for "guiding":* Zammattio, "Mechanics of Water and Stone," in *The Unknown Leonardo*, ed. Reti, pp. 204–6; Pedretti, *Chronology and Style*, p. 173.
45. *Leonardo consulted with Luca Fancelli:* Heydenreich, "The Military Architect," in *The Unknown Leonardo*, ed. Reti, p. 149; Bramly, *Leonardo*, p. 205. For Fancelli's 1487 project, see Baratta, *Leonardo da Vinci*, pp. 52–53.
45. *"On the 2nd of April":* Leonardo, *Notebooks*, vol. II, ed. J. P. Richter, #1370, p. 415. Pedretti indicates that the words "book entitled Of the Human Figure" were probably added around 1509 (*Literary Works*, vol. II, pp. 314–15), which suggests that Leonardo's date of April 2, 1489, recorded an intellectual event that led to a longer-term project. See the date of the passage in the next note.
45. *"And so may it please":* Leonardo, *Notebooks*, ed. J. P. Richter, #1362, vol. II, p. 414, italics added (c. 1509–10: Pedretti, *Literary Works*, vol. II, p. 311).
46. *Finally completed:* Bramly, *Leonardo*, pp. 228–33.

Chapter 4. Niccolò Achieves Power

49. *"Niccolò Piero Michele":* Roberto Ridolfi, *The Life of Niccolò Machiavelli*, p. 258 n. 10; NM, *Oeuvres Complètes*, ed. Pléiade, p. 14.
49. *According to one story:* Sebastian de Grazia, *Machiavelli in Hell*, p. 5.
49. *It is probable:* Ridolfi, *Machiavelli*, p. 257 n. 4.

50. *Alessandro Machiavelli died:* NM, *Oeuvres Complètes*, p. 15.; de Grazia, *Machiavelli in Hell*, p. 4.
50. *While not among the leading:* Christopher F. Black, *Italian Confraternities in the Sixteenth Century*, p. 238.
50. *"Niccolò" was a common name:* Born in 1472, Niccolò di Bernardo di Jacopo Machiavelli has sometimes been confused with *the* Niccolò, which led some scholars to believe that the future author of *The Prince* had been a banker in his youth. *Machiavelli and His Friends: Their Personal Correspondence*, p. 5; Mario Martelli, *L'altro Niccolò di Bernardo Machiavelli*, Quaderni di Rinascimento (Florence: Sansoni, 1975).
50. *At eleven, Bernardo records:* De Grazia, *Machiavelli in Hell*, p. 5.
50. *In return for compiling:* Ridolfi, *Machiavelli*, pp. 3–4, 257–58 n. 7; de Grazia, *Machiavelli in Hell*, pp. 5–6.
51. *"The conspiracy of the Pazzi":* NM, *Discourses on Titus Livy*, III, 67, ed. Mansfield and Tarcov, p. 228.
51. *In the* Florentine Histories: NM, *Florentine Histories*, VIII, 3–9, ed. Banfield and Mansfield, pp. 319–27.
51. *"there was no citizen":* NM, *Florentine Histories*, VIII, 9, ed. Banfield and Mansfield, p. 326.
53. *"had been successful around Perugia":* NM, *Florentine Histories*, VIII, 16, ed. Banfield and Mansfield, p. 336.
53. *First, Bernardo was a member:* John Henderson, "Le Confraternite Religiose nella Firenze del Tardo Medioevo: Patroni Spirituali e Anche Politici?," p. 93.
53. *One of the foremost flagellant societies:* Black, *Italian Confraternities;* John Henderson, *Piety and Charity in Late Medieval Florence*.
53. *"Exhortation to Penitence":* NM, "An Exhortation to Penitence," in *Machiavelli, Chief Works and Others*, ed. Allan Gilbert, vol. I, p. 170. Although Gilbert, like most commentators, assumes this text was written late in Niccolò's life, it begins with an introductory remark suited to the traditional youth oration: "Since this evening, *honored fathers and superior brothers,* I am to speak to Your Charities, in order *to obey my superiors* . . ." (p. 171, italics added).
53. *Conforming to the requirement:* NM, *Chief Works*, ed. Gilbert, vol. I, p. 170 (citing Oreste Tommasini's *Vita di Machiavelli*, vol. II, p. 734).
54. *Since Scala was responsible:* Felix Gilbert, *Machiavelli and Guicciardini*, pp. 162, 318–22.
54. *His publications included:* Poliziano was a participant as well as an observer of the playful and often frivolous life of Lorenzo's court, especially in the 1470s and 1480s (Bramly, *Leonardo*, p. 100). Given the importance of the charge of homosexuality against Leonardo, it is ironic that Poliziano's open homosexuality was apparently not a source of difficulty (cf. ibid., p. 129).
55. *"Cosimo was also a lover":* NM, *Florentine Histories*, VII, 6, ed. Banfield and Mansfield, p. 283.

55. *"He [Lorenzo the Magnificent] loved":* NM, *Florentine Histories,* VIII, 36, ed. Banfield and Mansfield, pp. 361–62.
55. *Apart from hints: Machiavelli and His Friends,* p. 433, n. 1 to letter #1.
56. *He knew Latin well:* Although many scholars have claimed that Niccolò was totally ignorant of Greek, there is some evidence he knew at least its rudiments. See Tommasini, *La Vita di Machiavelli,* vol. I, p. 98.
56. *The influence of long study:* See especially the *First Decennal* (1504), which uses a rhyming scheme akin to Dante's *Divine Comedy,* in NM, *Chief Works,* ed. Gilbert, vol. III, pp. 1444–57. For examples of the numerous allusions in his later correspondence, see *Machiavelli and His Friends,* pp. 499 (editorial note 1 to #208), 514 (editorial note 14 to #224), and 548 (editorial notes 7 and 10 to #300).
56. *Many other poets:* For examples in his correspondence, see *Machiavelli and His Friends,* pp. 500 (editorial note 2 to #210), 518 (editorial notes 3–5 to #229), 519 (editorial notes 6–7 to #231); 523 (editorial note to #238), 528–30 (editorial notes 1, 4, 13 to #247). See also Ridolfi, *Machiavelli,* pp. 89–90.
56. *"Dante or Petrarch":* NM to Francesco Vettori, December 10, 1513, *Machiavelli and His Friends,* #224, p. 264.
56. *This letter also contains:* See *Machiavelli and His Friends,* pp. 513–16 n. 1 (Petrarch, *Trionfo dell' eternità,* v. 13), n. 4 (the contemporary novella *Geta et Birra,* based on Plautus's *Amphytruo*), n. 22 (Juvenal and Plautus), n. 23 (Virgil and Lucretius).
56. *Niccolò also knew:* For example, Biagio Buonaccorsi to NM, October 21, 1502, *Machiavelli and His Friends,* #37, p. 55.
56. *During his term as second chancellor:* V. to NM, April 24, 1504, *Machiavelli and His Friends,* #89, p. 101. On the *First Decennale,* see Chapter 8, "The Aftermath."
56. *After the fall of the republic:* De Grazia, *Machiavelli in Hell,* p. 34.
56. *Years later, he was to write:* NM, *Mandragola,* ed. Flaumenhaft. See also NM, *The Comedies of Machiavelli,* ed. Sices and Atkinson.
56. *Under these circumstances:* Like Najemy (*Between Friends,* esp. chap. 9) and de Grazia (*Machiavelli in Hell*), Ridolfi also calls Niccolò a "poet" (*Machiavelli,* p. 13). Unfortunately, most scholars have not considered the implications of this identification.
56. *"Lately I have been reading":* NM to Ludovico Alamanni, December 17, 1517, *Machiavelli and His Friends,* #254, p. 318.
57. *The oldest surviving fragment:* NM to unknown addressee, December 1, 1497, *Machiavelli and His Friends,* #1, p. 6.
57. *The purpose of this text:* NM to Cardinal Lopez, December 2, 1497, *Machiavelli and His Friends,* #2, pp. 7–8.
57. *"Yet beset by ill health":* NM to unknown addressee, December 1, 1497, *Machiavelli and His Friends,* #1, pp. 6–7.
58. *Nothing seems to have prepared:* Or, to use another phrase of Niccolò's biographer, what was "the secret of his election"? (Ridolfi, *Machiavelli,* p. 17).

59. *Moreover, Niccolò also came to occupy:* NM, *Oeuvres Complètes,* p. 1469; Ridolfi, *Machiavelli,* p. 263 n. 21.
59. *The first and second chancellors:* Butters, *Governors and Governed in Early Sixteenth Century Florence,* chap. 1, esp. p. 22.
59. *For example, by this means:* See Butters, *Governors and Governed,* chap. 3–4 and appendices I, II, and III.
60. *By this same means:* See Butters, *Governors and Governed,* appendix VII, p. 320.
60. *But even granted that:* Trexler, *Public Life in Renaissance Florence,* pp. 11–12.
60. *The years of Savonarola's power:* Henderson, *Piety and Charity,* p. 401.
61. *For example, convictions and punishments:* Michael Rocke, *Forbidden Friendships: Homosexuality and Male Culture in Renaissance Florence,* esp. pp. 78–79 and chap. 6.
62. *A great deal can therefore:* NM to Ricciardo Becchi, March 9, 1498, *Machiavelli and His Friends,* pp. 8–9.
63. *"in my judgment":* ibid., italics added.
63. *Whatever else could be said:* Ridolfi, who treats Niccolò's remarks as an "unworthy letter" written "half in jest" to friends "for his own amusement and theirs" (*Machiavelli,* p. 9), was apparently unaware of Becchi's role in the curia.
63. *Contemporaries attributed this:* Francesco Guicciardini, *History of Florence,* chaps. xv–xvi, in *History of Italy and History of Florence,* ed. John R. Hale (New York: Twayne, 1964), pp. 57–83.
63. *In the official election register:* For the circumstances of Niccolò's election, see Rubenstein, "The Beginnings of Niccolò Machiavelli's Career in the Florentine Chancery." See also Black, "Machiavelli, Servant of the Florentine Republic," esp. pp. 85–86.
64. *The key document:* For a careful analysis, see Martelli, "Prehistoria (medicea) di Machiavelli."
65. *Becchi's family had long been:* For the relationship between Gentile Becchi and Lorenzo the Magnificent, see Trexler, *Public Life in Renaissance Florence,* p. 119 n. 130, pp. 429–32, 435. After 1502, another member of the Becchi family, Niccolò, was supported on election to the Signoria by Jacopo Salviati, an aristocrat who—after supporting Soderini's election—became one of his leading enemies and, after 1512, was closely allied with the Medici regime (Butters, *Governors and Governed,* p. 316 and passim).
65. *Corroborating evidence is provided:* Butters, *Governors and Governed,* pp. 63–65.
65. *"I am very happy":* Alamanno Salviati to NM, December 23, 1502, *Machiavelli and His Friends,* #67, p. 79 (italics added).
67. *"when Alamanno was in Bibbona":* Biaggio Buonaccorsi to NM, October 6, 1506, *Machiavelli and His Friends,* #127, p. 141.
67. *"Honored Patron":* NM to Alamanno Salviati, September 28, 1509, *Machiavelli and His Friends,* #G, p. 436.
67. *On November 3, 1503:* Battista Machiavelli to NM, November 9, 1503, *Machiavelli and His Friends,* #74, pp. 86–87.

68. *But some letters and texts:* See, for example, NM, *Chief Works*, vol. III, p. 1463.
68. *Conversely, when Soderini fell:* See Chapter 10.
68. *In twentieth-century terms:* Ridolfi, *Machiavelli*, p. 16; de Grazia, *Machiavelli in Hell*, p. 34. See also Black, "Machiavelli, Servant of the Florentine Republic."
68. *Niccolò's most serious rival:* Ridolfi, *Machiavelli*, p. 15.
68. *Such positions were thus:* Machiavelli and His Friends, p. 6; *Oeuvres Complètes*, p. 1469.
68. *"Your essay and the description":* Niccolò Valori to NM, October 22, 1502, *Machiavelli and His Friends*, #32, p. 49. Valori immediate adds: "I, in truth, discussing it with Piero Soderini, gave it its due."
69. *"I can scarcely express":* Bartolomeo Vespucci to NM, June 4, 1504, *Machiavelli and His Friends*, #92, p. 103.
69. *Not surprisingly, many Florentines:* See Michele Luzzati, *Una Guerra di Populo*. The tradition goes back at least to Dante: see *Inferno* XXXIII, 82.
69. *After the interlude of Savonarola:* Ridolfi, *Machiavelli*, p. 22.
70. *In May 1499, he wrote:* For the date, see Ridolfi, *Machiavelli*, pp. 23, 263.
70. *The Signoria decided the next step:* Ridolfi, *Machiavelli*, pp. 27–29. As Ridolfi notes, however, there is little reason "to attribute the machiavellian method of punishing Vitelli to Machiavelli himself" (p. 29).
71. *Then one of the commissioners:* Ridolfi, *Machiavelli*, pp. 30–33.
71. *It was necessary to renew:* See Ridolfi, *Machiavelli*, chap. 4, pp. 35–43.
72. *And by astute negotiation:* Ridolfi, *Machiavelli*, pp. 40–43.
72. *"Thus, King Louis lost":* NM, *The Prince*, chap. 3, ed. Mansfield, p. 15. "Rouen" was Georges d'Amboise, cardinal of Rouen—and brother of Charles d'Amboise, who became the French governor of Milan after 1506 and in that capacity was Leonardo's patron.

CHAPTER 5. THE MEETING

75. *And the populace was helpless:* This description of the situation of Florence in 1501–3 is drawn primarily from NM, *The Prince*, chap. 7.
75. *In April 1502:* Butters, *Governors and Governed*, pp. 49–50.
76. *Conflicts between the leading:* Butters, *Governors and Governed*, chap. 1, esp. pp. 38–40; Felix Gilbert, *Machiavelli and Guicciardini*, chap. 2, esp. pp. 62ff.
76. *"The illness of the city":* Gilbert, *Machiavelli and Guicciardini*, p. 69, citing Francesco Pepi of the Santa Croce quarter.
77. *Salai:* On Leonardo's decision to adopt the ten-year-old Giacomo Caprotti—nicknamed "Salai," or "devil," for his terrible behavior and his physical beauty—see Bramly, *Leonardo*, pp. 223–28.
77. *There he found himself:* Fra Pietro da Nuvolara to Isabella d'Este, April 3, 1501, in Rowden, *Leonardo da Vinci*, p. 158.
79. *Given the political uncertainties:* For Vasari's report on the *Virgin and Child with Saint Anne*, see Serge Bramly, *Leonardo*, p. 318.

79. *Rumors circulated:* Gilbert, *Machiavelli and Guicciardini*, p. 64.
79. *A Florentine force attacking:* Ridolfi, *Machiavelli*, pp. 44–48.
80. *"very dear friend":* Francesco Soderini to NM, August 10, 1502, *Machiavelli and His Friends*, #29, p. 47. On the mission, see also Ridolfi, *Machiavelli*, pp. 48–50.
80. *"To all our lieutenants":* Bramly, *Leonardo*, pp. 324–25.
81. *Bishop Soderini added:* Francesco Soderini to NM, September 29, 1502, *Machiavelli and His Friends*, #31, p. 48.
81. *In addition to proposing:* Heydenreich, "The Military Architect," in *The Unknown Leonardo*, ed. Reti, pp. 136–65.
82. *"so as to keep [Cesare]":* Francesco Guicciardini, *History of Florence*, trans. Mario Domandi (New York: Harper Torchbooks, 1970), p. 230, cited in *Machiavelli and His Friends*, p. 87. On this mission, see also Ridolfi, *Machiavelli*, chap. 6.
83. *"We have found":* Piero Soderini to NM, November 14, 1502, *Machiavelli and His Friends*, #54, pp. 68–69.
83. *"a clear, exact and sincere":* Niccolò Valori to NM, October 11, 1502, *Machiavelli and His Friends*, #32, p. 92.
85. *"it's part of my assignment":* NM to Signoria, October 7, 1502, cited in Masters, *Machiavelli, Leonardo, and the Science of Power*, p. 15. Because the Signoria and the Ten presumably knew what Niccolò's instructions were, this passage might well have been intended for Cesare's eyes: we know that messages were routinely intercepted, and by telling Cesare and his staff what he was required to do, Niccolò might expect to reduce their suspicions as he inquired of everyone in the court of Imola.
85. *His letters were indeed full:* NM to Signoria, November 1 and 3, 1502, cited in Masters, *Machiavelli, Leonardo, and the Science of Power*, pp. 15–16.
86. *By November 8, Niccolò wrote:* Masters, *Machiavelli, Leonardo, and the Science of Power*, p. 15.
86. *"Once the duke [Cesare]":* NM, *The Prince*, chap. 7, ed. Mansfield, pp. 30–31.
87. *"with a small escort":* Bramly, *Leonardo*. p. 329. See also Ridolfi, *Machiavelli*, pp. 62–63. Machiavelli himself described the events in detail in *A Description of the Method Used by Duke Valentino in Killing Vitellozzo Vitelli, Oliverotto da Fermo, and Others*, in NM, *Chief Works*, ed. Gilbert, vol. I, pp. 163–69.
87. *"their simplicity brought them":* NM, *The Prince*, chap. 7, ed. Mansfield, p. 29. Despite the understatement in *The Prince*, Niccolò witnessed at first hand the "elimination" of the condottieri in Sinigaglia just as he had been present at the "spectacle" of Remirro Lorqua in Cesena. Because the political theorists who comment on *The Prince* generally ignore his personal experiences, virtually none has bothered to notice that Niccolò was a firsthand witness to Cesare Borgia's brutalities.
87. *correspondence frequently makes mysterious:* Masters, *Machiavelli, Leonardo, and the Science of Power*, p. 278 n. 30.
88. *Mentioned by Vasari:* Vasari, *Lives*, vol. II, p. 372. On the discovery of the Madrid codices, see Pedretti, *Leonardo da Vinci Inedito: Tre Saggi*.

89. *Work for Cesare does not explain:* Although some have associated the map with the rebellion of Arezzo against Cesare Borgia's rule, there is little evidence supporting this view (Clayton, *Leonardo da Vinci: A Singular Vision*, pp. 97–98); Cesare's response to the uprising of Arezzo and the defection of his condotierri in 1502 was increased military preparation, luring rebellious captains back into his service, and securing new forces from other rulers, not an attempt to control rivers (Ridolfi, *Machiavelli*, p. 57).

89. *"I beg you":* Lorenzo di Niccolò Machiavelli to NM, September 7, 1502, *Machiavelli and His Friends*, #30, pp. 47–48.

89. *"beseech him . . . over and over":* Piero Soderini to NM, October 22, 1502, *Machiavelli and His Friends*, #40, p. 58.

89. *"make recommendations":* Piero Soderini to NM, November 14, 1502, *Machiavelli and His Friends*, #54, pp. 68–69.

91. *Florence needed an army:* See Ridolfi, *Machiavelli*, chaps. 6–7.

91. *In the spring and summer:* Frank Zöllner, "Leonardo's Portrait of Mona Lisa del Giocondo," *Gazette des Beaux-Arts*, March 1993, pp. 120–21.

91. *In the months that followed:* Pedretti, "La Verruca," pp. 417–25.

CHAPTER 6. THE COLLABORATION BEGINS

93. *Niccolò wrote a speech:* Ridolfi, *Machiavelli*, p. 66. For a selection from "A Provision for Infantry" (dated December 6, 1506), see NM, *Chief Works*, ed. A. Gilbert, vol. I, p. 3.

94. *After he drew money:* Bramly, *Leonardo*, pp. 329–30.

94. *"act quickly":* For the text of this message, written in Niccolò's own hand, see Pedretti, "La Verruca," pp. 421–22.

94. *On June 19:* Pedretti, "La Verruca," p. 422.

95. *"Leonardo da Vinci, himself":* Pedretti, "La Verruca," p. 417.

95. *Leonardo's* Notebooks *contain:* Heydenreich, "The Military Architect," in *The Unknown Leonardo*, ed. Reti, p. 148 (including Leonardo's sketch of Monte Verruca, from Madrid Codex II, folio 4 recto); Bramly, *Leonardo*, p. 459.

95. *On June 26:* Pedretti, "La Verruca," p. 422.

95. *Did others in the Florentine government:* Heydenreich, "The Military Architect," pp. 152–53.

95. *Officially, the chief military architect:* As evidence that Giuliano da Sangallo was contacted concerning La Verruca, Pedretti ("La Verruca," p. 422) cites G. Gaye, *Carteggio inedito di artisti* (Florence, 1840), vol. II, p. 61.

96. *Oddly enough: La Mandragola,* I, ii, ed. Flaumenhaft, p. 12. The dramatic date of the play's action is, incidentally, 1504.

96. *"Ex Castris, Franciscus":* Masters, *Machiavelli, Leonardo, and the Science of Power,* p. 237.

96. *"Leonardo's trip to the camp":* Masters, *Machiavelli, Leonardo, and the Science of Power,* p. 238.

96. *Confronted with the failure:* It is not known who first proposed the diversion of the Arno. Some say Machiavelli; others attribute the idea to the *gonfaloniere*, Piero Soderini; still others say Leonardo. Edmondo Solmi flatly asserts that the idea of the diversion came from Leonardo (*Scritti Vinciani*, p. 552). Others (including Heydenrich and Bramly) claim that Leonardo did no more than go to the field to consult on a project proposed by others. The idea of using water as a weapon was hardly new, though previous schemes of this sort—including one that Leonardo had suggested to the Venetians as a means of defense against the Turks—involved creating a flood rather than drying up the river (Heydenrich, "The Military Architect," p. 138; Bramly, *Leonardo*, pp. 330–31; Uzielli, *Le Deviazione dei Fiumi*). In the event, the Venetians did not adopt the flooding Leonardo proposed, even though—as a *defensive* measure—it was not subject to the tactical problems responsible for the failure of Brunelleschi's project at Lucca (see below, pp. 97–98).

97. *Critics who viewed the plan:* F. Villari, *Machiavelli e i suoi tempi*, pp. 213–15.

97. *"[In Florence] there were some":* G. Cavalcanti, *Istorie Fiorentine*, VI, xviii, ed. F. Polidore (Florence, 1838), vol. I, p. 328, cited in *Brunelleschi in Perspective*, ed. Isabelle Hyman (Englewood Cliffs, N.J.: Prentice Hall, 1974), p. 60.

97. *On July 1:* Villari, *Machiavelli*, pp. 212–13 (italics added).

97. *The capture of Librafatta:* See NM to Giovanni Ridolfi, June 1, 1504, *Machiavelli and His Friends*, #91, p. 103.

97. *as Dante had imagined:* See *Inferno* XXXIII, 82–89.

97. *"In those times":* NM, *Florentine Histories*, IV, 23, ed. Banfield and Mansfield, pp. 169–70.

98. *Presumably this is what:* See Guiducci's report, cited in Masters, *Machiavelli, Leonardo, and the Science of Power*, p. 237. The phrase "whether Arno turned there or remained with a channel" at first seems obscure: it becomes clear only in the light of Leonardo's alternative plan for the development of the Arno to carry seafaring ships as far inland as Florence. See Plate VIII and the discussion of the alternate routes for the diversion it proposes.

98. *Even today, some experts:* Heydenrich, "The Military Architect," p. 143. For the contrary view, see Uzielli, *Le Deviazione dei Fiumi*.

99. *"Master Leonardo da Vinci":* Bramly, *Leonardo*, p. 355. Cf. Leo Strauss, *On Tyranny*, rev. ed. (New York: Free Press, 1991), p. 237.

99. *The difficulty of the military diversion:* Oddly enough, Heydenrich—who called the military diversion "utopian"—speaks of the larger plan in very different terms: "Experienced scholars have examined it and investigated its practicability. The sensible calculations given of the daily working capacity of a digger, which serve as a basis for calculating the whole enterprise, are hardly consistent with an overly utopian conception. . . . Leonardo indicated in Codex Atlanticus an intention to tunnel through Serravalle—exactly where the builders of the modern *autostrada* from Florence to the sea did" ("The Military Architect," pp. 147–49).

100. *Another feature of the map:* I thank Martin Clayton, curator of the Windsor Collection, for showing me the details reported here.
100. *Among these are a pair:* Martin Clayton, *Leonardo da Vinci,* catalog #56 and 57, pp. 103, 105. Leonardo devoted a great deal of time to these carefully drawn maps. The finished version was obviously prepared to show to others.
101. *"56 miles by the Arno":* Leonardo, *Notebooks,* ed. J. P. Richter, #1006, vol. II, p. 229 (c. 1503–4?: Pedretti, *Literary Works,* vol. II, pp. 177–80).
101. *"By guiding the Arno":* Leonardo, *Notebooks,* ed. J. P. Richter, #1003, vol. II, p. 228 (c. 1503–4?: Pedretti, *Literary Works,* vol. II, pp. 176–77).
101. *In Niccolò's many messages:* Villari, *Machiavelli e i suoi tempi,,* pp. 213–14; Bramly, *Leonardo,* pp. 330–33; Solmi, *Scritti Vinciani,* pp. 545–46; Masters, *Machiavelli, Leonardo, and the Science of Power,* pp. 17–20 and appendix I.
102. *Indeed, two years earlier:* Poliziano to King John II of Portugal, quoted in Fernando Romero, "Sailing by Caravel," *Americas* 23 (1971): S7.
102. *Vespucci's goal:* Pohl, *Amerigo Vespucci: Pilot Major,* chap. 3. The pilot, Juan de la Cosa, had been on both Columbus's first voyage (as captain of the *Santa Maria*) and the second (as captain of the *Niña*). Although the admiral, Alonso de Hojeda, was nominally in command, Vespucci had authority to determine the route of the voyage.
102. *"since we were grievously wounded":* Pohl, *Amerigo Vespucci,* p. 84. See also Romero, "Sailing by Caravel," pp. S7–9.
103. *In addition to outlining:* Amerigo Vespucci to Lorenzo di Pierfrancesco de' Medici, July 18, 1500, in Pohl, *Amerigo Vespucci,* pp. 76–90.
103. *Columbus claimed:* Pohl, *Amerigo Vespucci,* p. 40.
103. *"we arrived at a new land":* Pohl, *Amerigo Vespucci,* p. 130.
104. *"Having no laws":* Pohl, *Amerigo Vespucci,* pp. 132–34.
104. *The government decreed a celebration:* De Grazia, *Machiavelli in Hell,* p. 21.
104. *By 1503, official documents:* For example, see Oreste Tommasini, *Vita di Machiavelli,* vol. I, p. 652.
104. *Leonardo also knew both:* On the portrait, see Vasari, *Lives,* ed. Blashfield, Blashfield, and Hopkins, vol. II, p. 382, and Pohl, *Amerigo Vespucci,* pp. 194–95. On Leonardo's references to a member of the Vespucci family and to Amerigo's patron Lorenzo di Pier Francesco de' Medici, see *Notebooks,* ed. J. P. Richter, #1452 and #1454, vol. II, pp. 436–7 (described further below in notes to p. 122).
104. *"had treasured Amerigo's letters":* Pohl, *Amerigo Vespucci,* p. 147.
105. *Throughout the spring and summer:* Zöllner, "Leonardo's Portrait of Mona Lisa del Giocondo," p. 120; Heydrenrich, "The Military Architect," pp. 142–51.
105. *Recently, however, an extensive study:* Zöllner, "Leonardo's Portrait," pp. 115–38, esp. nn. 8–23. I am indebted to Odile Taunay of the Cultural Services at the Louvre for bringing this work to my attention. For Vasari's account, see *Lives,* ed. Blasfield, Blasfield, and Hopkins, vol. II, pp. 395–97.
105. *Although no one knows:* It is conceivable that Leonardo met Francesco at the Santa Annunziata, where the artist had stayed between 1500 and 1502 and to

which the Giocondo family tomb was moved at some time in the early sixteenth century. Perhaps the artist met Lisa's father by chance at Santa Maria Nuova, where Gherardini filed his tax declaration and Leonardo kept his money. But such chance meetings scarcely explain an important commission. Is it conceivable that Niccolò, anxious to do his new friend a favor and get him a commission soon after his return to Florence, put Leonardo and Francesco Giocondo in touch with each other in the spring of 1503? Giocondo's election as one of the Twelve (*Buonomini*) in 1499 might have brought him to the second chancellor's attention. In addition, Francesco Giocondo's first wife (Camilla di Mariotto Rucellai) and Lisa del Giocondo's stepmother (Caterina di Mariotto Rucellai) were sisters (Zöllner, "Leonardo's Portrait," p. 119), and Niccolò was closely connected with the Rucellai family—most notably Cosimo Rucellai, to whom both the *Art of War* and the *Discourses on Titus Livy* are dedicated. Because both the Machiavelli and Gherardini families originally came from the parish of Santa Trinità, Niccolò might even have known Lisa as a girl ten years younger than himself. It is also possible, however, that Niccolò's assistant Agostino was involved in the commission as the result of Amerigo Vespucci's business contacts in Lisbon with Francesco's relative Giannetto Giocondo. Pohl, *Amerigo Vespucci*, pp. 31, 36, 43–44.

107. *He used it repeatedly:* Heydenrich, "The Military Architect," p. 147; Pedretti, "La Verruca," p. 424.

CHAPTER 7. THE ARNO DIVERSION FAILS

110. *Soderini, once elected:* Gilbert, *Machiavelli and Guicciardini*, p. 74; Butters, *Governors and Governed*, pp. 60–61.
110. *Instead of dividing Pisan:* Luzzati, *Una Guerra di Populo*.
110. *Compared to a a citizen army:* Tommasini, *La vita e gli scritti di Niccolò Machiavelli*, vol. I, p. 307.
110. *On August 18, 1503:* Ridolfi, *Machiavelli*, p. 66.
110. *This time, Niccolò was able:* The brief tenure of Pope Pius III is of importance for readers of Machiavelli's *Prince*. In chap. 7, Cesare Borgia is quoted as telling NM "on the day that Julius II was created, that he had thought about what might happen when his father was dying, and had found a remedy for everything, except that he never thought that at his death he himself would also be on the point of dying" (ed. Mansfield, p. 32). Machiavelli has written the chapter so that this remark seems to excuse Cesare's inability to prevent the election of Julius II as successor to Alexander VI, when in fact it was Pius III who was elected at his father's death. Generations of commentators have missed the irony. Niccolò did not meet Cesare in Rome until October, long after the immediate effects of illness would have passed; Cesare's remarks in chap. 7 of *The Prince* were self-serving rationalizations. As early as the autumn of 1502, when Niccolò was with Cesare's court in Imola, he wrote the Signoria that Borgia needed above all else to plan for the contingency of his father's death. As the last

110. sentence of chap. 7 puts it, Cesare made an "error" in the election of Julius II and it was the source of his "ruin." NM, *The Prince*, chap. 7, ed. Mansfield, p. 33, and Masters, *Machiavelli, Leonardo, and the Science of Power*, pp. 68–72.
110. *Niccolò left Florence:* Ridolfi, *Machiavelli*, p. 67.
111. *"My very dear compare":* Luca Ugolini to NM, November 11, 1503, *Machiavelli and His Friends*, #75, p. 87. The implication of the congratulatory remark is, of course, that Niccolò had not been cuckolded.
111. *On October 24:* Bramly, *Leonardo*, p. 326; Ridolfi, *Machiavelli*, p. 67.
111. *Leonardo had a formidable rival:* Michelangelo had previously accepted the challenge of sculpting his powerful *David* from a damaged block of marble. The statue was an immediate success, guaranteeing that Michelangelo would be a competitor for the commission to paint a mural in the Great Council Hall. Michelangelo was a jealous competitor too, having once taunted Leonardo as a failure in the streets of Florence. Bramly, *Leonardo*, p. 345.
111. *Ultimately, both were chosen:* Bramly, *Leonardo*, pp. 342–44.
112. *description of the event:* Bramly, *Leonardo*, pp. 336, 340.
112. *At least one other entry:* Leonardo, *Notebooks*, ed. J. P. Richter, #1552, vol. II, p. 465; corrected in Leonardo, *Literary Works*, ed. J. P. Richter and I. A. Richter, rev. ed. (Oxford University Press, 1939), vol. II, p. 386 (c. 1504: Pedretti, *Literary Works*, vol. II, p. 384): "Stephano Iligi, Canonico of Dulcigno, servant of the honorable cardinal Grimani at S. Apostoli.'
112. *And in another note:* Leonardo, *Notebooks*, ed. J. P Richter, #1048, vol. II, p. 242 (c. 1504: Pedretti, *Literary Works*, vol. II, p. 191). Niccolò also knew Latin and could have translated the passage—but since he was frequently away from Florence on diplomatic missions, perhaps Leonardo had to remind himself of another way to translate a technical passage.
112. *They met on January 25:* Leonardo, *Notebooks*, ed. I. Richter, p. 354; Bramly, *Leonardo*, p. 343.
114. "Item dicti Domini": The text is in the Florentine archives (*Signori e Collegi, Deliberazioni fatte in forza di ordinaria autorità*, 106, cc. 40v–41r) and was published in Fachard, *Biagio Buonaccorsi*, pp. 259–60. For the English translation, see Masters, *Machiavelli, Leonardo, and the Science of Power*, pp. 239–40.
114. *"by next February 1504 [1505]":* In Florence, the calendar in use began the counting of the new year on March 25 (*Machiavelli and His Friends*, pp. 433–34).
115. *Thereafter, Soderini's policies:* Butters, *Governors and Governed*, pp. 60–67, 83–87.
116. *Niccolò went to Piombino:* Ridolfi, *Machiavelli*, p. 76.
116. *"Although many things are":* Francesco Soderini to NM, May 29, 1504, *Machiavelli and His Friends*, #90, p. 102.
116. *"it is not possible":* Luzzati, *Una Guerra di Popolo*, p. 152.
116. *Because poor citizens:* Luzzati, *Una Guerra di Popolo*, esp. chaps. 5–6.
117. *Leonardo therefore designed:* The texts and drawings for this plan have been dated to 1504 by Pedretti (*Literary Works*, vol. II, pp. 62–63); consistent with this dating, on the back of Fig. 7.1 are studies for the *Battle of Anghiari*.

117. *"let the charges at once"*: Pedretti, *Literary Works*, vol. II, p. 63.
117. *"And if you do not want"*: Pedretti, *Literary Works*, vol. II, p. 63, citing Codex Atlanticus, 24v–a (the text in Fig. 7.2). By "mines" (*cave*) here, Leonardo clearly means "guns" placed in underground or protected bunkers, described as "hidden guns" (*le artiglierie coperte*) in the passage cited previously (Pedretti, *Literary Works*, vol. II, p. 64). As these passages indicate, Leonardo was specifically concerned with the need to reduce Florentine casualties during the final attack on the city—a central issue that was debated at the time.
117. *"The prisoners said"*: Butters, *Governors and Governed*, p. 88.
120. *"these are not troops"*: NM to Giovanni Ridolfi, June 1, 1504, *Machiavelli and His Friends*, #91, pp. 102–3. For the passage of this letter linking the "campaign against Librafratta" to the overall "victory," see Butters, *Governors and Governed*, pp. 60–67, 83–87.
120. *Around this time, what purports:* The text is described as a Latin translation of a letter in Italian from Amerigo Vespucci to Lorenzo di Pierfrancesco de' Medici by someone called Jocundus (which may be a Latin spelling of "Giocondo"). The work, usually called a forgery, is perhaps best described as plagiarism or unauthorized publication of the sort typical in Renaissance Italy. Many historians use the errors in the text to dismiss Amerigo Vespucci's importance as an explorer. In fact, the publication of *Mundus Novus* may be connected to Florentine politics and was never a claim that Vespucci was the first European to set foot on the American mainland. See Pohl, *Amerigo Vespucci*, pp. 149–50.
120. *"On a former occasion"*: Amerigo Vespucci, *Mundus Novus, Letter to Lorenzo Pietro di Medici*, p. 1.
121. *After describing the route:* For these errors, see Pohl, *Amerigo Vespucci*, pp. 149–50. For example, in *Mundus Novus* Vespucci speaks of his "fourth journey" (pp. 23–24).
121. *"they have another custom"*: Vespucci, *Mundus Novus*, pp. 5–6.
121. *"live according to nature"*: Vespucci, *Mundus Novus*, p. 6. The actual texts of Amerigo Vespucci's letters do not compare the natives of the New World to Epicureans.
121. *Mundus Novus describes the different constellations:* The image demonstrating that the earth cannot be flat shows two men standing on the surface of the earth at different latitudes, with the straight lines from the heavens through their bodies to the center of the earth forming a triangle (Vespucci, *Mundus Novus*, p. 12). This illustration is probably based on the observation that, at a given time and day, a man's shadow differs depending on the latitude at which he is standing. Cf. Leonardo, *Notebooks*, ed. J. P. Richter, #863, vol. II, p. 130: "Each man is always in the middle of the surface of the earth and under the zenith of his own hemisphere, and over the centre of the earth" (c. 1487–90: Pedretti, *Literary Works*, vol. II, p. 121). Elsewhere, Leonardo is explicit in his statements that the earth is a "globe," or sphere: *Notebooks*, ed. J. P. Richter, #857 and #861, vol. II, p. 137–38 (respectively 1503–5 and 1508: Pedretti, *Literary Works*, vol. II, p. 121).

122. *Bartolomeo also acknowledges:* Bartolomeo Vespucci to NM, June 4, 1504, *Machiavelli and His Friends,* #92, pp. 103–4.

122. *"Vespuccio will give me":* Leonardo, *Notebooks,* ed. J. P. Richter, #1452, vol. II, p. 436 (c. 1503–5: Pedretti, *Literary Works,* vol. II, p. 346). Although Pedretti concludes that Leonardo's "Il Vespuccio" refers to Agostino, Solmi ("Le fonti dei Manuscritti di Leonardo da Vinci," *Giornale Storico della Letteratura Italiana* [1908], Suppl., pp. 291–92) thought the note referred to Bartolomeo, the professor of astronomy who corresponded with NM.

122. *"boxes of Lorenzo":* Leonardo, *Notebooks,* ed. J. P. Richter, #1454, vol. II, pp. 436–37. Pedretti has dated this list to 1504, while admitting it might be from 1506–7 (*Literary Works,* vol. II, p. 346). A conjunction of mathematical, geometrical, and astronomical research is involved in the attempt to determine longitude.

122. *More important, at just this time:* On Leonardo's attempt to develop a ship's log around 1504, see : "On Movements:—How Much a Ship Advances in an Hour," in Leonardo, *Notebooks,* ed. J. P Richter, #1113, vol. II, pp. 273–74, and the comments by Pedretti, *Literary Works,* vol. II, p. 218, as well as his comments on #918 (ibid., p. 135) and #1156 (ibid., p. 239)—all dated either 1504 or 1506–7. On Leonardo's concerns for computing longitude and nautical distance, see also *Notebooks,* ed. J. P. Richter, #864, vol. II, p. 139 (c.1506–9: Pedretti, *Literary Works,* vol. II, p. 121) as well as the citations several notes above.

122. *"I saw things incompatible":* Vespucci, *Mundus Novus,* p. 10.

122. *And the evidence that a Florentine:* Perhaps this explains the preparation of yet another plagiarism or unauthorized publication, this time in Italian hastily translated from a Spanish original. Dated September 1504 but not published until 1505, this *Letter of Amerigo Vespucci on the Islands Newly Found in His Four Voyages* combines the inaccuracies of *Mundus Novus* with further imprecisions. It is often called the *Letter to Soderini* because, in one manuscript version, copied on February 10, 1505, it is called a letter to Piero Soderini. For a careful account of the *Letter* as well as the text, unraveling the many problems of philology in the original Italian (which is marred by multiple hispanicisms), see *Amerigo Vespucci, Letter to Piero Soderini,* ed. George Tyler Northup.

123. *"At this time it was considered":* Biagio Buonaccorsi, *Sunmario,* trans. Francesca Roselli, in Masters, *Machiavelli, Leonardo, and the Science of Power,* pp. 245–46.

123. *Upon completion, it would be:* "The ditch, of 40 braccia [about 80 feet] in width at the mouth and of 32 [braccia, or about 64 feet] at the end is 16 [braccia—that is, about 32 feet] in depth; (its surface) 576 braccia; (it is the length of a mile)" (Leonardo, Codex Atlanticus, 210 recto and verso, cited in Edmondo Solmi, *Scritti Vinciani,* pp. 554–55). In Florence at the time, a braccio was 21.7 inches in land survey measurement and 23 inches in a builder's measure (*Machiavelli and His Friends,* p. 448). For simplicity, I have estimated the measurements as approximately two feet per braccio. Without understating the massive nature of the project, it is not the seven-mile-long canal that some critics of the diversion

claimed was involved. Compare Heydenrich, "Military Architect," p. 141, citing the arguments of Bentivogli and Giacomini against the project.

125. *He realized that to lift:* Solmi, *Scritti Vinciani,* p. 555.
127. *Should manpower be a problem:* Solmi, *Scritti Vinciani,* p. 555.
127. *"With regard to Colombino":* NM to Antonio Giacomini, September 3, 1503, cited in Masters, *Machiavelli, Leonardo, and the Science of Power,* p. 240.
128. *"Colombino cannot be held":* Giuliano Lapi to committee of Ten, September 10, 1504, in Masters, *Machiavelli, Leonardo, and the Science of Power,* p. 241.
128. *"Colombino is an excellent expert":* NM to Antonio Giacomini, September 11, 1504, in Masters, *Machiavelli, Leonardo, and the Science of Power,* p. 241.
128. *"Your letter of yesterday":* NM to Giuliano Lapi, September 20, 1504, in Masters, *Machiavelli, Leonardo, and the Science of Power,* pp. 242–43.
129. *"The greater of the two":* Buonaccorsi, *Sunmario,* in Masters, *Machiavelli, Leonardo, and the Science of Power,* p. 246.
130. *"Your delay makes us fear":* NM to Giuliano Lapi, September 21, 1504, in Masters, *Machiavelli, Leonardo, and the Science of Power,* p. 242.
130. *Niccolò probably recognized:* After his study of the manuscripts, Solmi concluded that Leonardo and Niccolò talked on a daily basis at this time (*Scritti Vinciani,* p. 557).
130. *"they ought to go forward":* For the text, see Solmi, *Scritti Vinciani,* pp. 558–59. See also Villari, *Machiavelli e i suoi tempi,*, p. 216.
130. *Soderini and Niccolò were:* Solmi, *Scritti Vinciani,* p. 558.
130. *A specialist, Marcantonio Colonna:* Solmi, *Scritti Vinciani,* p. 559.
130. *"and above all other things"*: Solmi, *Scritti Vinciani,* p. 560.
131. *"And since the workers":* Tommaso Tosinghi to committee of Ten, September 28, 1504, in Masters, *Machiavelli, Leonardo, and the Science of Power,* pp. 244–45.
131. *"And the undertaking":* Buonaccorsi, *Sunmario,* in Masters, *Machiavelli, Leonardo, and the Science of Power,* pp. 245–46.
132. *As Buonaccorsi adds:* Buonaccorsi, *Sunmario,* in Masters, *Machiavelli, Leonardo, and the Science of Power,* pp. 245–46.
132. *Leonardo's* Notebooks *show:* Zammattio, "Mechanics of Water and Stone," pp. 200–201.
133. *"This undertaking came to cost":* To keep the cost in perspective, however, recall that the Florentines had spent twenty thousand gold ducats to purchase a cardinal's hat for Francesco Soderini. The annual cost of the alliance with France in these years was often around one hundred thousand ducats.

Chapter 8. The Aftermath

135. "Notable man": Francesco Soderini (in Rome) to NM, October 26, 1504, *Machiavelli and His Friends,* #94, pp. 106–7.
136. *"this undertaking, begun":* Francesco Guicciardini, *Storia d'Italia,* VI, cited in *Machiavelli and His Friends,* p. 98 (italics added).
136. *Piero Soderini, who had supported:* Butters, *Governors and Governed,* p. 91.

136. *Niccolò, now widely viewed:* F. Gilbert, *Machiavelli and Guicciardini*, p. 173.
136. *In the Dedication: First Decennale,* in NM, *Chief Works,* ed. A. Gilbert, vol. III, p. 1444.
136. *Niccolò's citizen army, a plan supported by Soderini: Machiavelli and His Friends,* p. 463 (n. 3 to #109).
136. *In the poem, which borrows:* Ridolfi, *Machiavelli,* pp. 82–83.
136. *"Nor did you desist": First Decennale,* 499–507, in NM, *Chief Works,* ed. Gilbert, vol. III, p. 1456.
137. *In apparently the only explicit:* To my knowledge, the closest thing to another reference occurs in the *Art of War,* which notes that "many generals have poisoned waters and *turned rivers aside in order to take cities,* even though *in the end they might not succeed." Art of War,* book 7, ed. Gilbert, vol. II, p. 713, italics added. See also Masters, *Machiavelli, Leonardo, and the Science of Power,* appendix III, pp. 257–58.
137. *At the end of his poem: First Decennale,* 547–50, in *Chief Works,* ed. Gilbert, vol. III, p. 1457.
137. *Although he stayed in Piombino for six or seven weeks:* Bramly, Leonardo, p. 342; Pedretti, *Literary Writings,* vol. I, pp. 191, 193, 194, 294, 330, 351, 382; vol. II, pp. 24, 51, 55, 64–70, 80, 189, 192, 199–200, 221, 277, 319–20, 342, 352, 355, 382; Pedretti, *Leonardo: A Study in Chronology and Style,* p. 95; Heydenreich, "The Military Architect," in Reti, *Unknown Leonardo,* esp. pp. 156–57, 163–64; Zammatio, "Mechanics of Water and Stone," in Reti, *Unknown Leonardo,* pp. 200–201.
139. *The Great Council Hall was made ready:* Leonardo, *Notebooks,* ed. Irma Richter, p. 357.
139. *"On 6 June 1505":* Serge Bramly, *Leonardo,* pp. 347–48.
139. *Leonardo was not given:* For a reproduction of this page of Leonardo's *Notebooks,* see Anna Maria Brizio, "The Painter," in *The Unknown Leonardo,* ed. Reti, p. 45.
139. *Leonardo, who was one:* On the introduction of oil painting in Italian painting and Leonardo's development of the technique, see Bramly, *Leonardo,* pp. 101–7.
139. *Discouraged, he apparently:* Bramly, *Leonardo,* pp. 347–50.
141. *But the paint continued:* Bramly, *Leonardo,* p. 350.
141. *The science and technology of controlling water:* See Leonardo da Vinci, *Codex Leicester: A Masterpiece of Science,* ed. Claire Farago (New York: American Museum of Natural History, 1996), p. 135 (reproducing page 13 recto of the codex). This codex, with its remarkable record of Leonardo's scientific research, has recently been published in facsimile edition and made available on CD-ROM: *Leonardo da Vinci* (Bellevue, Wash.: Corbis, 1996), CD-ROM #011N–D01. For the date of this manuscript, see Carlo Pedretti, "The Structure and Dating of the Codex Leicester," in *Codex Leicester,* ed. Farago, pp. 31–32. Leonardo's procedure was to write a number of related "cases" on a single large sheet, folded in four pages. As a result, a single page contains distinct

observations laid down over a period of time, with sketches along the margins to illustrate the text. For example, one sheet of the codex (reproduced in Farago, p. 134) contains three apparently disparate matters: on the top, "a geometric method for determining the speed of a boat" along with a description of a "seagoing clock" and ways of measuring a ship's course; in the middle, illustration of "underwater vortices created when something blocks the current" and below, sketches showing "the course of the Arno at four different points on its route toward Florence."

141. *In addition to continued studies:* Zammattio, "Mechanics of Water and Stone," pp. 196–207. The most extensive work on hydraulics is the Codex Leicester itself, which has been dated between 1508 and 1510: Pedretti, "Structure and Dating of the Codex Leicester," p. 31. See also the reproductions in *Leonardo da Vinci: Scientist, Inventor, Artist,* eds. Letze and Buchsteiner, pp. 126–27, 140–41, 150–55.

141. *Leonardo further explored means of improving:* On the cosmology associated with navigation, see Leonardo, *Notebooks,* vol. II, ed. J. P. Richter, #864, p. 139 (c. 1506–9) as well as #861, #862, #866, and #867, pp. 138–40 (c. 1508: Pedretti, *Literary Works,* vol. II, p. 121). For Leonardo's work with clocks, see Silvio A. Bedini and Ladislao Reti, "Horology," in *The Unknown Leonardo,* ed. Reti, pp. 242–63.

141. *Scholars explain that this:* Leonardo, *Notebooks,* ed. I. Richter, p. 357; Bramly, *Leonardo,* pp. 346–47, 461.

142. *After the failure:* Butters, *Governors and Governed,* pp. 92–94.

142. *Niccolò did not return:* Ridolfi, *Machiavelli,* pp. 83–86. For the fee offered by Florence, the marquis was willing to provide only 150 men-at-arms and 500 foot soldiers, and he placed impossible restrictions on which enemies he would fight (Butters, *Governors and Governed,* pp. 94–95). These negotiations make it more obvious why Niccolò sought to create a civilian militia.

143. *These complications were aggravated:* Butters, *Governors and Governed,* pp. 94–95.

143. *"we here find ourselves":* Biagio Buonaccorsi to NM, July 25, 1505, *Machiavelli and His Friends,* #102, pp. 112–13.

143. *"Keep what I am writing":* NM to Antonio Tebalducci [Giacomini], August 27, 1505, *Machiavelli and His Friends,* #103, p. 113.

143. *And so, again, Florence:* For Machiavelli's account of this event, see *Discourses on Titus Livy,* I, 53, ed. Mansfield and Tarcov, p. 108.

144. *They feared that Soderini:* Guicciardini, *Storie Fiorentine,* cited in Ridolfi, *Machiavelli,* p. 277.

144. *He was not to return:* Ridolfi, *Machiavelli,* pp. 84–91.

144. *By late April:* Bramly, *Leonardo,* pp. 353–55.

145. *In 1513, after Giovanni:* Butters, *Governors and Governed,* pp. 217–18.

145. *In fact, although the exiled:* Piero Soderini to NM, April 13, 1521, in *Machiavelli and His Friends,* #267, p. 334. Soderini's offer was a position managing the affairs of "Lord Prospero" for two hundred ducats plus expenses, far more than the payments Niccolò was receiving to write the *Florentine Histories.*

146. *"That night when Piero"*: Epigram, "Piero Soderini," in NM, *Chief Works*, ed. Gilbert, vol. III, p. 1463.
146. *"Pluto roared: 'Why'"*: See Dante, *Inferno* XXXI, 70.
146. *"there is no easier way"*: NM, *Discourses on Titus Livy*, I, 53, ed. Mansfield and Tarcov, p. 108.
147. *Though gunpowder and cannon:* For Machiavelli's mature view of technology, political power, and warfare, see Masters, *Machiavelli, Leonardo, and the Science of Power*, pp. 186–95.
147. *"virtue" and "one's own arms"*: NM, *The Prince*, chap. 6, ed. Mansfield, p. 25.
147. *"good arms" and "good laws"*: NM, *The Prince*, chap. 12, ed. Mansfield, p. 48. Compare "A Provision for Infantry," in *Chief Works*, ed. Gilbert, vol. I, p. 3.

CHAPTER 9. LEONARDO IN THE COURTS OF POWER

149. *Despite pressure from Soderini:* Bramly, *Leonardo*, pp. 348–50.
150. *Leonardo seemed assured:* Bramly, *Leonardo*, p. 335.
150. *"received a large sum"*: Bramly, *Leonardo*, pp. 353–54.
150. *"The excellent works accomplished"*: Bramly, *Leonardo*, p. 355.
150. *Leonardo did just that:* Bramly, *Leonardo*, pp. 355–56.
150. *Niccolò was unlikely:* See *Machiavelli and His Friends*, pp. 116–17, 127–48.
151. *"We singularly desire"*: Bramly, *Leonardo*, pp. 356–57, 462.
151. *On August 15, 1507:* For the text, see Pedretti, *Literary Works*, vol. II, p. 298.
151. *Leonardo set up a temporary:* Trexler, *Public Life in Renaissance Florence*, p. 435.
151. *Leonardo joined this fun-loving group:* Bramly, *Leonardo*, pp. 357–58. Martelli, who was a mathematician and a familiar in the discussions of the Rucellai gardens, was known to both Niccolò and Leonardo as early as 1502: see Masters, *Machiavelli, Leonardo, and the Science of Power*, p. 286 n. 59.
152. *Leonardo had apparently:* Leonardo had also been befriended by Isabella d'Este, Il Moro's sister-in-law, at the Sforza court in Milan—and, indeed, had been repeatedly opportuned to come to her court in Mantua or at least to paint her portrait. Cf. Bramly, *Leonardo*, p. 309–10.
152. *This text is the only surviving letter:* Bramly, *Leonardo*, pp. 356–57.
152. *"I arrived from Milan"*: Leonardo, *Notebooks*, ed. J. P. Richter, #1348, vol. II, pp. 402–3, and Pedretti, *Literary Works*, vol. II, p. 298.
152. *Rafaello Girolami, had twice:* Butters, *Governors and Governed*, p. 320.
152. *Niccolò, back in Florence:* Filippo Casavecchia to NM, September 22, 1507, *Machiavelli and His Friends*, #148, p. 164.
153. *Around the same time, the marquis:* Pedretti, *Literary Works*, vol. II, p. 300.
153. *Because he had settled:* Pedretti, *Literary Works*, vol. II, p. 299.
153. *As time went on:* When Leonardo was in Rome in December 1514, he had a friendly visit from his stepbrother Ser Giuliano da Vinci (Bramly, *Leonardo*, p. 389; Pedretti, *Literary Works* vol. II, p. 300), and in his will, Leonardo left a sub-

stantial sum to his stepbrothers (Leonardo, *Notebooks*, ed. J. P. Richter, #1566, vol. II, pp. 468–71, at 470).

153. *"I am afraid lest":* Leonardo, *Notebooks*, ed. J. P. Richter, #1349, vol. II, pp. 403–4 (c. 1508: Pedretti, *Literary Works*, vol. II, p. 302–3).

154. *This issue was extremely:* Bramly, *Leonardo*, pp. 356, 359.

154. *Although Leonardo's* Notebooks *contain:* For Leonardo's letter to "Messer Niccolò," see Raymond S. Stites, *The Sublimation of Leonardo*, p. 321, and Pedretti, *Literary Works*, vol. II, pp. 300–301. See also Masters, *Machiavelli, Leonardo, and the Science of Power*, pp. 20, 285–86.

154. *Back in Milan:* Bramly, *Leonardo*, pp. 367–79. On Leonardo's paintings at this time, see Pedretti, *Leonardo: A Study in Chronology and Style*, pp. 103–10.

155. *It is not impossible:* Bramly, *Leonardo*, p. 397.

155. *From the summer of 1512:* Bramly, *Leonardo*, pp. 381–82.

155. *"I left Milan":* Leonardo, *Notebooks*, ed. J. P. Richter, #1465, vol. II, p. 441.

156. *"like a brother":* Bramly, *Leonardo*, pp. 383–84.

156. *In Rome, Leonardo worked:* Responding to the needs of his patron Giuliano and a friend (Antonio Segni, an artist responsible for the papal mint's production of a new coin around 1515), Leonardo designed a press for stamping out coins (c. 1515: Pedretti, *Literary Works*, vol. II, pp. 17–18, explaining Leonardo, *Notebooks*, ed. J. P. Richter, #726, vol. II, pp. 17–18). A recent exhibition of Leonardo's scientific and technological genius at the Boston Museum of Science showed an excellent model of this press. As is often the case, however, the legend for the display did not inform the viewer of the specific context that elicited Leonardo's inventiveness. The outstanding exhibit catalog, while invaluable for an understanding of Leonardo's inventions, does not picture this model (*Leonardo da Vinci: Scientist, Inventor, Artist*, eds. Letze and Buchsteiner), p. 219.

158. *"with this one can supply":* Pedretti, *Literary Works*, vol. II, pp. 19–20.

158. *In December 1514:* Pedretti, *Literary Works*, vol. I, p. 117; vol. II, pp. 388–90.

158. *Once a group had come:* Bramly, *Leonardo*, p. 388.

158. *"The Magnifico Giuliano":* Leonardo, *Notebooks*, ed. J. P. Richter, # 1377, vol. II, p. 417 (Pedretti, *Literary Works*, vol. II, p. 323). Philiberta of Savoy was the daughter of the duke of Savoy and the aunt of the new French king, Francis I.

159. *"I was so greatly rejoiced":* Leonardo, *Notebooks*, ed. J. P. Richter, #1352, vol. II, p. 409 (alternative drafts: ibid., #1351, pp. 407–8). For these texts, written in 1515, see Pedretti, *Literary Works*, vol. II, p. 303–5.

159. *Ill, angry, and frustrated:* Bramly, *Leonardo*, pp. 386–87, 397. For drafts of Leonardo's anguished letter to his patron Giuliano de' Medici, complaining of his German assistants, see Leonardo, *Notebooks*, ed. J. P. Richter, #1351–53, vol. II, pp. 407–10 (July–August 1515: Pedretti, *Literary Works*, vol. II, pp 303–6).

160. *As soon as he could:* Bramly, *Leonardo*, p. 397.

160. *For the young Francis:* Bramly, *Leonardo*, p. 8.

160. *"Be it known to all":* Leonardo, *Notebooks,* ed. J. P. Richter, #1566, vol. II, p. 468.
161. *His bank account:* Leonardo, *Notebooks,* ed. J. P. Richter, #1566, vol. II, pp. 468–71.
161. *Less than a month later:* Bramly, *Leonardo,* pp. 407–8.
161. *He left these manuscripts:* Bramly, *Leonardo,* p. 407.
162. *"Avoid studies":* Leonardo, *Notebooks,* ed. J. P. Richter, #1169, vol. II, p. 293 (c. 1493–6: Pedretti, *Literary Works,* vol. II, p. 242).

CHAPTER 10. NICCOLÒ'S STRUGGLE, VICTORY, AND DEFEAT

164. *"Niccolò Machiavelli, historian":* NM to Francesco Guicciardini, October 21, 1525, *Machiavelli and His Friends,* #300, p. 371.
164. *"here the idea":* Marcello Virgilio di Adriano Berti to NM, February 6, 1506, *Machiavelli and His Friends,* #105, p. 117.
164. *"your new military idea":* Cardinal Francesco Soderini to NM, March 4, 1506, *Machiavelli and His Friends,* #109, p. 120.
164. *Sometimes powerful people:* Giovanni Ridolfi to NM, April 20, 1507, *Machiavelli and His Friends,* #141, p. 155.
164. *"went astray":* Giovan Batista Soderini to NM, September 26, 1506, *Machiavelli and His Friends,* #123, p. 137.
165. *"Hell's Bells, Luigi":* NM to Luigi Guicciardini, December 8, 1509, *Machiavelli and His Friends,* #178, p. 190.
165. *He was also often helpful:* Many who asked for help wrote as *compare* and might have been fellow members in Niccolò's confraternity (in all probability, the youth group of Sant' Antonio de Padova, and then La Pietà). Others came from the Machiavelli family. Most frequent were requests from Niccolò's younger brother Totto, who was an entrepreneur before ultimately taking religious orders. Like other businessmen, Totto sometimes requested Niccolò's help when shipments of valuable merchandise were hijacked. Totto also sought help in arranging a benefice, smoothing an angered acquaintance, and assisting a newfound friend. No matter how pressing public affairs, Niccolò, patient, seemed to have time.
166. *"I shall be happy":* Biagio Buonaccorsi to NM, October 21, 1502, *Machiavelli and His Friends,* #37, p. 55.
166. *"tell that asshole":* Biagio Buonaccorsi to NM, February 10, 1509, *Machiavelli and His Friends,* #162, p. 177.
166. *"I am so sick":* Biagio Buonaccorsi to NM, October 6, 1506, *Machiavelli and His Friends,* #127, p. 141.
166. *Biagio's letters combine:* As an example, see Biagio Buonaccorsi to NM, September 9, 1506, *Machiavelli and His Friends,* #117, pp. 131–32. In this one letter, as in many others, Biagio discussed favors for others and concern for family; foreign policy; ambitious rivalries as others seek a "counterweight" to Niccolò; and progress in forming the militia. The chanceries were busy. And

Biagio reminded his superior—in code—that others "adapt better than you." On the relationship between Niccolò and Biagio, see Fachard, *Biagio Buonaccorsi*.

166. *Lacking copyright protection:* Agostino Vespucci to NM, March 14, 1506, *Machiavelli and His Friends*, #110, p. 121.

166. *"I have just come back":* Agostino Vespucci to NM, March 14, 1506, *Machiavelli and His Friends*, p. 122. Then as now, it was hard to disentangle favors for friends, concern for family, personal ambition, and government business.

166. *a reference in his correspondence:* In a letter concerning business and family affairs, NM's brother-in-law reports, when speaking of letters that NM sent from Rome to Florence for further forwarding, "The letter was sent to the painter. . . ." (Piero de Francesco del Nero to NM, October 6, 1506, *Machiavelli and His Friends*, #128, pp. 143–44). It is, of course, possible that another artist was involved. A month earlier, NM's assistant Buonaccorsi wrote him, "You must have received, by the hand of the *sculptor* Michelangelo, the money for the courier" (Biagio Buonaccorsi to NM, September 5, 1506, *Machiavelli and His Friends*, #115, p. 129, italics added). In a second letter sent that day, Buonaccorsi mentioned using Michelangelo as a courier again, adding, "he told me he would be there next Sunday and would find you, since he also has some of his own business to do," and asking NM to confirm receipt of the money (Biagio Buonaccorsi to NM, September 5, 1506, *Machiavelli and His Friends*, letter C, p. 424). Four days later, Buonaccorsi repeated the request: "Let me know if you got that money from Michelangelo" (Biagio Buonaccorsi to NM, September 9, 1506, *Machiavelli and His Friends*, #117, p. 132). Nothing came of this, however, since two days later Buonaccorsi wrote again: "Just when I thought that Michelangelo had given you that money, it was brought back to me by one of his men, who told me that he had turned back for good reason: I see that I can find no way of sending it safely to you, unless some trusted person comes along" (Biagio Buonaccorsi to NM, September 11, 1506, *Machiavelli and His Friends*, #118, p. 132). Not only does this exchange refer to Michangelo as a *sculptor*, but there seems no reason for NM to have written him in October—or to have asked his brother-in-law to forward a letter that could have been sent directly. In contrast, NM had need of knowing Leonardo's intentions in Milan and could well have lacked a means to send a letter there. After losing office, Niccolò had contact with Andrea del Sarto and Aristotele Sangallo (the artists who painted the scenery for performances of *Mandragola* and *Clizia*), but there is no evidence of his relationship with these painters while he was in office. See below, second note to p. 187.

167. *"there were many decent":* Guicciardini, *History of Florence*, cited in *Machiavelli and His Friends*, p. 153; Butters, *Governors and Governed*, p. 116.

167. *"My good, and not unfortunate":* Alessandro Nasi to NM, July 30, 1507, *Machiavelli and His Friends*, #143, pp. 158–59, italics added. The same day, another friend wrote expressing grief that "I should hear you come out with

things of such a sort" as were in a letter (now lost) from Niccolò about his loss of the German mission (Filippo Casavecchio to NM, July 30, 1507, *Machiavelli and His Friends*, #142, p. 157).

169. *Niccolò himself went:* Butters, *Governors and Governed*, pp. 135–37.

169. *"wish to recognize your authority":* Ridolfi, *Machiavelli*, p. 107.

169. *Niccolò, sent in March: Machiavelli and His Friends*, pp. 154–55; Luzzati, *Una Guerra di Populo*.

169. *The final surrender:* For the text of this document, see Tommasini, *La Vita di Machiavelli*, vol. I, pp. 685–701.

169. *"in some measure":* Agostino Vespucci to NM, June 8, 1509, in *Machiavelli and His Friends*, #167, p. 180.

170. *His friends congratulated him:* In his letter of June 8, Agostino Vespucci went on to say: "If I did not think it would make you too proud, I should dare say that you with your battalions accomplished so much good work, in such a way that, not by delaying but by speeding up, you restored the affairs of Florence" (*Machiavelli and His Friends*, #167, p. 181).

170. *"I wish you a thousand":* Filippo Casavecchia to NM, June 17, 1509, *Machiavelli and His Friends*, #169, p. 182.

170. *Salviati had agreed:* Casavecchia's messenger reported that he saw Niccolò "at Pontedera with Alamanno and the Pisan ambassadors" (Filippo Casavecchia to NM, June 17, 1509, *Machiavelli and His Friends*, #169, p. 182), so it was public knowledge that they had worked together.

170. *"if a word should need":* Niccolò di Alessandro Machiavelli to NM, June 9, 1509, *Machiavelli and His Friends*, #168, p. 181.

170. *"Honored Patron":* Niccolò used this deferential term in addressing only four correspondents. In addition to Salviati, the others were Antonio Tebalducci—also called Antonio Giacomini (*Machiavelli and His Friends*, #103, #104, pp. 113, 114); Giovanni Ridolfi (ibid., #112, p. 223); and—after Niccolò's fall from power—Francesco Vettori (ibid., #210, #219, #224, pp. 370, 399, 423). I am indebted to James Atkinson for confirming this information from his review of the correspondence. Like Alamanno Salviati, Ridolfi was one of the leading aristocrats in Florentine politics; Tebalducci was the condottiere in charge of the Florentine army during the siege of Pisa in the summer of 1504; Vettori was serving as Florence's ambassador to the papal court when he and Niccolò entered into their famous exchange of letters after 1512 (see Najemy, *Between Friends*). The career of NM's assistant Agostino Vespucci provides further evidence of the clientelismo they shared. Elected to the Second Chancery with NM in 1498, he was secretary to Tebalducci in 1503–4. After the fall of Soderini and his dismissal from office in 1512, Agostino went to Rome, where he was secretary to Giacomo Salviati and Francesco Vettori. Pedretti, *Literary Works*, vol. I, p. 382n.

170. *The letter is a detailed:* NM to Alamanno Salviati, September 28, 1509, *Machiavelli and His Friends*, #G, pp. 426–29.

170. *"My dearest Niccolò":* Alamanno Salviati to NM, October 4, 1509, *Machiavelli and His Friends,* #171, pp. 186–87.

171. *Perhaps his reputation:* For Alamanno Salviat's public criticism of Niccolò, see Buonaccorsi to NM, October 8, 1506, *Machiavelli and His Friends,* #127, p. 1412. Alamanno's cousin Jacopo Salviati also had a reputation as "extremely strict about manners and morals" (Ridolfi, *Machiavelli,* p. 212).

172. *The pope and the Spanish forces:* Butters, *Governors and Governed,* pp. 159–63. During this time, Cardinal Giovanni de' Medici was kept informed of communications to Soderini by Giovanni Vespucci, who communicated through Niccolò d'Este (ibid., p. 161). Given Niccolò's contacts with the Vespucci family and with Isabella d'Este, he seems to have had personal connections on both sides.

172. *Some were later:* Paolo Vettori's brother Francesco had befriended Niccolò during their embassy to Emperor Maximilian. Another leader of the plot was Antonfrancesco degli Albizzi, who became one of a group of Niccolò's friends. For correspondence demonstrating these connections, see, among others, NM to Paolo Vettori, October 10, 1516, *Machiavelli and His Friends,* #251, p. 315; NM to Ludovico Alamanni, December 17, 1517, ibid., #254, pp. 317–18; Zanobi Buondelmonte to NM, September 6, 1520, ibid., #263, p. 328.

173. *To the astonishment of the Signoria:* Rocke, *Forbidden Friendships.* On Niccolò's later relations with Giovanni delle Bande Nere (the son of Giovanni di Pierfrancesco de' Medici and Caterina Sforza), who became a leading condottiere, see *Machiavelli and His Friends,* pp. 376, 552; Ridolfi, *Machiavelli,* p. 323 n. 34.

173. *Overcoming the* gonfaloniere's *resistance:* See the exchange of correspondence between Francesco Vettori and NM, April 21, 1513, *Machiavelli and His Friends,* #211, p. 229, as well as Najemy, *Between Friends.*

173. *His description of the coup:* NM to a Noblewoman, after September 16, 1512, *Machiavelli and His Friends,* #203, pp. 214–17.

173. *"everyone's fear intensified":* NM to a Noblewoman, after September 16, 1512, *Machiavelli and His Friends,* #203, pp. 216–17. On these events, see Butters, *Governors and Governed,* pp. 163–67. Niccolò does not point out that he and Francesco Vettori were the "citizens" who arranged the *gonfaloniere's* departure, thereby preventing violence between Soderini's supporters and his enemies.

174. *"On the sixteenth":* NM to a Noblewoman, after September 16, 1512, *Machiavelli and His Friends,* #203, pp. 216–17. On these events, see Butters, *Governors and Governed,* pp. 163–67.

174. *Niccolò made it clear:* The document is entitled "Ai Pallesci: Notate bene questo scripto"; for the text, see NM, *Arte della guerra e scritti politici minori,* pp. 225–27. Presumably directed to Cardinal Giovanni de' Medici—the future Pope Leo X—this memorandum warned against any policy aligned with the aristocratic "moderates" who were seeking to attack Piero Soderini personally as a "wicked" leader. For the likelihood that this document was written before September 16, when a coup d'état brought the Medici officially to power, see ibid., p. 222. (I have never seen an English translation of this important text.)

175. *"city is quite peaceful":* NM to a Noblewoman, after September 16, 1512, *Machiavelli and His Friends,* p. 217.

175. *"I therefore believe":* NM to Giovanni de' Medici, September 29, 1512, *Machiavelli and His Friends,* #D, p. 424.

175. *His friend and assistant:* Ridolfi, *Machiavelli,* p. 133. On Agostino Vespucci, see the fifth note to p. 170, above.

175. *The action was not merely:* Ridolfi, *Machiavelli,* p. 134.

176. *"Fortune has seen to it":* NM to Franceso Vettori, April 9, 1513, *Machiavelli and His Friends,* #208, p. 225.

177. *"Giuliano, I have a pair":* Ridolfi, *Machiavelli,* p. 137. For a different translation, see "Two Sonnets to Giuliano, Son of Lorenzo de' Medici," I, 1–4, in NM, *Chief Works,* ed. Gilbert, vol. II, p. 1013.

177. *"Now let them go":* "First Sonnet to Giuliano," 19–20, in Ridolfi, *Machiavelli,* p. 137, or NM, *Chief Works,* ed. Gilbert, vol. II, p. 1013. The existing text is questionable.

177. *"You are not Niccolò":* "Second Sonnet to Giuliano," in Ridolfi, *Machiavelli,* p. 138; NM, *Chief Works,* ed. Gilbert, vol. II, p. 1014.

177. *"Give her [the muse] proof":* "Second Sonnet to Giuliano," line 17, NM, *Chief Works,* ed. Gibert, vol. II, p. 1014. The last words (*"ma sono io"*) may also be intended as a clever blasphemy, since Yahweh identifies himself in the Torah by saying, "I am I."

177. *Niccolò's first act:* NM to Francesco Vettori, March 13, 1513, *Machiavelli and His Friends,* #204, p. 221.

177. *"take heart against" . . . "because I can say":* Francesco Vettori to NM, March 15, 1513, *Machiavelli and His Friends,* #205, p. 221; NM to Francesco Vettori, March 18, 1513, ibid., #206, p. 222.

178. *"I hear that Cardinal":* NM to Francesco Vettori, April 9, 1513, *Machiavelli and His Friends,* #108, p. 225. The newly elected Florentine pope had in fact sought to reconcile the Soderini and Medici clans, relying on Niccolò's old friend Francesco, the cardinal of Volterra, for numerous administrative functions.

178. *"because, although he is":* Francesco Vettori to NM, April 9 (19?) 1513, *Machiavelli and His Friends,* #209, p. 226.

178. *When it became clear:* NM to Francesco Vettori, April 16, 1513, *Machiavelli and His Friends,* #210, p. 228.

178. *"I myself did not":* NM to Francesco Vettori, December 19, 1513, *Machiavelli and His Friends,* #225, p. 267.

178. *While the accusation had been dismissed:* See *Machiavelli and His Friends,* p. 492.

178. *"the fame of your revelries":* Filippo de' Nerli to NM, February 22, 1525, in *Machiavelli and His Friends,* #286, p. 354. Around the same time, Nerli wrote Niccolò's brother-in-law Francesco del Nero, "Since Machia is a friend and relative of yours and a very good friend of mine, I cannot help saying, on this occasion that you have given me to write you, how aggrieved I am about what daily reaches my ears concerning him" (March 1, 1525, ibid., p. 542).

178. *His friend Donato:* NM to Francesco Vettori, August 25, 1513, *Machiavelli and*

179. *His Friends*, #221, p. 256; and December 19, 1513, #225, pp. 265–66. For the follow-up, see Francesco Vettori to NM, July 27, 1514, ibid., #237, pp. 291–92.

179. *"you never set eyes"*: Francesco Vettori to NM, January 18, 1514, *Machiavelli and His Friends*, #228, p. 276.

179. *"take off the saddlepacks"*: NM to Francesco Vettori, February 4, 1514, *Machiavelli and His Friends*, #229, p. 278.

179. *"I shall agree"*: Francesco Vettori to NM, April 21, 1513, *Machiavelli and His Friends*, #211, p. 231.

179. *"I send you, Giuliano"*: "A Third Sonnet to Giuliano, Son of Lorenzo de' Medici," in NM, *Chief Works*, ed. Gilbert, vol. II, p. 1015.

179. *"Physically I feel well"*: NM to Giovanni Vernacci, August 4, 1513, *Machiavelli and His Friends*, #217, p. 244.

180. *Originally entitled* On Principalities: NM, *De Principatibus*, ed. Giorgio Inglese, esp. chap. 1. For a longer discussion of the significance of the handwritten copies distributed prior to the posthumous publication of *The Prince* in 1532, see Chapter 11, "The Legacy."

180. *"a certain work"*: Francesco Vettori to NM, December 24, 1513, *Machiavelli and His Friends*, #226, p. 269.

180. *"His Magnificence Giuliano"*: NM to Francesco Vettori, April 16, 1513, *Machiavelli and His Friends*, #210, p. 228. The dedication to Lorenzo de' Medici, which we find in surviving manuscript copies and published editions, was a change—probably dating from 1515 or 1516.

180. *"through this study of mine"*: NM to Francesco Vettori, December 10, 1513, *Machiavelli and His Friends*, #224, p. 265. Since Niccolò had been elected second chancellor fifteen years before, it seems that he began "studying the art of the state" only in 1498. This is consistent with the evidence that his academic training was primarily in poetry and literature.

180. *"amid my lice"*: NM to Francesco Vettori, June 10, 1514, *Machiavelli and His Friends*, #236, p. 290.

182. *"I have laid aside"*: NM to Francesco Vettori, August 3, 1514, *Machiavelli and His Friends*, #239, p. 293.

182. *"sordid and ignominious"*: NM to Francesco Vettori, December 4, 1514, *Machiavelli and His Friends*, #240, p. 295.

182. *"I have not yet shown"*: Francesco Vettori to NM, December 15, 1514, *Machiavelli and His Friends*, #242, p. 302.

182. *"has been seen by the pope"*: Francesco Vettori to NM, December 30, 1514, *Machiavelli and His Friends*, #245, p. 307.

182. *"Your Paolo has been here"*: NM to Francesco Vettori, January 31, 1515, *Machiavelli and His Friends*, #247, p. 313.

183. *"whoever becomes prince"*: NM to Francesco Vettori, January 31, 1515, *Machiavelli and His Friends*, #247, p. 313.

183. *Niccolò proposes Paolo Vettori*: NM to Francesco Vettori, January 31, 1515, *Machiavelli and His Friends*, #247, p. 313.

183. *"Cardinal de' Medici questioned"*: Ridolfi, *Machiavelli*, p. 162.

184. *In 1515, Francis I:* Butters, *Governors and Governed,* pp. 264–65. On the effect of these events on Leonardo, see Bramly, *Leonardo,* p. 397. Among those whom Lorenzo de' Medici appointed to positions of importance was Francesco Vettori, who had finally returned from Rome in May 1515.

184. *Moreover, his principal task:* Butters, *Governors and Governed,* p. 289.

184. *"the Magnificent Lorenzo":* Ridolfi, *Machiavelli,* p. 164.

184. *Not surprisingly, Niccolò:* Ridolfi, *Machiavelli,* p. 164.

184. *Niccolò would use his pen:* See Mansfield, *Machiavelli's Virtue,* and Sullivan, *Machiavelli's Three Romes.*

184. *"I have become useless":* NM to Giovanni Vernacci, February 15, 1516, *Machiavelli and His Friends,* #250, p. 315.

185. *traveling to Leghorn:* NM to Paolo Vettori, October 10, 1516, *Machiavelli and His Friends,* #251, p. 315.

185. *and to Genoa to untangle:* Francesco _____ to NM, April 15, 1518, *Machiavelli and His Friends,* #257, p. 320.

185. *"the times . . . have made me":* NM to Giovanni Vernacci, August 18, 1515, *Machiavelli and His Friends,* #248, p. 314.

185. *The play was probably written:* Ridolfi, *Machiavelli,* pp. 301–3. In April, one of the participants in conversations at the Rucellai gardens, while in Rome, wrote Niccolò of the pope's interest in a performance of *La Mandragola* (Battista della Palla to NM, April 26, 1520, *Machiavelli and His Friends,* #260, p. 325).

185. *In 1519, Niccolò's young friend:* Cosimo was buried in Santa Maria Novella on November 2, 1519: Ridolfi, *Machiavelli,* p. 304.

185. *The* Art of War: See NM, *Chief Works,* vol. II, pp. 563–65. Book I of the *Art of War* begins with praise of Cosimo, "after his death," as one who had "those qualities desired in a good friend by his friends and in a citizen by his native city" (p. 568). For an analysis of this work, see Mansfield, *Machiavelli's Virtue.*

185. *In 1520, Lorenzo Strozzi:* At this time, Lorenzo's brother Filippo Strozzi wrote him: "I am quite pleased that you introduced Machiavelli to the Medici because, should he gain the confidence of the masters, he is a person on the rise" (*Machiavelli and His Friends,* p. 322).

185. *Always alert to opportunity: Machiavelli and His Friends,* p. 322. For a commentary, see Theodore Sumberg, *Political Literature of Europe* (Lanham, Md.: University Press of America, 1996), pp. 52–61.

186. *"was very well disposed":* Battista della Palla to NM, April 26, 1520, *Machiavelli and His Friends,* #260, p. 325.

186. *Another commercial mission:* For the *Life of Castruccio Castracani,* see NM, *Chief Works,* ed. Gilbert, vol. II, pp. 533–59.

186. *The latter was intended:* Zanobi Buondelmonte wrote Niccolò in Lucca, sharing the praise of a number of their friends for the *Life of Castruccio Castracani,* calling it "this model of a history of yours" and urging him to return so he could

discuss with Battista della Palla the "notion of ours that you know about" to write a history of Florence (Zanobi Buondelmonti to NM, September 6, 1520, *Machiavelli and His Friends*, #263, pp. 328–29).

186. *Niccolò himself drafted:* NM to Francesco del Nero, September 10–November 7, 1520, *Machiavelli and His Friends*, #264, p. 329.

186. *"this book for the common welfare":* Cardinal Giovanni Salviati to NM, September 6, 1521, *Machiavelli and His Friends*, #275, p. 342.

186. *During the next three years:* Even when traveling, as on his mission to Carpi in May 1521, he reports learning useful background information. See NM to Francesco Guicciardini, May 19, 1521, *Machiavelli and His Friends*, #274, p. 342.

186. *By March 1525:* Francesco Vettori to NM, March 8, 1525, *Machiavelli and His Friends*, #287, pp. 354–55.

187. *They fled along with most:* Ridolfi, *Machiavelli*, p. 203.

187. *Niccolò's* La Mandragola *was performed:* Ridolfi, *Machiavelli*, p. 208. These painters had been associated with Leonardo in the mock confraternity called the Company of the Cauldron, which met in Pierro Martelli's house in 1507–8: Bramly, *Leonardo*, pp. 357–58. Andrea del Sarto and Aristotele de Sangallo were also close to Niccolò's friends Luigi Alamanni and Zanobi Buondelmonte, and after Giuliano de' Medici's return to Florence in 1512, they joined another playful group called the Company of the Trowel, which included Niccolò and performed *La Mandragola*. Tommasini, *Machiavelli*, vol. II, pp. 385–86.

188. *"I cannot complain":* Ridolfi, *Machiavelli*, p. 209.

188. *According to one historian:* Ridolfi, *Machiavelli*, p. 210.

188. *"Fornaciaio and you":* Filippo de' Nerli to NM, February 22, 1525, *Machiavelli and His Friends*, #286, p. 354. Among the "fine things" is the scene in which the seventy-year-old Nicomaco is in bed with a person he erroneously thinks is the beautiful Clizia: the manservant impersonating her repulses his sexual advances and, when he falls asleep, sodomizes him.

189. *The same friend wrote:* Filippo de' Nerli to Francesco del Nero, March 1, 1515, *Machiavelli and His Friends*, p. 542.

189. *"As a secretary":* Ridolfi, *Machiavelli*, p. 212. Jacopo Salviati's relationship with Niccolò probably went back to the epoch of his original election as second chancellor, in 1498, and clearly survived the twists and turns of Florentine politics, not to mention the enmity of Alamanno Salviati after 1504.

189. *Pope Clement decided:* "We shall have to give up Niccolò Machiavelli, because I see that the Pope is reluctant" (Jacopo Salviati to Cardinal Salviati, May 17, 1525, in Ridolfi, *Machiavelli*, p. 212).

189. *Things were looking up:* Ridolfi, *Machiavelli*, pp. 216–17.

190. *This time, Niccolò's play:* Ridolfi, *Machiavelli*, p. 224.

190. *"brainless Charles":* NM, *Chief Works*, ed. Gilbert, vol. III, p. 1463.

190. *the new post:* Ridolfi, *Machiavelli*, pp. 225–27.

191. *When asked which he preferred:* Ridolfi, *Machiavelli*, pp. 249–50.

191. *"Machia"*: On "Machia" as Niccolò's nickname, see Filippo de' Nerli to Francesco del Nero, March 1, 1525, *Machiavelli and His Friends*, p. 542, as well as Ridolfi, *Machiavelli*, p. 249

192. *"I love Messer Francesco"*: NM to Francesco Vettori, April 16, 1527, *Machiavelli and His Friends*, #331, p. 416. Atkinson and Sices translate *mia patria* as "my native city," but the Italian suggests Italy and is rendered "my country" by Ridolfi, *Machiavelli*, p. 241.

Chapter 11. The Legacy

193. *When a flash flood: Ricordanze di Bartolomeo Masi*, pp. 249–50.

194. *"With Leonardo modern art"*: Lionello Venturi and Rosabianca Skira-Venturi, *Italian Painting: The Creators of the Renaissance* (Geneva: Albert Skira, 1950), p. 204.

194. *"Heaven sometimes sends:"* Bramly, *Leonardo*, p. 411.

194. *"This gentleman has written"*: Giorgio Nicodemi, "The Life and Works of Leonardo," in *Leonardo*, ed. Istituto Geografico d'Agostino, p. 86. The Spanish cleric visiting Leonardo's studio was Cardinal Louis of Aragon, and his secretary was Antonio de Beatis.

195. *innumerable ideas that he sketched:* Those who have visited Florence and crossed the Ponte Vecchio have seen an example. In the 1560s, the architect and artist Vasari designed a covered walkway leading from the Pitti Palace across the Arno to the Palazzo Vecchio. Vasari had studied Leonardo's architectural projects, which include the concept in drawings for Ludovico Sforza in Milan as early as the 1490s. Whether by direct influence or not, Vasari was implementing Leonardo's approach to urban planning. Today, the result is becoming commonplace, as skyways separating pedestrian from vehicular levels have been introduced in cities as different as Minneapolis and Atlanta.

195. *"Wisdom is the daughter"*: Leonardo, *Notebooks*, ed. J. P. Richter, #1150, vol. II, p. 288 (c. 1493: Pedretti, *Literary Works*, vol. II, p. 236).

195. *"The greatest deception"*: Leonardo, *Notebooks*, ed. J. P. Richter, #1180, vol. II, p. 295 (c. 1505: Pedretti, *Literary Works*, vol. II, p. 244).

195. *"we ought not to desire"*: Leonardo, *Notebooks*, ed. J. P. Richter, #1190, vol. II, p. 297 (c. 1513–15: Pedretti, *Literary Works*, vol. II, p. 246).

195. *"necessity is the theme"*: Leonardo, *Notebooks*, ed. J. P. Richter, #1135, vol. II, p. 285 (c. 1493–99: Pedretti, *Literary Works*, vol. II, p. 233).

195. *"All our knowledge"*: Leonardo, *Notebooks*, ed. J. P. Richter, #1147, vol. II, p. 288 (c. 1487–90: Pedretti, *Literary Works*, vol. II, p. 236).

195. *"Nature is full"*: Leonardo, *Notebooks*, ed. J. P. Richter, #1150, vol. II, p. 288 (c. 1487–90: Pedretti, *Literary Works*, vol. II, p. 236).

195. *"There is no certainty"*: Leonardo, *Notebooks*, ed. J. P. Richter, #1158, vol. II, p. 289 (c. 1510–11: Pedretti, *Literary Works*, vol. II, p. 239).

195. *"Instrumental or mechanical science"*: Leonardo, *Notebooks*, ed. J. P. Richter, #1154, vol. II, p. 289 (c. 1505: Pedretti, *Literary Works*, vol. II, p. 239).

195. *"Those who fall":* Leonardo, *Notebooks,* ed. J. P. Richter, #1161, vol. II, p. 290 (c. 1510–11: Pedretti, *Literary Works,* vol. II, p. 239).
196. *"The water you touch":* Leonardo, *Notebooks,* ed. J. P. Richter, #1174, vol. II, p. 294 (c. 1487–90: Pedretti, *Literary Works,* vol. II, p. 243).
196. *"As a day well spent":* Leonardo, *Notebooks,* ed. J. P. Richter, #1173, vol. II, p. 293. "Life, if well spent, is long": ibid., #1174, vol. II, p. 294. Both are dated 1487–90 (Pedretti, *Literary Works,* vol. II, p. 243).
196. *In pure science:* Under Leonardo in the listing of Sources, see the works in the second paragraph of "Secondary Sources."
196. *"Some there are who":* Leonardo, *Notebooks,* ed. J. P. Richter, #1179, vol. II, p. 295 (c. 1493–96: Pedretti, *Literary Works,* vol. II, p. 244).
196. *"virtue is our true good":* Leonardo, *Notebooks,* ed. J. P. Richter, #1183, vol. II, p. 296 (c. 1492: Pedretti, *Literary Works,* vol. II, p. 245).
196. *"The man who does not restrain":* Leonardo, *Notebooks,* ed. J. P. Richter, #1192, vol. II, p. 297 (c. 1493–94: Pedretti, *Literary Works,* vol. II, p. 246).
197. *"Justice requires power":* Leonardo, *Notebooks,* ed. J. P. Richter, #1191, vol. II, p. 297 (c. 1493–94: Pedretti, *Literary Works,* vol. II, p. 246).
197. *"To preserve nature's chiefest boon":* Leonardo, *Notebooks,* ed. J. P. Richter, #1204, vol. II, p. 300 (c. 1487–90: Pedretti, *Literary Works,* vol. II, p. 251).
197. *"There will be eternal fame":* Leonardo, *Notebooks,* ed. J. P. Richter, #1203, vol. II, p. 299 (c. 1493: Pedretti, *Literary Works,* vol. II, p. 249–51). This note is from what appears to have been a memorandum to Ludovico Sforza, proposing Leonardo's scientific plans for the expansion of the city of Milan.
197. *"Science is the captain":* Leonardo, *Notebooks,* ed. J. P. Richter, #1160, vol. II, p. 290 (c. 1497: Pedretti, *Literary Works,* vol. II, p. 239).
198. *"Yet nature is made better":* Shakespeare, *The Winter's Tale,* IV, iv, 89–92.
198. *Most intellectuals and philosophers:* E. M. W. Tillyard, *The Elizabethan World Picture* (New York: Vintage Books, 1942).
198. *"brave new world":* Shakespeare, *The Tempest,* V, i, 183.
198. *"so potent art":* Shakespeare, *The Tempest,* V, i, 50.
198. *But in the end, Prospero:* Shakespeare, *The Tempest,* V, i, 51–57.
199. *"Because life is brief":* NM, *The Prince,* chap. 17, ed. Mansfield, p. 66.
200. *"For one can say":* NM, *La Mandragola,* ed. Flaumenhaft, Song, p. 7.
200. *"wicked and do not observe faith":* NM, *The Prince* chap. 18, ed. Mansfield, p. 69.
200. *"Many times underneath":* NM, *Discourses on Titus Livy,* III, 28, ed. Mansfield and Tarcov, p. 276.
200. *"The sins of peoples":* NM, *Discourses on Titus Livy,* III, 29, ed. Mansfield and Tarcov, p. 277.
200. *"in the actions of all":* NM, *The Prince,* chap. 18, ed. Mansfield, p. 71.
200. *Piero Soderini, for example:* NM, *Discourses on Titus Livy,* III, 3, ed. Mansfield and Tarcov, p. 215.
200. *"when the deed accuses":* NM, *Discourses on Titus Livy,* I, 9, ed. Mansfield and Tarcov, p. 29.

200. *"He is prosperous" . . . "lets herself"*: NM, *The Prince*, chap. 25, ed. Mansfield, pp. 99, 101.

200. *"respect for the laws"*: NM, *Discourses on Titus Livy*, I, 58, ed. Mansfield and Tarcov, p. 117.

200 *"in the election of magistrates"*: NM, *Discourses on Titus Livy*, III, 34, ed. Mansfield & Tarcov, p. 290.

200. *Republics are therefore:* NM, *Discourses on Titus Livy*, I, 20, ed. Mansfield and Tarcov, p. 54. Cf. *The Prince*, chap. 3, ed. Mansfield, p. 9: defensively, republics are also stronger than principalities because citizens have self-interested reasons to fight against foreign conquest.

201. *This should be taken:* NM, *Discourses on Titus Livy*, I, 9, ed. Mansfield and Tarcov, p. 29.

201. *"there cannot be good laws"*: NM, *The Prince*, chap. 12, ed. Mansfield, p. 48. See also NM, *Discourses on Titus Livy*, I, 21, ed. Mansfield and Tarcov, p. 55.

201. *"a republic with its own arms"*: NM, *The Prince*, chap. 12, ed. Mansfield, p. 50.

201. *"The Fatherland ought"*: NM, *Discourses on Titus Livy*, III, 41, ed. Mansfield and Tarcov, p. 300.

201. *Such changes as artillery:* "If you defend a great town, . . . artillery is nonetheless beyond comparison more useful to whoever is outside than to whoever is inside. . . . So the defense of the city has to be reduced to defending it with one's arms [NM says *"braccia"*—the upper limbs of the body, not weapons]. . . . One ought to found oneself more on infantry than on horse" or "artillery." NM, *Discourses on Titus Livy*, II, 17, ed. Mansfield and Tarcov, pp. 164–65, 166.

201. *"In Italy at present"*: NM, *The Prince*, chap. 16, ed. Mansfield, p. 101.

202. *"Thus, one should not"*: NM, *The Prince*, chap. 16, ed. Mansfield, p. 105.

202. *Under its original title:* Nineteen of these manuscript copies, including three in the hand of Niccolò's former assistant and friend Biagio Buonaccorsi, are still extant. Just as the diffusion of Leonardo's style in drawing and painting influenced a number of artists, who copied from one another, the manuscript of *On Principalities* spread through a network of readers. Careful comparison of errors and variants in the nineteen remaining copies shows that there is no single line of descent. Instead, several different manuscripts apparently served as the basis of further copies. And in some instances, a single copy was the product of a careful comparison between at least two earlier versions. See Giorgio Inglese, "Introduction," NM, *De Principatibus*, especially pp. 10–18. This variorum edition, with extensive critial annotations, resolves numerous puzzles that have confronted earlier editors, and should be indispensable for anyone with a serious interest in Machiavelli's most famous work.

202. *In 1524:* Inglese, "Introduction," NM, *De Principatibus*, pp. 18–23.

202. *was increasingly read:* For the spread of NM's works in England, see Raab, *The English Face of Machiavelli*.

203. *Pole asserted, moreover:* Reginald Pole, *Apologia Reginaldi Poli ad Carolum V. Caesarem, De Unitate Ecclesiae,* § xxx, in *Epistolarum Reginaldi Poli,* pp. 136ff.
204. *"I am Machevill":* Christopher Marlowe, *The Jew of Malta,* Prologue, 13–21.
204. *In the decade after:* In all three, the reference is anachronistic (since the events occurred before Niccolò's lifetime). In *Henry VI, Part 1*—probably written around 1591–93—the duke of Alençon refers to "that notorious Machiavel" (V, iv). In *Merry Wives of Windsor,* usually dated between 1599 and 1602, the Host of the Inn associates Machiavelli with one who is "politic" and "subtle" (III, i). But it is in *Henry VI, Part 3,* in current form dating from after 1595, that Shakespeare gives us his fullest view of Niccolò's reputation.
204. *"Why, I can smile":* Shakespeare, *Henry VI, Part III,* III, ii, 182–93.
205. *according to some Shakespearean scholars:* See Joseph Alulis and Vickie Sullivan, eds., *Shakespeare's Political Pageant* (Lanham, Md: Rowman and Littlefield, 1995), esp. chap. 7.
205. *Of particular importance:* On this tradition, see Vickie Sullivan, "The Civic Humanist Portrait of Machiavelli's English Successors," *History of Political Thought* 15 (1994): 73–96.
206. *While some continued to decry:* In France, compare Louis Machon's *Apologie pour Machiavel* (1640), arguing for the independence of the French monarch from the pope's religious or moral control.
206. *"last or furthest end":* Francis Bacon, *The Proficience and Advancement of Learning,* book 1, in *Francis Bacon: A Selection,* ed. Sidney Warhaft, pp. 234–35.
206. *"Nature to be commanded":* Bacon, *The New Organon,* book I, aphorism iii, in *Francis Bacon: A Selection,* ed. Warhaft, p. 331
206. *"natural philosophy be carried on":* Bacon, *The New Organon,* book I, lxxx, ed. Warhaft, p. 353.
206. *"the mechanical arts":* Bacon, *The New Organon,* book II, lxxvii, ed. Warhaft, p. 352.
206. *"'Things are preserved'":* Bacon, *De Dignitate et Augmentis Scientiarum,* in *Francis Bacon: A Selection,* ed. Warhaft, p. 413. Bacon refers to Machiavelli's *Discourses on Titus Livy,* III, i.
207. *Bacon's project of a "conquest":* The result was an approach to politics that diverged in a basic way from Machiavelli's teachings. On the differences between Machiavelli and Hobbes, see Masters, *Machiavelli, Leonardo, and the Science of Power,* pp. 195–202.
207. *While America's founding fathers:* Gerard Stourzh, *Alexander Hamilton and the Idea of Republican Government* (Stanford: Stanford University Press, 1970), esp. pp. 34–36, 63–75.
207. *For example, Alexander Hamilton:* Alexander Hamilton, *The Farmer Refuted,* citing Hume's essay "On the Independency of Parliament," in Stourzh, *Hamilton and the Idea of Republican Government,* p. 77.
207. *Hume was referring:* See NM, *The Prince,* chap. 17: "For one can say this gener-

ally of men: that they are ungrateful, fickle, pretenders and dissemblers, evaders of danger, eager for gain" (ed. Mansfield, p. 66).
208. *"And although [rivers]":* NM, *The Prince,* chap. 25, ed. Mansfield, p. 98.
208. *Washington soon became active:* James Thomas Flexner, *Washington: The Indispensable Man* (Boston: Little Brown, 1974), pp. 196–99, 232, 313.
209. *"I wanted to see":* Ridolfi, *Machiavelli,* p. 236.
209. *"At that time the Arno":* NM, *Life of Castruccio Castricani,* in *Chief Works,* vol. II, ed. Gilbert, pp. 550–52.
210. *To them were opposed:* Ibid.
211. *Is our control over:* John McPhee, *The Control of Nature* (New York: Farrar, Straus, Giroux, 1989).
211. *"There is no other news":* Giustiniano and "Your Comrade" to NM, October 1, 1506, *Machiavelli and His Friends,* #125, p. 139. I believe the "comrade in Imola" who wrote this letter may have been Jacopo Salviati, who offered to pay NM's taxes when the second chancellor was in Imola and then succeeded him as emissary to Cesare Borgia. See Jacopo Salviati to NM, October 27, 1502, *Machiavelli and His Friends,* #43, pp. 60 and 449n, as well as the references to Giustiniano in Biagio Buonaccorsi to NM, September 1, 1506, #113, p. 128, and September 21, 1506, #122, p. 136. On the phrase "let the water run down the hill," see *Clizia,* III, 2, in *Chief Works,* ed. Gilbert, vol. II, p. 840.

Sources

The list of references below does not pretend to be exhaustive; rather, it provides an indication of the principal sources on which I have relied, and a guide to readers seeking more information about the life and works of Leonardo and Machiavelli.

Although most people are surprised to learn that Leonardo da Vinci and Niccolò Machiavelli knew each other and worked together, their collaboration has not been completely unknown among scholars. Interestingly enough, however, there is an asymmetry among those who have studied the Italian Renaissance. Art historians, especially if they specialize in the life and works of Leonardo, generally agree that Leonardo collaborated with Machiavelli between 1503 and 1505 in the service of the Florentine republic. In contrast, because political theorists and intellectual historians usually focus on written texts and pay little attention to philosophers' lives, most specialists in the thought of Machiavelli are unaware of the diversion of the Arno and do not consider the possibility that Machiavelli knew Leonardo da Vinci or worked with him.

A number of the documents that link Leonardo and Machiavelli, including the contract for the *Battle of Anghiari* and official reports to and from the camp at Pisa, have been reproduced in Roger D. Masters, *Machiavelli, Leonardo, and the Science of Power* (Notre Dame: University of Notre Dame Press, 1996), Appendix II. Additional evidence, reproduced or cited in the present book, includes maps and notes by Leonardo (principally from the Madrid Codex II in the Royal Library of Madrid and the Royal Collection in Windsor Castle) and a number of documents by or to Machiavelli (from the Florentine archives). Many relevant documents were published in *Scritti Inediti di Niccolò Machiavelli,* ed. Giuseppi Canestrini (Florence: Barbara, Bianchi, & Co., 1857). Also important is the report by Machiavelli's friend and assistant Biagio Buonaccorsi in his *Sunmario,* of which the key passage is translated in Masters, *Machiavelli, Leonardo, and the Science of Power,* pp. 245–46.

Of those who have studied Leonardo's life and works, Edmondo Solmi was the first to use some of these materials as the basis for a detailed study of the collaboration, in "Leonardo e Machiavelli," *Archivio storico lombardo* XVII (1912): 231, reprinted in *Scritti Vinciani,* rev. ed. (Firenze: La Nuova Italia, 1976). Shortly before this article, however, several other Italian scholars had presented communications touching on the collaboration: see Mario Baratta, *Leonardo da Vinci negli Studi per la Navigazione dell'Arno* (Roma: Società Geografica Italiana, 1905), and Gustavo Uzielli, *Le Deviazioni dei Fiumi negli assedi di Lucca (1430) di Pisa (1509) et in altre Imprese Guerresche* (Roma: Accademia dei Linci, 1906).

In more recent years, numerous art historians and biographers have weighed the evidence. The most complete discussion is found in Carlo Pedretti's careful analyses of the *Notebooks* and manuscripts of Leonardo. See especially Carlo Pedretti, *Literary Works of Leonardo da Vinci,* 2 vols. (Berkeley: University of California Press, 1977). For a detailed discussion of the collaboration on the fortress at La Verruca, see Pedretti's "La Verruca," *Renaissance Quarterly* 25 (1972): 417–25. For Leonardo's maps and their relationship to Machiavelli's role in the siege of Pisa, see the works edited by Ladislao Reti; Martin Clayton; Otto Letze and Thomas Buchsteiner; Paolo Galluzzi; and the Istituto Geografico de Agostini, listed below under Leonardo's iconography.

As a result of these analyses, virtually all of Leonardo's contemporary biographers treat the collaboration with Machiavelli as accepted fact (see the works of Bramly, Vallentin, Clark, Rowden, Stites, and Merejkowski, listed below under biographical studies of Leonardo). Even a recent biography of Michelangelo makes the same assumption: see George Bull, *Michelangelo* (New York: St Martin's Press, 1996).

Among those who have studied Machiavelli, in contrast, only a few—primarily Italian biographers—have emphasized his career between 1498 and 1512 as second chancellor of the republic. Of those, a number have discussed, in more or less detail, his responsibility for the siege of Pisa, the fortification of La Verruca, and the diversion of the Arno (see the works of Villari, Tomassini, and Ridolfi, cited among biographies of Machiavelli). Denis Fachard, the French biographer of Buonaccorsi (see below), recognized that the events took place, but expressed doubt that Machiavelli and Leonardo worked together closely. Among English and American editors of Machiavelli's writings, only David Wootton seems to have noted the collaboration with Leonardo; and he mentions it briefly without discussion: see Niccolò Machiavelli, *Selected Political Writings*, ed. David Wootton (Indianapolis: Hackett Classics, 1994).

Leonardo da Vinci

Editions. Many texts from Leonardo's *Notebooks* were published in the late nineteenth century and, most widely available, with Italian and English on facing pages, in Leonardo da Vinci, *Notebooks*, ed. J. Richter, 2 vols. (New York: Dover, 1970). References in the notes are to this edition. Scholars will prefer to consult the second revised edition, *The Literary Works of Leonardo da Vinci*, ed. Jean Paul Richter and Irma A. Richter (London: Oxford University Press, 1939; reprint, Phaidon, 1970); page references for the revised edition will be found in the notes on the World Wide Web. Other editions of the *Notebooks* were published by George Braziller (New York, 1958) and Raynal and Hitchcock (ed. Edward MacCurdy; New York, 1938). For scholarly work, the indispensable complement to these editions is Carlo Pedretti, *Literary Works of Leonardo da Vinci*, 2 vols. (Berkeley: University of California Press, 1977), which dates and comments on texts by the number in Richter's edition, adding a large number of passages not previously available. For those interested in a less comprehensive selection, see Irma Richter, ed., *Leonardo's Notebooks* (New York: Penguin, 1980).

Iconography. There are numerous volumes of art or history of science containing collections of images from Leonardo's paintings, maps, and drawings, often accompanied by valuable discussions of his life and work. For works now found in the Royal Collection at Windsor Castle, see Martin Clayton, *Leonardo da Vinci: A Singular Vision* (New York: Abbeville Press, 1996). For the Codex Leicester, see Claire Farago, ed., *Leonardo da Vinci, Codex Leicester: A Masterpiece of Science* (New York: American Museum of Natural History, 1996). Among other volumes, see Otto Letze and Thomas Buchsteiner, eds., *Leonardo da Vinci: Scientist, Inventor, Artist* (Tübingen: Institut für Kulturaustausch, 1997), the catalog of a major exhibition at the Boston Museum of Science; Paolo Galluzzi, ed., *Leonardo da Vinci, Engineer and Architect* (Montreal: Montreal Museum of Fine Arts, 1987), the catalog of an exhibition in Montreal; *Leonardo da Vinci*, ed. Istituto Geografico de Agostini (New York: Reynal, 1956); *The Unknown Leonardo*, ed. Ladislao Reti (New York: McGraw Hill, 1974); and Maria Costantino, *Leonardo: Artist, Inventor, Scientist* (New York: Crescent Books, 1993).

Biography. The best currently available biography of Leonardo is Serge Bramly, *Leonardo: Discovering the Life of Leonardo da Vinci*, trans. Siân Reynolds (New York: Edward Berlingame Books, 1991). See also Antonina Vallentin, *Leonardo da Vinci* (New York: Viking, 1938), and Kenneth Clark, *Leonardo da Vinci: An Account of His Development as an Artist* (New York: Macmillan, 1939). It is also useful to consult the fictionalized but carefully researched biography by Dmitri Merejkowski, *The Romance of Leonardo da Vinci*, trans. Bernard Guilbert Guerney (New York: Random House, 1928). The most famous contemporary account is Vasari's brief summary, though it is focused on Leonardo as an artist, and specialists often question its accuracy: see Giorgio Vasari, *Lives of Seventy of the Most Eminent Painters, Sculptors and Architects*, ed. E. H. and E. W. Blashfield and A. A. Hopkins (New York: Charles Scribner, 1917), vol. II, pp. 367–407.

Secondary Sources. On Leonardo's career, Carlo Pedretti's works have been especially comprehensive and detailed: see Carlo Pedretti, *Studi Vinciani* (Genève: E. Droz, 1957); *Leonardo da Vinci Inedito: Tre Saggi* (Firenze: G. Barbèra, 1968); *Leonardo da Vinci: The Royal Palace at Romorantin* (Cambridge, Mass.: Harvard University Press, 1972); *Leonardo: A Study in*

Chronology and Style (London: Thames and Hudson, 1973; reprint, New York: Johnson Reprint, 1982); *Leonardo: Architect* (New York: Rizzoli, 1981). Much valuable information is contained in Edmondo Solmi's somewhat dated *Scritti Vinciani*, rev. ed. (Firenze: La Nuova Italia, 1976). Among the multitude of other studies, see Morris Philipson, ed., *Leonardo da Vinci: Aspects of the Renaissance Genius* (New York: George Braziller, 1966); Vasilii Zubov, *Leonardo da Vinci* (Cambridge, Mass.: Harvard University Press, 1968); Cesare Laporini, *La Mente da Leonardo* (Firenze: G. C. Sansone, 1953); Girolamo Calvi, *I Manuscritti di Leonardo de Vinci* (Bologna: Nicola Zanichelli, 1928); Maurice Rowden, *Leonardo da Vinci* (London: Widenfeld and Nicolson, 1975); and Raymond S. Stites, *The Sublimation of Leonardo* (Washington: Smithsonian Institution Press, 1970). For a careful account of Leonardo's most famous painting, see Frank Zöllner, "Leonardo's Portrait of Mona Lisa del Giocondo," *Gazette des Beaux-Arts*, March 1993, pp. 115–38.

On Leonardo's scientific contributions, perhaps the most valuable single study is Ernst Cassirer, *The Individual and the Cosmos in Renaissance Philosophy*, trans. Mario Domandi (New York: Barnes and Noble, 1963). See also Pierre Duhem, "De l'accélération produite par une force constante," *Congrès Internationale de Philosophie*, 2nd session (Geneva, 1904), vol. III, pp. 514ff., and *Etudes sur Léonard de Vinci*, vol. III (Paris: Herman, 1913); Paul Valéry, *Introduction to the Method of Leonardo da Vinci*, trans. Thomas McGreevy (London: John Rodker, 1929); Boris Kouznetsov, "The Rationalism of Leonardo da Vinci and the Dawn of Classical Science," *Diogenes* 69 (1970): 1–11; Jacob Klein, *Lectures and Essays* (Annapolis: St. John's University Press, 1985); John Herman Randall Jr., "The Place of Leonardo da Vinci in the Emergence of Modern Science," *Journal of the History of Ideas* 14 (1953): 191–202; Alexandre Koyré, *Galileo Studies*, trans. John Mepham (Atlantic Highlands, N.J.: Humanities Press, 1978), esp. part II; Giorgio de Santillana, "Man Without Letters," in Morris Philipson, *Leonardo da Vinci: Aspects of the Renaissance Genius* (New York: George Braziller, 1966); Giovanni Gentile, "The Thought of Leonardo," in *Leonardo da Vinci*, ed. Istituto Geografico de Agostini, p. 163.

Fiction. Jack Dann's recent novel, *The Memory Cathedral: A Secret History of Leonardo da Vinci* (New York: Bantam, 1995) explicitly takes liberties with chronology, making Machiavelli older to allow for collaboration with Leonardo between 1482 and 1486. Another new fictional work uses detailed knowledge of Leonardo's biography as the basis of a dual plot, combining a twentieth-century story with an account of Leonardo; it too assumes that Leonardo and Machiavelli worked together: R. M. Berry, *Leonardo's Horse* (Chicago: Fc2/Black Ice Books, 1997), pp. 17, 65, 124.

NICCOLÒ MACHIAVELLI

Editions: Of the numerous English translations of Machiavelli's writings, I have relied primarily on the following, each of which has excellent notes: *The Prince,* ed. Harvey C. Mansfield Jr. (Chicago: University of Chicago Press, 1985); *Discourses on Titus Livy,* ed. Harvey C. Mansfield and Nathan Tarcov (Chicago: University of Chicago Press, 1996); *Florentine Histories,* ed. Laura F. Banfield and Harvey C. Mansfield Jr. (Princeton, N.J.: Princeton University Press, 1988); *Mandragola,* trans. Mera J. Flaumenhaft (Prospect Heights, Ill.: Waveland, 1981). Machiavelli's personal correspondence is now available in an English translation that is indispensible for those who seek direct evidence of his career: *Machiavelli and His Friends: Their Personal Correspondence,* ed. James Atkinson and David Sices (DeKalb, Ill.: Northern Illinois University Press, 1996). The most extensive edition of Machiavelli's collected writings now available in English is Machiavelli, *Chief Works and Others,* ed. Allan Gilbert, 3 vols. (Durham, N.C.: Duke University Press, 1965). All three of Machiavelli's plays, including *The Woman from Andros* and *Clizia,* are available in a bilingual edition: *The Comedies of Machiavelli,* ed. David Sices and James B. Atkinson (Hanover, N.H.: University Press of New England, 1985).

The definitive variorum edition of Machiavelli's *Prince,* under its original title, is *De Principatibus,* ed. Giorgio Inglese (Rome: Istituto Storico Italiano, 1994). For the collected works in Italian, see Niccolò Machiavelli, *Opere,* ed. Mario Bonfantini (Milan: Riccardo Ricciardi, 1954). For the most extensive English excerpts of Machiavelli's dispatches to the Signoria of 1502 and 1503—the so-called *Legazioni al Duca Valentino*—see *Chief Works*, ed. Gilbert, vol. I, pp. 121–60; for the complete text, see Machiavelli, *Legazioni, Commissarie, Scritti di Governo*, ed. Fredi Chiappelli (Roma: Gius. Laterza & Figli, 1973), vol. II, pp. 192–401. Selections are available in Machiavelli, *The Prince*, ed. Robert M. Adams (New York: W. W. Norton, 1977), pp. 83–92, which also contains useful information on Machiavelli's influence. For Machiavelli's advice to the Medici after the fall of the Florentine republic in 1512, see "Ai Pallesci: Notate bene questo scripto," in Niccolò Machiavelli, *Arte della guerra e scritti politici minori*, ed. Sergio Bertelli (Milano, Feltrinelli, 1961), pp. 225–27. Much useful information and some texts not available in English are found in the French edition of Machiavelli's *Oeuvres Complètes* (Paris: Bibliothèque de la Pléiade, 1952)

Biography. The standard source is Roberto Ridolfi, *The Life of Niccolò Machiavelli*, trans. C. Grayson (Chicago: University of Chicago Press, 1963). See also Sebastian de Grazia, *Machiavelli in Hell* (Princeton: Princeton University Press, 1989). Among influential and valuable works of Italian biographers, see Oreste Tommasini, *La vita e gli scritti di Niccolò Machiavelli*, 2 vols. (Roma: Ermanno Loescher, 1911); F. Villari, *Niccolò Machiavelli e i suoi tempi* (Firenze, 1877–82); Nino Borsellino, *Machiavelli* (Roma: Editori Laterza, 1973); Francesco Nitti, *Machiavelli nella vita e nelle dottrine* (Napoli: Società Editrice Il Mulino, 1991).

On Machiavelli's life and political career, see M. Martelli, "Preistoria (medicea) di Machiavelli," *Studi di filologia italiana* 29 (1971): 377–405; Nicolai Rubenstein, "The Beginnings of Niccolò Machiavelli's Career in the Florentine Chancery," *Italian Studies* 11 (1956): 72–91; Robert Black, "Machiavelli, Servant of the Florentine Republic," in Gisela Bock, Quentin Skinner, and Maurizio Viroli, eds., *Machiavelli and Republicanism* (Cambridge: Cambridge University Press, 1990), pp. 71–99; John H. Najemy, *Between Friends* (Princeton: Princeton University Press, 1993); Charles Tarlton, *Fortune's Circle: A Biographical Interpretation of Machiavelli* (Chicago: Quadrangle Books, 1970); Felix Gilbert, *Machiavelli and*

Guicciardini (Princeton: Princeton University Press, 1965). For the biography of Machiavelli's assistant and friend Buonaccorsi, see Denis Fachard, *Biagio Buonaccorsi: sa vie—son temps—son oeuvre* (Bologna: Massimiliano Boni, 1976).

Secondary Scholarship. For comprehensive analyses, see especially Leo Strauss, *Thoughts on Machiavelli* (Glencoe, Ill.: Free Press, 1958); Harvey Mansfield Jr., *Machiavelli's New Modes and Orders* (Ithaca: Cornell University Press, 1979) and *Machiavelli's Virtue* (Cambridge: Harvard University Press, 1996); Vickie Sullivan, *Machiavelli's Three Romes* (DeKalb, Ill.: Northern Illinois University Press, 1996). See also J. Whitfield, *Machiavelli* (Oxford: Blackwell, 1947); Theodore A. Sumberg, "Belfagor: Machiavelli's Short Story," *Interpretation* 19 (Spring 1992): 243–50; Roger D. Masters, *Machiavelli, Leonardo and the Science of Power* (Notre Dame: University of Notre Dame Press, 1996); Hanna F. Pitkin, *Fortune Is a Woman* (Berkeley: University of California Press, 1984); and Mark Hulliung, *Citizen Machiavelli* (Princeton: Princeton University Press, 1983).

On the premodern elements in Machiavelli, see J. G. A. Pocock, *The Machiavellian Moment: Florentine Political Thought and the Atlantic Republican Tradition* (Princeton, N.J.: Princeton University Press, 1975); Jack H. Hexter, *On Historians* (Cambridge, Mass.: Harvard University Press, 1979); Anthony J. Parel, *The Machiavellian Cosmos* (New Haven: Yale University Press, 1992); Jacob Burkhardt, *The Civilization of the Renaissance in Italy*, vol. I (New York: Harper Torchbooks, 1958); and Sammy Basu, "In a Crazy Time the Crazy Come Out Well: Machiavelli and the Cosmology of His Day," *History of Political Thought* XI (1990): 213–39.

On Machiavelli as the originator of modernity, see Anthony Parel, ed., *The Political Calculus: Essays on Machiavelli's Philosophy* (Toronto: University of Toronto Press, 1972), pp. 3–32; Leonardo Olschlei, *Machiavelli the Scientist* (Berkeley: University of California Press, 1945); and Pierre Manent, *An Intellectual History of Liberalism*, trans. Rebecca Balenski (Princeton: Princeton University Press, 1994).

For Machiavelli's influence in England and the United States, see Felix Raab, *The English Face of Machiavelli* (London: Routledge, Kegan Paul, 1964); Victoria Kahn, *Machiavellian Rhetoric from the Counter-Reformation to Milton* (Princeton: Princeton University Press, 1994); Vickie Sullivan, "The Civic Humanist Portrait of Machiavelli's English Successors," *History of Political Thought* 15 (1994): 73–96; Gerard Stourzh, *Alexander Hamilton and the Idea of Republican Government* (Stanford: Stanford University Press, 1970). See also Reginald Pole, *Apologia Reginaldi Poli ad Carolum V. Caesarem, Super Quatuor Libris a Se Scriptis, De Unitate Ecclesiae,* § xxx, in *Epistolarum Reginaldi Poli* (Brixiae: Joannes Maria Rizzardi, 1744; reprint Farnborough: Gregg Press, 1967), pp. 136ff.; Christopher Marlowe, *The Jew of Malta,* Prologue, 13–21, ed. T. W. Craik (New York: Hill and Wang, 1966), p. 9; Shakespeare, *3 Henry VI* III, ii, 182–193; and Francis Bacon, *The Proficience and Advancement of Learning,* book 1, in Sidney Warhaft, ed., *Francis Bacon: A Selection* (New York: Odyssey, 1965), pp. 234–35.

The Context

On the milieu and politics of Florence, an excellent survey is provided by Richard C. Trexler, *Public Life in Renaissance Florence* (Ithaca: Cornell University Press, 1980). For the best historical account, see H. C. Butters, *Governors and Governed in Early Sixteenth Century Florence, 1502–1509* (Oxford: Clarendon Press, 1985). See also Felix Gilbert, "Florentine Political Assumptions in the Age of Savonarola and Soderini," *Journal of the Warburg Cultural Institute;* 20 (1957); William J. Connell, "The Republican Tradition, in and out of Florence," in *Girolamo Savonarola: Piety, Prophecy and Politics in Renaissance Florence,* ed. Donald Weinstein and Valerie R. Hotchkiss (Dallas: Bridwell Library, 1994), pp. 95–105; Nicolai Rubenstein, "Cradle of the Renaissance," in Denys Hay, ed., *The Age of the Renaissance* (New York: McGraw Hill, 1967), pp. 18ff; J. N. Stephens, *The Fall of the Florentine Republic* (Oxford: Clarendon Press, 1983); Peter Burke, *The Italian Renaissance: Culture and Society in Italy* (Princeton: Princeton University Press, 1987). For a contemporary account by one of Machiavelli's friends, see Francesco Guicciardini, *History of Florence*, ch. xv–xvi, in John R. Hale, ed., *History of Italy and History of Florence* (New York: Twayne, 1964).

Confraternities, which provide an excellent view of social life in Florence, are carefully analyzed by Ronald F. D. Weissman, *Ritual Brotherhood in Renaissance Florence* (New York: Academic Press, 1982); John Henderson, *Piety and Charity in Late Medieval Florence* (Oxford: Clarendon Press, 1994); Christopher F. Black, *Italian Confraternities in the Sixteenth Century* (Cambridge: Cambridge University Press, 1989); John Henderson, "Le Confraternite Religiose nella Firenze del Tardo Medioevo: Patroni Spirituali e Anche Politici?" *Richerche storiche* 15 (1985), esp. p. 93. On homosexuality, see Michael Rocke, *Forbidden Friendships: Homosexuality and Male Culture in Renaissance Florence* (New York: Oxford University Press, 1996). For a contemporary diary, see *Ricordanze di Bartolomeo Masi, Calderaio Fiorentino, dal 1478 al 1526* (Firenze: Sansoni, 1906). On the war between Florence and Pisa from the Pisan perspective, see Michele Luzzati, *Una Guerra di Populo, Lettere private del tempo dell'assedio di Pisa, 1494–1509* (Pisa: Pacini Editore, 1973).

On the role of Florence in the discovery of the New World, see Consuela Varela, *Colon y los Florentinos* (Madrid: Alianza Editorial, 1988); Frederick J. Pohl, *Amerigo Vespucci* (New York: Columbia University Press, 1944); Amerigo Vespucci, *Mundus Novus, Letter to Lorenzo Pietro di Medici*, trans. George Tyler Northup (Princeton: Princeton University Press, 1916); *Amerigo Vespucci, Letter to Piero Soderini*, ed. George Tyler Northup (Princeton: Princeton University Press, 1916); Pedro Mártir de Anglería, *Cartas sobre el Nuevo Mundo* (Madrid: Ediciones Polifemo, 1990); Fernando Romero, "Sailing by Caravel," *Americas* 23 (1971): S7; and Stelio Cro, "Italian Humanism and the Myth of the Noble Savage," *Annali d'Italianistica* 10 (1992): 46–68.

CREDITS

❖

TEXT

Frontispiece (p. viii). Leonardo da Vinci, Self-portrait (ca. 1516). Turin, Biblioteca Reale. Reproduced with permission of the Biblioteca Reale di Torino. Text: Leonardo, *Notebooks,* ed. I. Richter, pp. 26–27, 351–52.

Frontispiece (p. ix). Niccolò Machiavelli, by Santi di Tito, Palazzo Vecchio, Florence. Reproduced by permission of the Headquarters for Italian Local Museums, Florence. Text: Machiavelli, *Prince,* ch. 25, ed. Mansfield, pp. 98–99.

Figure 2.1. Leonardo da Vinci, Aerial view of the Arno (ca. 1502). Windsor, Royal Library #12277. Reproduced by permission of The Royal Collection; ©1997 Her Majesty Queen Elizabeth II.

Figure 2.2. S. Bonsignori, Map of Florence called "della Catena." Museo de Firenze. Reproduced by permission of Scala/Art Resource, New York.

Figure 3.1. Leonardo da Vinci, Defense against ladders attacking a wall. Codex Atlanticus, folio 49, verso b. Reproduced by permission of Biblioteca Veneranda Ambrosiana, Milan. Property of Biblioteca Ambrosiana. All rights reserved. No reproductions allowed.

Figure 3.2. Leonardo da Vinci, *Adoration of the Magi* (ca. 1481–82). Galleria degli Uffizi, Florence. Reproduced by permission of the Italian Ministry of Culture. All rights reserved. No reproductions allowed.

Figure 3.3. Leonardo da Vinci, Wooden bridges. Manuscript B, folio 23, recto. Paris, Bibliothèque de l'Institut de France. Reproduced with permission.

Figure 3.4. Leonardo da Vinci, Siege equipment. Codex Atlanticus, folio 16, verso a. Reproduced by permission of Biblioteca Veneranda Ambrosiana, Milan. Property of Biblioteca Ambrosiana. All rights reserved. No reproductions allowed.

Figure 3.5. Leonardo da Vinci, Shrapnel-firing cannon. Codex Atlanticus, folio 9, verso a. Reproduced by permission of Biblioteca Veneranda Ambrosiana,

Milan. Property of Biblioteca Ambrosiana. All rights reserved. No reproductions allowed.

Figure 3.6. Leonardo da Vinci, Double-hulled structure and mysterious vessel for sinking enemy ships. Manuscript B, folio 11, recto. Paris, Bibliothèque de l'Institut de France. Reproduced with permission.

Figure 3.7. Leonardo da Vinci, Scythed chariot and covered armored car. London, British Museum. Reproduced by permission of the British Museum (© British Museum).

Figure 3.8. Leonardo da Vinci, Study for the tiburio of Milan Cathedral. Codex Atlanticus, folio 850 recto / 310 recto. Reproduced by permission of Biblioteca Veneranda Ambrosiana, Milan. Property of Biblioteca Ambrosiana. All rights reserved. No reproductions allowed.

Figure 3.9. Leonardo da Vinci, Communications and buildings of city with raised streets. Manuscript B, folio 16, recto. Paris, Bibliothèque de l'Institut de France. Reproduced with permission.

Figure 3.10. Leonardo da Vinci, Study for the monument to Francesco Sforza (ca. 1488–89). Windsor, Royal Library #12358 recto. Reproduced by permission of The Royal Collection; ©1997 Her Majesty Queen Elizabeth II.

Figure 4.1. Leonardo da Vinci, Bernardo di Bandini Baroncelli (1479). Musée Bonnat, Bayonne. Reproduced with permission of the Musée Bonnat and the Réunion des Musées Nationaux de France.

Figure 4.2. Pamphlet in calligraphy by Biagio Buonaccorsi, poem by Machiavelli with sketch attributed to Botticelli (ca. 1492–94?). Florence, Biblioteca Medicea Laurenziana, ms. Plut. 41.33, c. 7v. Reproduced by permission of the Italian Ministry of Culture.

Figure 5.1. Leonardo da Vinci, Cartoon, *Virgin and Child with Saint Anne* (ca. 1501?). London, National Gallery. Reproduced by courtesy of the Trustees, The National Gallery, London.

Figure 5.2. La Rocca, the fortress at Imola. Ladislao Reti, ed., *The Unknown Leonardo* (1974), p. 152 (photo Gian Franco Fontana).

Figure 5.3. Leonardo da Vinci, Fortress at Imola (ca. 1502). Codex Atlanticus, folio 48, recto b. Reproduced by permission of Biblioteca Veneranda Ambrosiana, Milan. Property of Biblioteca Ambrosiana. All rights reserved. No reproductions allowed.

Figure 5.4. Leonardo da Vinci, Working sketches for map of Imola. Windsor, Royal Library #12686. Reproduced by permission of The Royal Collection; ©1997 Her Majesty Queen Elizabeth II.

Figure 6.1. Ruins of La Verruca. Ladislao Reti, ed., *The Unknown Leonardo* (1974), p. 146 (photo Alinari).

Figure 6.2. Leonardo da Vinci, *Mona Lisa* or *La Gioconda* (ca. 1503–7). Louvre, Paris. Reproduced by permission, Musée du Louvre and Réunion des Musées Nationaux, France.

Figure 7.1. Leonardo da Vinci, Sketch of the right-hand group of the *Battle of*

Anghiari (ca. 1504–5). Windsor, Royal Library #12339. Reproduced by permission of The Royal Collection; ©1997 Her Majesty Queen Elizabeth II.

Figure 7.2. Leonardo da Vinci, Fortification studies (ca. 1504). Codex Atlanticus, folio 24, verso a. Reproduced by permission of Biblioteca Veneranda Ambrosiana, Milan. Property of Biblioteca Ambrosiana. All rights reserved. No reproductions allowed.

Figure 7.3. Leonardo da Vinci, Fortification studies and sketch of a horse for the *Battle of Anghiari* (ca. 1504). Codex Atlanticus, folio 2, recto and verso c. Reproduced by permission of Biblioteca Veneranda Ambrosiana, Milan. Property of Biblioteca Ambrosiana. All rights reserved. No reproductions allowed.

Figure 7.4. Biagio Buonaccorsi, *Sunmario,* Plan of the diversion of the Arno (1504). Biblioteca Riccardiana, Florence, ms. 1920, cc. 83 verso, 84 recto. Reproduced by permission of the Biblioteca Riccardiana and the Italian Ministry of Culture.

Figure 7.5. Leonardo da Vinci, Men digging a ditch (ca. 1504). Reproduced by permission of the Biblioteca Nacional, Madrid.

Figure 7.6. Leonardo da Vinci, Machine (ca. 1504). Codex Atlanticus, folio 4, recto. Reproduced by permission of Biblioteca Veneranda Ambrosiana, Milan. Property of Biblioteca Ambrosiana. All rights reserved. No reproductions allowed.

Figure 8.1. Leonardo da Vinci, Fortifications at Piombino (1504). Additional sketches from Leonardo's military assistance mission to Piombino. Codex Madrid II, folio 24, verso. Reproduced by permission of the Biblioteca Nacional, Madrid.

Figure 8.2. Peter Paul Rubens, Copy of the battle around the standard from Leonardo's *Battle of Anghiari* (ca. 1604). Louvre, Paris. Reproduced by permission. Département des Arts Graphiques, Musée du Louvre and Réunion des Musées Nationaux, France.

Figure 9.1. Leonardo da Vinci, Pontine swamps (ca. 1514–15). Windsor, Royal Library #12684. Reproduced by permission of The Royal Collection; ©1997 Her Majesty Queen Elizabeth II.

Figure 10.1. Niccolò Machiavelli, *De Principatibus,* page from a manuscript copy by Biagio Buonaccorsi (ca. 1518–20). Paris, Salle des Manuscrits, Bibliothèque Nationale. Reproduced with permission of the Bibliothèque Nationale.

INSERT

Plate I. Map drawn by Joan E. Thompson.

Plate II. Leonardo da Vinci, Sketch of the Arno (1473). Galleria degli Uffizi, Florence. Reproduced by permission of the Italian Ministry of Culture. All rights reserved. No reproductions allowed.

Plate III. Leonardo da Vinci, Bird's-eye view of the Arno (ca. 1502–3). Windsor Royal Library #12683. Reproduced by permission of The Royal Collection; ©1997 Her Majesty Queen Elizabeth II.

Plate IV. Leonardo da Vinci, Arno from Empoli to Pisa. Codex Madrid II, folio 2. Reproduced by permission of the Biblioteca Nacional, Madrid.

Plate V. Leonardo da Vinci, Two routes of canal from Arno to the sea. Codex Madrid II, folio 22 verso and 23 recto. Reproduced by permission of the Biblioteca Nacional, Madrid.

Plate VI. Leonardo da Vinci, Map of Imola. Windsor, Royal Library #12284. Reproduced by permission of The Royal Collection; ©1997 Her Majesty Queen Elizabeth II.

Plate VII. Leonardo da Vinci, Val di Chiana (ca. 1502–3). Windsor, Royal Library #12278. Reproduced by permission of The Royal Collection; ©1997 Her Majesty Queen Elizabeth II.

Plate VIII. Leonardo da Vinci, Map of Pisa region and the estuary of the Arno (ca. 1503–4). Codex Madrid II, folio 52 verso and 53 recto. Reproduced by permission of the Biblioteca Nacional, Madrid.

Plate IX. Leonardo da Vinci, Sketch for Arno canal to sea (ca. 1503–4). Windsor, Royal Library #12279. Reproduced by permission of The Royal Collection; ©1997 Her Majesty Queen Elizabeth II.

Plate X. Leonardo da Vinci, A stretch of the Arno (1504). Windsor, Royal Library #12677. Reproduced by permission of The Royal Collection; ©1997 Her Majesty Queen Elizabeth II.

Plate XI. Leonardo da Vinci, A stretch of the Arno (1504). Windsor, Royal Library #12678. Reproduced by permission of The Royal Collection; ©1997 Her Majesty Queen Elizabeth II.

Acknowledgments

This book would not have been written without the support of two people: Bruce Nichols, who suggested and shaped the project (guiding me through the editing process), and Susanne Masters, who kept life on an even keel (tolerating a husband who frequently disappeared into the early sixteenth century without warning). A number of scholars have been generous with their knowledge and their time. I have particularly benefited from the insights of Martin Clayton (who shared his expert knowledge of the maps in the Royal Collection and the career of Leonardo), James Atkinson and David Sices (who patiently and carefully answered many questions elicited by their invaluable edition of Machiavelli's correspondence), William Connell (who reminded me of crucial pitfalls and suggested resources for avoiding them), and Heinrich Meier (who at an early stage helped me think through the form of the issues). Very special gratitude is due to colleagues who read the manuscript and caught numerous specific errors: in addition to the first two named above, Hanna Holborn Gray, Debora Spini, Vickie Sullivan, and Michael T. McGuire. I came to understand the importance of Machiavelli—and the care with which his words must be read—thanks to my teacher Leo Strauss. Others who have been especially helpful through their scholarship and correspondence include (in alphabetical order) the late Allan Bloom, Sebastian de Grazia, Harvey Mansfield, Carlo Pedretti,

Maria Grazie Pernis, John T. Scott, Tracy Strong, Theodore A. Sumberg, and Nathan Tarcov. The original impetus to write a book on Machiavelli came from the late Richard Hartigan, whose invitation to give the Covey Lectures at Loyola University of Chicago led to an unexpectedly long and complex line of research. Thanks are also due to Roger Bingham, who induced me to visit the Art Institute of Chicago and left me in its bookshop long enough to make the critical discovery. (As Machiavelli teaches, accident plays a crucial role in human affairs.)

It is conventional to end acknowledgments with a disclaimer that the author alone is responsible for the faults of his work. Such a statement is especially necessary here, because many of the scholars mentioned above have reservations on points of my interpretation and analysis. It could hardly be otherwise, for—like a detective investigating a puzzling murder—I have been forced to reconcile mutually contradictory accounts of events for which there is no living witness. Despite my best efforts to get at the truth, I have no doubt that errors remain.

R. D. M.

INDEX

❖

Acqua Claudia, 13
Adams, John, 207
Adda River, 44, 156
Adoration of the Magi (Leonardo), 31, 33–34, *33*
Adrian VI, Pope, 187
Adriani, Marcello Virgilio, 68, 112, 164, 169, 175
aerial perspective, 107
Agobito, Messer, 85
Alamanni, Luigi, 187, 243n
Albizzi, Alexandro degli, 101
Albizzi, Antonfrancesco degli, 172, 239n
Alexander VI, Pope: and Borgia's conquests, 70; death of, 110; Florence as threatened by, 76; Florentine negotiations on taxing the clergy, 93; Savonarola opposed by, 61–62; shifting his alliance to Spain, 90
Alviano, Bartolomeo d', 142, 143
Amadori, Albiera di Giovanni, 23, 24
Amboise, Charles d': and Georges d'Amboise, 222n; death of, 155; as having adequate resources, 145; invites Leonardo to Milan, 144, 149; Leonardo given leave to settle his lawsuit, 151; on Leonardo's talents, 99, 150; requesting permission for Leonardo to remain in Milan, 99, 150

Amboise, Georges d', 222n
Andrea del Sarto, 151, 187, 237n, 243n
Archimedes, 156
Ardinghelli, Piero, 183
Arezzo, 7, 76, 79, 88, 224n
Argyropoulos, John, 30, 55
Ariosto, Ludovico, 56–57
Aritmetico, Benedetto, 30
Arles (Arelate), 13
armored vehicles, 38, *41*
Arno, the: aerial view of, *8,* 10; bird's-eye view of valley, 101; course of, 7; Dante's plan to dam, 11; floods of, 7, 16, 44, 193, 211; Florence seeking to control, 69; Leonardo's plan to straighten at Florence, 99–100; in Leonardo's Val di Chiana map, 88; in Machiavelli's *Life of Castruccio Castracani,* 209–10; Pisa blocking free use of, 20; source of, 7; valley of, 7
Arno diversion project: abandonment of, 3, 131; Brunelleschi's plan compared with, 97–98; Buonaccorsi's report on, 122–23, *124,* 129; Colombino as changing Leonardo's plan, *124,* 127, 129–30; Colombino as directing, 122, 123; controlling Arno's flow required for, 88; cost of, 133, 231n; discovery of maps for, 88; ditch-digging

Arno diversion project: *(cont.)*
machine for, *126;* ditches in Leonardo's plan for, 123–27, 230n; economic benefits of, 101; failure of, 109–33; Florence made a seaport by, 3, 90; Guicciardini on failure of, 136; Lapi as commissioner for, 122; Leonardo's master plan for the Arno, 2, 99, 101–2, 123, 225n; and Leonardo's Val di Chiana map, 88–89; Leonardo working on in Milan, 44; as little known, 4; Machiavelli as supervising, 2, 20, 101; Machiavelli as supporting, 96–97; Machiavelli on failure of, 147; Machiavelli's justification of, 137; Milanese experts on failure of, 132; as militarily defensible, 98; New World's discovery as reason for, 104–5, 122; opposition to, 20–21, 117; Pisa deprived of water by, 2, 20, 97; the Pisans as fearing, 117; the Pisans filling up the canals, 131; reasons for failure of, 131–33; the river returning to its old course, 130; Signoria approves, 122; Soderini attempts to continue, 130–31; Soderini supporting, 96–97, 100; Soderini's weakness in failure of, 145; source of, 225n; temporary weir for, 127, 130, 131; time-and-motion studies for, 123, 125, *125*, 127; as utopian, 98

artillery: in Leonardo's plan for assaulting Pisa, 117, *119;* in Leonardo's proposal to Sforza, 37, *40;* Machiavelli on, 201, 246n

Art of War (Machiavelli), 147, 185, 186, 227n, 232n, 242n

assassination, 5

Auvergne, Madeleine de la Tour d', 160

Avignon, 12–13

Bacon, Sir Francis, 197, 199, 205, 206–7, 210

Baglioni, Giampaolo, 142

Bande Nere, Giovanni delle (Giovanni di Pierfrancesco de' Medici), 173, 239n

Barbegal, 13

Baroncelli, Bernardo di Bandini, 52, *52*

Battle of Anghiari, The (Leonardo), 111–15; abandonment and destruction of, 3, 133, 139, 141; cartoon for, 112, *113*, 139, 141; experimental use of oils in, 3, 133, 139; Leonardo begins to paint, 139; Leonardo lacking the heart to return to, 149; Leonardo repaying money spent on, 150, 151; Leonardo's agreement with Signoria, 114–15, 137; Machiavelli's role in, 2, 111, 114–15; Rubens's copy of, 139, *140;* sketches for, *118*, *119;* work resumed on, 139

Becchi, Gentile, 65, 221n

Becchi, Niccolò, 221n

Becchi, Ricciardo, 62–63, 65, 221n

Belfagor (Machiavelli), 185

Belle Ferronière, La (Leonardo), 45

Benci, Genevra de', 30

Bene, Tommaso del, 172

Benois Madonna (Leonardo), 30

Bentivoglio, Ercole, 143

Berardi, Giovanni, 128

Bernoulli's principle, 132

Bibbiena, Cardinal, 182

Blado, Antonio, 202

Bologna, 166, 172

Bonsignori, S., *9*

Borgia, Cesare: condottieri executed by, 87, 223n; Faenza taken by, 79; Florence pressured to ally with, 79–80; Florentine mule train seized by, 89; Imola and Forlì taken by, 70; Leonardo as informant for Machiavelli on, 85–87; Leonardo as military engineer to, 1, 10, 38, 79, 80, 81, 89; Leonardo declines position with, 77; Leonardo leaves service of, 91; Lorqua executed by, 86, 223n; Machiavelli's diplomatic mission to, 1, 81–87, 90–91; Piero de' Medici allied with, 72, 76; Piombino taken by, 79; poisoning of, 110; power lost with election of Julius II, 116, 227n; *The Prince* on, 86, 87; raising an army, 76; Romagna under control of, 72, 76, 79, 86; Soderini's mission to, 79–80; Urbino taken by, 79

Boscoli, Pietropaolo, 176, 177

Botticelli, Sandro, 28, 31, 65, *66*, 112

Braccesi (Bracci), Alessandro, 62, 63

bridges: Leonardo's military, 37, *38;* Pont d'Avignon, 12–13; Ponte Vecchio, 8, 244n; on the Rhône River, 12

Bruges, 15

Brunelleschi, Filippo, 11, 19, 30, 97–98

Bruni, Leonardo, 17, 19, 112

Buonaccorsi, Biagio: Arno diversion project report, 122–23, *124*, 129; correspondence with Machiavelli, 166, 236n, 237n; on Florentine position in face of Venetian coalition, 143; manuscript copy of *The Prince, 181;* manuscript of Machiavelli's Carnival poems, 64–65, *66;* on reasons for Arno diversion's failure, 131–33; removal from office, 175; on Salviati, 67

Buondelmonte, Zanobi, 185, 187, 242n, 243n

Buonomini (Twelve Good Men), 17

Capponi, Agostino, 176, 177

Caprina, Luca del, 95

Caprotti, Giacomo (Salai), 77, 94, 155, 222n

Casavecchia, Filippo, 170, 238n

Caterina (mother of Leonardo), 23

Cavalcanti, Giovanni, 97

Cavallo, Il (Leonardo), 46–47; clay model of, 46; French destruction of, 47; Leonardo's proposal for, 36–37; study for, *47*

Cellini, Benvenuto, 141

Charles V, Emperor, 187, 190, 203

Charles VIII (king of France), 69

Clement VII, Pope (Giulio de' Medici): contesting papacy with Soderini, 187; election of, 187; *Florentine Histories* commissioned by, 186; Machiavelli contacts regarding brother Totto, 67; Machiavelli presents *Florentine Histories* to, 189; Machiavelli's opinion on papal policy requested by, 182; meets Machiavelli in Rucellai garden, 185; plot to assassinate when Cardinal, 187; publication of Machiavelli's works approved by, 202; Spanish attack on, 190–91

Clizia (Machiavelli), 188–89, 243n, 248n

Colleoni, Bartolomeo, 46

Colombino: as doubting he could carry out the project, 131; as engineer for Arno diversion project, 122, 123; Lapi as defending, 127–28; Leonardo's plan changed by, *124,* 127, 129–30; Machiavelli's criticism of, 127, 128–30; reasons for failure of Arno diversion, 131–32, 145; as underestimating labor involved, *125,* 127

Colonna, Marcantonio, 130

Columbus, Christopher, 102, 103, 104, 120

"Commentary on Florentine Affairs after the Death of Lorenzo de' Medici the Younger" (Machiavelli), 185

Company of the Caldron, 151

Company of the Trowel, 243n

confraternities, 18

Confraternity of Saint Paul, 18

Confraternity of San Girolamo sulla Costa (La Pietà), 53, 236n

Confraternity of Sant' Antonio da Padova, 53, 236n

Confraternity of the Immaculate Conception, 35, 144

Corno, Donato del, 172, 178–79

Corsini, Marietta, 77

Council of Eighty, 18, 59

Credi, Lorenzo di, 28

Cromwell, Thomas, 203

Cronaca, Il, 112

Dante, 11, 56, 136

David (Michelangelo), 112, 228n

Dazzo, Andrea, 177
De Divina Proportione (Pacioli), 35
della Casa, Francesco, 71, 72
Della Robbia, Andrea, 112
Dieci (Ten of War), 17, 59, 70
Discourse on the Pisan War (Machiavelli), 70
Discourses on Titus Livy (Machiavelli): dedication to Cosimo Rucellai, 185, 227n; on failure of siege of Pisa, 146; influence of, 199, 205; on Pazzi conspiracy, 51; publication of, 202; as written after Machiavelli's removal from office, 185
ditch-digging machine, *126*
double-hulled vessel, *40*
equestrian statue of Francesco Sforza (Leonardo). *See Cavallo, Il*

Este, Beatrice d', 37
Este, Ippolito d', 151–53
Este, Isabella d', 77, 153, 234n

Fable of the Bees, The (Mandeville), 207
Faenza, 79
Fancelli, Luca: Arno canal proposal, 44; and dome for cathedral of Milan, 40, *42;* meets Leonardo, 10, 214n
Fermo, Oliverotto da, 87
Ficino, Marsilio, 24, 54, 55
First Chancery, 59
First Decennale (Machiavelli), 56, 67, 136–37, 166, 220n
floods: as acts of God, 9; agricultural effects of, 12; of the Arno, 7, 16, 44, 193, 211; destructiveness of, 9, 44; Florentine control projects, 16; of 1997, 210–11
Florence: Arno diversion making a seaport of, 3, 90; the Arno flowing through, 7, 14; as bankrupt and defenseless after Savonarola, 75; battle of Poggio Imperiale, 53; Borgia demands alliance with, 79–80; Borgia's seizure of goods from, 89; Catholic doctrine as honored in, 20; control of the Arno sought by, 69; Council of Eighty, 18, 59; coup against Medicis of 1527, 191; decision making in, 17; della Catena map of, *9;* emerging as major center, 7–8; flood control projects, 16; floods in, 16, 44, 193, 211; *gonfaloniere,* 17, 59; Great Council, 17, 59, 60, 110, 173; in Julius II's war with the French, 171–72; Leonardo returns to in 1500, 77; Leonardo's plan to straighten the Arno at, 99–100; Machiavelli as curator of walls, 190; Giuliano de' Medici becomes ruler of, 156; men of letters in governing of, 68; origins of, 14; parties in, 60; Pazzi conspiracy, 51–52; Pisan countryside laid waste by, 109–10; Pisan revolt, 69–71; Pisa taken in 1509, 3, 163, 169; Ponte Vecchio, 8, 244n; population in fifteenth century, 18; priors, 17; republican self-government in, 17; during Roman Empire, 14–15; under Savonarola, 17–18, 58–63; Signoria, 17, 59, 61; site of, 14; Sixteen Standard-bearers *(Gonfalonieri),* 17, 18; Spanish attack rumored, 117, 120; Spanish defeat of republican, 163; taxes 1498–1502, 75–76; Ten of War *(Dieci),* 17, 59, 70; Twelve Good Men *(Buonomini),* 17; Venetian coalition defeated by, 142–43; Vespucci's discoveries' significance for, 104–5, 122; voting requirements, 18; wool workers uprising of 1378, 50. *See also* Medici family; Soderini, Piero
Florentine Histories (Machiavelli): on Brunelleschi's plan to flood Lucca, 97–98; on Florence during Roman Empire, 15; influence of, 205; Machiavelli asks Vettori about presenting to the pope, 186; on Medici associations with scholars, 55; Giulio de' Medici commissioning, 186; on

murder of Giuliano de' Medici, 51; on origins of Florence, 14; presented to Clement VII, 189
Fornaciaio, Jacopo, 187, 188
fortifications: Leonardo advising Florentines on, 39; Leonardo's defense against ladders attacking, 32; Leonardo's plan for breaching Pisan, 2, 117, *118*, *119;* Leonardo works on Piombino's, 116, 137–38, *138;* Machiavelli as curator of Florentine walls, 190
Francis I (king of France): becomes king, 184; capture at Pavia, 189; Charles V releases, 190; Leonardo at court of, 4, 145, 159–61; Leonardo's canalization projects financed by, 44; Marignano victory, 159
Freud, Sigmund, 215n

Galileo, 197
Gherardini, Lisa di Anton Maria di Noldo, 105, 227n
Ghirlandaio, Domenico, 28, 31, 33
Giacomini, Antonio, 127, 128, 146, 238n
Gioconda, La (Leonardo). *See Mona Lisa*
Giocondo, Francesco di Bartolomeo di Zanobi del, 105, 227n
Giocondo, Giannetto, 227n
Giorgio, Master, 158, 159
Giovanni of the Mirrors, Master, 158–59
Girolami, Rafaello, 152
Giuliano da Vinci, 153, 158, 235n
Golden Ass, The (Machiavelli), 56–57, 185
gonfaloniere, 17, 59
Gonfalonieri (Sixteen Standard-bearers), 17, 18
Gordan, Thomas, 205
Great Council, 17, 59, 60, 110, 173
Grimaldi, Count, 171
Gualanda, Isabella, 105
guasto, the, 109
Guicciardini, Francesco, 82, 136, 172, 189, 190, 192
Guicciardini, Luigi, 165, 172

Guicciardini, Piero, 172
Guiducci, Francesco, 98, 100, 101
Gutenberg, Johannes, 16

Hamilton, Alexander, 207
Harrington, James, 205
Henry VI, Part 3 (Shakespeare), 204–5, 247n
Henry VIII (king of England), 202–3
Hobbes, Thomas, 207
humanists: artisans contrasted with, 24–25; astrology as interest of, 20; and Leonardo, 20, 24–25; and Machiavelli, 20; scientists distinguished from, 18
Hume, David, 207, 247n
hydraulic engineering: Bernoulli's principle, 132; Leonardo on canalizing rivers, 9–10, 141; in Leonardo's *Notebooks*, 141, 203n; in Leonardo's urban planning, 43; Leonardo's water meter, 149; mobile locks, 38, 39; Pontine Marshes project, 156, *157;* Roman, 12, 13, 15; in United States, 209; in Western civilization, 208. *See also* Arno diversion project

Imola: Borgia's conquest of, 70; Borgia taking up residence in, 81; La Rocca, 81, *82*, *83*, *84;* Leonardo and Machiavelli meeting in, 3; Leonardo's map of, 81, *84*
Italy: battle of Marignano, 159; battle of Pavia, 189; Charles VIII's invasion of, 69; hydraulic engineering in thirteenth century, 15; Louis XII's invasion of, 70; Machiavelli on unity of, 201; Maximilian's invasion of, 171; power relations transformed by election of Julius II, 116; social mobility in cities of, 17; spirit of enquiry and innovation in, 17; urban rivalry in, 16–17. *See also cities and regions by name*

Jacopo IV d'Appiano, 2, 70, 79, 116, 137
Jew of Malta (Marlowe), 204

Julius II, Pope: campaign against Bologna, 166; in coalition against Venice, 169; death of, 177; Italian power relations transformed by election of, 116; *The Prince* on election of, 227n; war with the French, 171–72

Lady with an Ermine (Leonardo), 45
La Gioconda (Leonardo). See *Mona Lisa*
Lanfredini, Francesca, 24
Lanfredini, Lanfredino, 143
Lapi, Giuliano, 122, 127–28, 130, 131
La Pietà (Confraternity of San Girolamo sulla Costa), 53, 236n
La Rocca (fortress), 81, *82, 83, 84*
Last Supper (Leonardo), 45
La Verruca (Verrucola): for defense of Arno diversion, 98; Florentine capture of, 2, 94–95; Leonardo's analysis of, 2, 95–96; Monte Verruca in background of *Mona Lisa*, 107; ruins of, *94*
Leda (Leonardo), 154
Leo X, Pope (Giovanni de' Medici): alliance with Charles V, 187; communication with Machiavelli authorized by, 186; death of, 187; elected pope, 156, 177; Giuliano de' Medici made ruler in Romagna, 182; in Medici restoration, 174, 175; Soderinis pardoned by, 145; in Soderini's removal, 172, 239n
Leonardo da Vinci
  anatomical studies: for painting, 25, 35; prohibited by the pope, 159
  architecture and planning, 39–41; city with multiple levels, 41–43, *43;* Milan cathedral dome project, 39–41, *42,* 44
  Arno diversion project: aftermath of, 137–42; Colombino changing plan of, *124,* 127, 129–30; as disaster for, 132; ditch-digging machine for, *126;* time-and-motion studies for, 123, 125, *125,* 127; working on in Milan, 44
  as artist: *Adoration of the Magi,* 31, 33–34, *33;* aerial perspective invented by, 107; angel in Verrocchio's *Baptism of Christ,* 28; apprenticed to Verrocchio, 24, 26, 28–29; art studies, 25; *La Belle Ferronière,* 45; *Benois Madonna,* 30; *Lady with an Ermine,* 45; *Last Supper,* 45; *Leda,* 154; *Madonna Litta,* 45; *Musician,* 45; as musician, 34; at de Predis studio, 35; *Saint Jerome,* 30; shield for his father, 28; *Virgin and Child with Saint Anne,* 77, *78,* 154; *Virgin of the Rocks,* 35, 144, 217n
  festivals produced by: for Lorenzo di Piero de' Medici's marriage, 160; for Louis XII's visit to Milan, 151; for Sforza, 37
  as hydraulic engineer: on canalizing rivers, 9–10, 141; mapping the Arno, *8,* 10, 99–100; master plan for the Arno, 2, 99, 101–2, 123, 225n; mobile locks, 38, *39;* Pontine Marshes project, 156, *157;* on rivers' destructive power, viii, 8–9; skills as unknown in 1503, 99; on straightening the Arno at Florence, 99–100
  as inventor: as ahead of his time, 21; coin press, 235n; flying machines, 141–42; navigational aids, 122; parabolic mirror, 156, 158–59; secrecy regarding inventions, 4; at Sforza court, 35; water meter, 149
  legacy of, 194–98; Bacon as influenced by, 195, 206–7; eighteenth-century view of, 207
  life: achieves fame, 23–48; anonymous accusations against, 5, 29; birth of, 23; career stages of, 26; childhood of, 26–27; in Company of the Caldron, 151; in the courts of power, 149–62; death of, 161; education of, 26; at Francis I's court, 4, 145, 159–61; and the humanists, 20, 24–25; lawsuit over disputed inheritance, 2, 3–4, 34, 145, 151–53, 167; in

Giuliano de' Medici's service, 4, 145, 155–59; with Melzi in Vaprio, 155; Milanese water tax income, 149, 153–54; moves to Milan in 1482 or 1483, 34; patrons after 1506, 145, 147; as raised by his grandparents, 24; returns to Florence in 1500, 77; returns to Milan in 1506, 3, 144, 149; and Salai, 77, 94, 155, 222n; at Sforza court, 35–48; after Sforza's fall, 77; Vespuccis as known to, 104, 122; will of, 160–61

and Machiavelli, 1–6; after 1506, 145; as informant on Borgia, 85–87; Machiavelli and letter to Cardinal d'Este, 152–53, 167; Machiavelli as aware of technical expertise of, 95–96; Machiavelli in *Battle of Anghiari* negotiations, 2, 111, 114–15, 137; Machiavelli in *Mona Lisa* commission, 227n; meets Machiavelli, 1, 87

as military engineer: armored vehicles, 38, *41*; on artillery, 37, *40*, 117, *119*; in Borgia's service, 1, 10, 38, 79, 80, 81, 89; bridges, 37, *38*; on fortifications, 2, 31, *32*, 116, 117, *118*, 119, 137–38, *138*; in Jacopo d'Appiano's service, 2, 116, 137–38, *138*; La Verruca studied by, 2, 95–96; leaves Borgia's service, 91; map of Imola, 81, *84*; Pisan assault studied by, 2, 96, 116–17, *118*, *119*, 229n; in Sforza's service, 35–39; siege equipment, 37, *39*; in Trivulzio's service, 155; Venetian flooding of Friuli proposed by, 39, 225n; in Venetian service, 77

personal characteristics: aspirations of, 25–26; as left-handed, 26; as Prospero, 198; as Renaissance man, 24; as secretive, 4; sexuality of, 29, 215n; visual memory of, 27

views of: on human nature, 196–97; political views, 197; on scientific method, 195–96; on Soderini, 145

See also Battle of Anghiari, The; Cavallo, Il; Mona Lisa; Notebooks; Treatise on Painting

Letter of Amerigo Vespucci on the Islands Newly Found in His Four Voyages, 230n

Letter to Soderini, 230n

Librafatta, 94, 97, 116

Life of Castruccio Castracani (Machiavelli), 186, 209–10, 242n

Lippi, Filippino, 33, 112

Livy, 56

Locke, John, 199, 207

Lombardy, 16, 72

Lorqua, Remirro, 86, 223n

Louis XII (king of France): Alexander VI shifting his alliance from, 90; death of, 158; festivities during visit to Milan, 151; Italy invaded by, 70; Machiavelli's missions to, 71–72, 171; urging that Leonardo remain in Milan, 150, 151

Lucca, 11, 39, 94, 97–98, 186

Machiavelli, Alessandro, 50
Machiavelli, Bernardo (father), 49, 50–54
Machiavelli, Francesco, 57
Machiavelli, Giralamo, 50
Machiavelli, Guido, 50
Machiavelli, Lorenzo, 89
Machiavelli, Niccolò

Arno diversion project: aftermath of, 135–37; attempts to continue, 130–31; Colombino criticized by, 127, 128–30; as disaster for, 132; justification of, 137; proposal attributed to, 225n; on reasons for failure of, 147; supervision of, 2, 20, 101; support of, 96–97

correspondence, 166; with Buonaccorsi, 166, 236n, 237n; "Honored Patron" in, 168, 238n; letters to Vernacci, 184–85; letter to Cardinal Lopez, 57–58; with Vettori, 56, 176, 177–78, 180, 182, 192

Machiavelli, Niccolò *(cont.)*
  diplomatic missions: to Baglioni, 142; to Borgia at Imola, 1, 81–87, 90–91; election of Julius II, 110–11; to Grimaldi, 171; to Jacopo d'Appiano, 116, 137; to Julius II, 166; to Louis XII, 71–72, 171; to Emperor Maximilian, 154, 167, 168; to Minorite Friars, 186; to Petrucci, 93, 142; with Francesco Soderini to Borgia, 79–80
  legacy of, 202–7; Bacon as influenced by, 197, 206–7; eighteenth-century view of, 207; Marlowe's portrayal of, 204; Shakespeare's portrayals of, 204–5, 247n
  and Leonardo, 1–6; after 1506, 145; as aware of Leonardo's technical expertise, 95–96; in *Battle of Anghiari* negotiations, 2, 111, 114–15, 137; Leonardo as informant on Borgia for, 85–87; Leonardo's letter to Cardinal d'Este, 152–53, 167; meets Leonardo, 1, 87; in *Mona Lisa* commission, 227n
  life: achieves power, 49–73; anonymous accusations against, 5; astronomical inquiries of, 121–22; baptism of, 49; birth of first son, 111; business commissions, 185, 186; death of, 191; education of, 50–51, 54, 55–56; final illness of, 191; and the humanists, 20; in La Pietà, 53; marriage to Marietta Corsini, 77; and Barbera Salutati, 187–89; Vespucci's discoveries as known to, 104
  as man of letters, 164, 191; *Belfagor*, 185; Carnival poems of, 64–65, 66; *Clizia*, 188–89, 243n, 248n; *The Golden Ass*, 56–57, 185; literary ability of, 68–69; poem on Charles V, 190; poems from prison to Giuliano de' Medici, 56, 176–77; poem to Giuliano de' Medici seeking a position, 179; as poet, 56–57, 220n; writings on *Index of Prohibited Books*, 203
  military affairs: on artillery, 201, 246n; citizen militia, 3, 93, 133, 136, 137, 142, 143–44, 164, 172, 190, 201; on Florentine siege of Pisa, 146; in La Verruca siege of 1503, 2, 94; in Pisan defeat of 1509, 3, 163, 169–70; Pisan revolt, 69–71; on rumors of Spanish attack on Florence, 120; Spanish rout militia of, 3, 133
  personal characteristics: devious methods of, 143; licentiousness of, 164–65, 171, 178, 240n; as secretive, 4
  political and historical writings: *Art of War*, 147, 185, 186, 227n, 232n, 242n; "Commentary on Florentine Affairs after the Death of Lorenzo de' Medici the Younger," 185; *Discourse on the Pisan War*, 70; *First Decennale*, 56, 67, 136–37, 166, 220n; *Life of Castruccio Castracani*, 186, 209–10, 243n; "A Summary of Matters in the City of Lucca," 186
  political career: as administrator under Florentine republic, 18; adversaries as numerous, 5; arrest in plot to kill Giuliano de' Medici, 3, 176; attempted reconciliation with Salviati, 170–71; and Borgia's seizure of Florentine mule train, 89; Chancery work before 1498, 54; connections of, 64; as curator of Florentine walls, 190; and the Medici family, 64–67, 163, 182, 185, 187, 202; in Medici return to power, 172–74, 239nn; papal position sought through Vettori, 177–79; removed from office, 3, 133, 175–76; salary as second chancellor, 59, 216n; Salviati as hostile toward, 163, 167, 168, 169; Savonarola opposed by, 62–63; as second chancellor, 58–64; as secretary of Ten of War, 59, 70; as Soderini ally, 64, 67–68, 81; on Soderini as weak, 68, 145–46, 174; and Soderini–Salviati conflict, 110,

115, 168; Soderini's offer of job to, 146, 234n; torture of, 176; Paolo Vettori advised by, 182–83; Francesco Vettori requests opinion on papal policy, 182

political theory, 21; basic principles of, 199–201; as Italian patriot, 192; on republics as superior to monarchies, 200; the river as a metaphor for, 10–11, 209

See also *Discourses on Titus Livy*; *Florentine Histories*; *Mandragola, La*; *Prince, The*

Machiavelli, Niccolò di Alessandro, 170
Machiavelli, Niccolò di Bernardo di Jacopo, 219n
Machiavelli, Niccolò di Buoninsegno (grandfather), 49
Machiavelli, Totto (brother), 67, 177, 236n
"Machiavellian," 203
Machon, Louis, 247n
Madison, James, 207
Madonna Litta (Leonardo), 45
Mandeville, Bernard, 207
Mandragola, La (Machiavelli): as greatest comedy of Italian theater, 56, 185; Guicciardini plans to produce, 189, 190, 199; La Verruca reference, 96; Monteloro performance, 187, 243n; Venetian production, 189–90
Mannelli, Luigi, 90
Mantua, marquis of, 142, 153
Marignano, battle of, 159
Marlowe, Christopher, 204
Martelli, Piero di Braccio, 151, 234n
Martelli, Ugolino de, 64
Masque of the Planets, 37, 160
Maximilian, Emperor: in coalition against Venice, 169; Florentine republic as threatened by, 167; Italy invaded by, 171; Machiavelli's mission to, 154, 167, 168; Salviati's pro-imperial policy, 167, 170
Medici, Catherine de', 203
Medici, Clarice de', 168
Medici, Cosimo de', 50, 55
Medici, Giovanni de'. *See* Leo X, Pope
Medici, Giovanni di Pierfrancesco de', 60–61, 63, 64
Medici, Giovanni di Pierfrancesco de' (Giovanni delle Bande Nere), 173, 239n
Medici, Giuliano de': death of, 160; Leonardo in service of, 4, 145, 155–59; Machiavelli arrested in plot against, 3, 176; Machiavelli dedicates poem to, 65; Machiavelli's poem requesting a position, 179; Machiavelli's poems from prison to, 56, 176–77; marriage to Philiberta of Savoy, 158; in Medici restoration, 174; *The Prince* as dedicated to, 180; rule in Romagna, 182–83; as ruler of Florence, 156; as Vangelista, 18
Medici, Giuliano di Piero de', 5, 51
Medici, Giulio de'. *See* Clement VII, Pope
Medici, Lorenzo (the Magnificent) de': Becchi as tutor to, 65; confraternities supported by, 18; Fancelli's canal proposal to, 44; Florentine politics under, 17; and intellectuals, 55; Pazzi plot to assassinate, 51; poems in Machiavelli manuscript, 65; and Savonarola, 58; silver lute given to Sforza, 34, 36
Medici, Lorenzo di Pierfrancesco de': death of, 104; in elections of 1498, 63; in Medici family divisions, 60–61; poems in Buonaccorsi manuscript, 65; Vespucci in service of, 64, 102; Vespucci's reports from New World, 103, 104, 120, 229n
Medici, Lorenzo di Piero de': death of, 185; as duke of Urbino, 184; Leonardo's marriage festivities for, 160; Machiavelli presents *The Prince* to, 184; *The Prince* as dedicated to, 180, 184, 241n; Vettori negotiating marriage for, 184
Medici, Pierfrancesco de', 60

Medici, Piero de': Borgia as seeking restoration of, 72, 76; deposed, 58, 60, 69; in Medici family divisions, 60; Pisa lost by, 69; rising against Savonarola, 61; as successor to Lorenzo, 58; Venetian coalition supporting, 142

Medici family: as bankers, 16; coup against of 1527, 191; divisions within, 60–61; humanists at court of, 54; Machiavelli seeking employment from, 163; Machiavelli's ties to, 64–67, 182, 187, 202; opponents of, 60; Pazzi conspiracy against, 51–52; political manipulation by, 17; return to power, 133, 163, 172–74. *See also family members by name*

Melzi, Francesco, 154, 155, 160, 161

Merry Wives of Windsor (Shakespeare), 247n

Michelangelo: battle of Cascina project, 111, 139, 141; Buonaccorsi mentions in letter to Machiavelli, 237; *David*, 112, 228n; on Leonardo's *Adoration of the Magi*, 33; as rival of Leonardo, 111

Michele, Don, 144

Michelozzi, Niccolò, 175

Migliorotti, Atalante, 34

Milan: canal network, 16; cathedral dome, 39–41, *42*, 44; crossroads site of, 14; designs on Pisa, 69; Leonardo moves to in 1482 or 1483, 34; Leonardo returns to in 1506, 3, 144, 149; Leonardo's flood control projects, 44; Leonardo's water meter for, 149; plague of 1484, 41; Massimiliano Sforza restored in, 155. *See also* Sforza, Ludovico

military technology: armored vehicles, 38, *41*; Leonardo's interest in, 31, 36; Leonardo's proposals to Sforza, 36, 37–39; Renaissance developments in, 16; siege equipment, 37, *39*. *See also* artillery; fortifications

Minorite Friars, 186

mobile locks, 38, 39

Modena, 182

Mona Lisa (Leonardo), 105–7, *106*; dating of, 105; identity of sitter, 105; Machiavelli's involvement in commission for, 227n

Montaigne, 205

Mundus Novus, 104, 120–22, 229nn

Musician (Leonardo), 45

Nelli, Bartolomea (mother of Machiavelli), 50

Nerli, Filippo de', 240n

Nero, Francesco del, 240n

New Organon, The (Bacon), 206

Notebooks (Leonardo): on Arno development project, 100–101; Bernoulli's principle anticipated in, 132; dismantling of, 161; on the earth as a globe, 229n; on hydraulic engineering, 141, 232n; on Leonardo's early life, 26–27; letter to "Messer Niccolò," 154, 235n; Melzi's attempt to edit, 161; mirror writing in, 4; "Of the Human Figure" entry, 45, 218n; publication assumed by Leonardo, 162; on the Vespuccis, 30, 122

Ombrone River, 7

Pacioli, Luca, 35, 77

parabolic mirror, 156, 158–59

Parma, 182

Pavia, 189

Pazzi conspiracy, 51–52

Perugia, 142

Perugino, 24–25, 28, 31, 112

Petrarch, 56

Petrucci, Pandolfo, 93, 142

Philiberta of Savoy, 158, 235n

Piacenza, 182

Pico della Mirandola, Giovanni, 19, 54–55

Piero da Vinci (father of Leonardo), 23–24, 27–28, 31, 60

Piero di Cosimo, 151
Piombino: Borgia takes, 79; Jacopo IV d'Appiano, 2, 70, 79, 116, 137; Leonardo visits while in Borgia's service, 79, 138; Leonardo works on fortifications of, 116, 137–38, *138*; Machiavelli's mission to, 116, 137
Pisa: Arno diversion project depriving of water, 2, 20, 97; blocking Florentine use of the Arno, 20, 69; Dante's plan to flood, 11; as fearing Arno diversion, 117; Florence laying waste to countryside, 109–10; Florentine conquest of 1509, 3, 163, 169; Florentine siege of 1504, 116–17; Florentine siege of 1505–6, 143, 146; Florentine strategy of isolating, 97; French conquest of, 69; Leonardo's scheme to blow up walls of, 2, 117, *118*, 119; Machiavelli on siege of, 146; proposed consistory at, 171; revolt against Florence, 69–71; Soderini urging direct assault on, 116–17; Vitelli's failure to take, 70
Pistoia, 10, 76, 101
Pius III, Pope, 110, 227n
Poggio Imperiale, battle of, 53
Pole, Reginald, 202–3
Poliziano, Angelo, 24, 54, 55, 65, 102, 219n
Pollaiuolo, Antonio, 31
Pont d'Avignon, 12–13
Pont du Gard, 13
Ponte Vecchio (Florence), 8, 244n
Pontine Marshes, 156, *157*
Potomac Company, 208
Po Valley, 16
practica, 17
Prato, 2, 172
Predis, Ambrogio de, 35, 144
Predis, Evangelista de, 35
Prince, The (Machiavelli), 179–84; on Borgia, 86, 87; on Borgia and the election of Julius II, 227n; copies made of, 202, 246n; as dedicated to Giuliano de' Medici, 180; as dedicated to Lorenzo di Piero de' Medici, 180, 184, 241n; on Fortune as a river, ix, 10, 208; on history as written by the winners, 200; influence of, 202–3; on Louis XII failing to hold Lombardy, 72; Machiavelli presents copy to Lorenzo de' Medici, 184; opening page of manuscript copy, *181*; on political success, 147; publication of, 202; Spinoza on, 205; traditional interpretation of, 180
printing, 16, 201
priors, 17

Quaratesi, Francesco di Bernardo, *181*

Raphael, 33, 105, 141
Reggio, 182
Renaissance: engineering and trade as foundation of, 16; Leonardo as Renaissance man, 24; letters as not secure during, 5–6, 87; *The Prince* on political practices of, 180. *See also* humanists
Rhône River, 12–13
Ridolfi, Giovanni, 67, 120, 238n
Romagna: Borgia taking control of, 72, 76, 79, 86; Julius II desiring to recapture, 166; Leo X's projected state in, 158; Giuliano de' Medici ruling cities in, 182
Romans: Acqua Claudia, 13; hydraulic engineering of, 12, 13, 15; Pont du Gard, 13; Rhône River bridges, 12
Rome: Acqua Claudia, 13; Leonardo working in, 156–59; Pontine Marshes project, 156, *157*; Sistine Chapel, 31; Spanish attack on, 190–91
Rubens, Peter Paul, 139, *140*
Rucellai, Camilla di Mariotto, 105, 227n
Rucellai, Caterina di Mariotto, 227n
Rucellai, Cosimo di Cosimo, 174, 184, 185, 227n, 242n
Rustici, Giovanni Francesco, 151

Saint Bartholomew's Day Massacre, 203
Saint Jerome (Leonardo), 30
Salai (Giacomo Caprotti), 77, 94, 155, 222n
Salutati, Barbera, 187–89
Salviati, Alamanno: Baglioni supported by, 142; death of, 171; *First Decennale* dedicated to, 67, 136; as "Honored Patron" for Machiavelli, 168, 170, 238n; insults Machiavelli at Pisa, 169; letter to Machiavelli, 65, 67; Machiavelli disliked by, 163, 167, 168; Machiavelli's attempted reconciliation with, 170–71, 238n; Medici connections of, 65; pro-imperial policy of, 167, 170; Soderini opposed by, 110, 115, 168; and Soderini's Pisan strategy, 169, 170
Salviati, Giacomo, 238n
Salviati, Giovanni, 186, 189
Salviati, Jacopo: financial assistance to Machiavelli, 168, 248n; as patron of Machiavelli, 189, 221n, 243n; and Soderini, 110; as strict about manners and morals, 239n
Sangallo, Antonio da, the Elder, 95
Sangallo, Aristotele, 151, 187, 188, 237n, 243n
Sangallo, Giuliano da, 95
Santa Croce, Church of, 50
Santa Maria Novella, 111
Santa Maria Nuova, 91, 144, 155
Savonarola: Alexander VI as hostile toward, 61–62; excommunication of, 62; execution of, 5, 58, 63; Florence left bankrupt and defenseless by, 75; Florentine government under, 17–18, 58–63; Machiavelli as opposed to, 62–63; opponents of, 60; Pico della Mirandola influenced by, 54; puritanism of, 60, 61
Scala, Bartolomeo, 53–54, 65
Second Chancery, 59
Segni, Antonio, 235n
Serchio River, 11

Serravalle, Mount, 2, 99, 226n
Sforza, Caterina, 70, 72
Sforza, Francesco, 36–37, 46–47
Sforza, Gian Galeazzo, 37
Sforza, Ludovico (Il Moro): Charles VIII invited into Italy by, 69; *Last Supper* sponsored by, 45; Leonardo at court of, 35–48; Leonardo delivers silver lute to, 34, 36; driven from power by Louis XII, 70; marriage to Beatrice d'Este, 37
Sforza, Massimiliano, 155
Shakespeare, William, 197–98, 204–5, 247n
Sidney, Algernon, 205
siege equipment, 37, *39*
Siena, 93, 142
Sieve River, 7
Signorelli, Luca, 31
Signoria, 17, 59, 61
Sistine Chapel, 31
Sixteen Standard-bearers *(Gonfalonieri)*, 17, 18
Smith, Adam, 207
Snow, C. P., 208
Soderini, Francesco: cardinal's hat purchased for, 93–94; consoling Machiavelli over Arno project, 135; contesting papacy with Giulio de' Medici, 187; diplomatic mission to Borgia, 79–80; expectation of victory over Pisa, 116; and Machiavelli's attempt to secure papal position, 178, 240n; on Machiavelli's citizen militia plan, 164; replying to Machiavelli's letter to Piero Soderini, 81; Vatican post for, 145
Soderini, Giovan Batista, 164
Soderini, Piero: Arno project failure as disaster for, 132, 136; Arno project proposal attributed to, 225n; Arno project supported by, 96–97, 100; attempts to continue diversion project, 130–31; and *Battle of Anghiari*, 112, 115; on Borgia's seizure of

Florentine goods, 89; on citizen militia plan, 93, 136, 144; on a condottiere for Florence, 142–43; at consultative meeting on Florentine crisis, 90; correspondence with Machiavelli at Imola, 82–83; expulsion from office, 163; as *gonfaloniere* of justice, 60, 80–81; offers job to Machiavelli, 146, 234n; Leonardo on, 145; Leonardo's departure for Milan opposed by, 149, 150; and Leonardo's letter to Cardinal d'Este, 152; *Letter to Soderini* attributed to Vespucci, 230n; Machiavelli as ally of, 64, 67–68, 81; Machiavelli family as critical of, 60; Machiavelli recalled from Imola by, 91; Machiavelli's criticism of, 68, 145–46, 174; Machiavelli's epitaph for, 146; Maximilian as threat to, 167; Michelangelo as protégé of, 111; Pisan assault urged by, 116–17; Pisan strategy of 1509, 169, 170; removal of, 172, 173; and Salviati family, 81, 110, 115, 168, 221n; as turning his back on his aristocratic supporters, 110, 115

sodomy: in *Clizia* scene, 243n; in demands of Medici supporters, 173; Leonardo accused of, 5, 29; Savonarola's campaign against, 61

Spinoza, 205

Stagno di Livorno, 99–100, 123

strappado, 176

Strozzi, Filippo, 168, 172, 242n

Strozzi, Lorenzo di Filippo, 185, 242n

"Summary of Matters in the City of Lucca, A" (Machiavelli), 186

Tacitus, 15, 56

Tebalducci, Antonio, 238n

Tempest, The (Shakespeare), 198

Ten of War *(Dieci)*, 17, 59, 70

Tiber River, 88

Toscanelli, Paolo del Pozzo, 30, 103, 217n

Tosinghi, Pier Francesco, 95

Tosinghi, Tommaso, 131

Treatise on Painting (Leonardo): on humanists, 25; Melzi's editing of, 161; writing of, 35

Trenchard, John, 205

Trivulzio, Marshal, 155, 159

Tuscany, 7, 53, 76, 120

Twelve Good Men *(Buonomini)*, 17

Ugolini, Luca, 111

underwater swimming equipment, 40

urban planning, Leonardo's conceptions of, 41–43, *43*, 197

Urbino, 79, 184

Val di Chiana, 15, 79, 88–89

Valori, Francesco, 61, 63

Vangelista youth confraternity, 18

Vasari, Giorgio: on cartoon for *Virgin and Child with Saint Anne*, 77; covered walkway of Ponte Vecchio, 244n; on *La Gioconda*, 107; on Leonardo, 24, 194; on Leonardo playing jokes on papal entourage, 158; on Leonardo's angel in *Baptism of Christ*, 28; on Leonardo's death, 161; on Leonardo sketch of Vespucci, 104; on performance of *La Mandragola*, 187; on Raphael studying Leonardo, 141; on scenery for *Clizia*, 188; on young Leonardo's shield, 28

Venice: designs on Pisa, 69; Florence defeats coalition led by, 142–43; French defeat at Marignano, 159; Leonardo's advice on flooding the Friuli, 39, 225n; Leonardo's visit to, 77; *La Mandragola* produced in, 189–90; Pisa abandoned by, 70; pope, emperor, and Spanish combine against, 169; ship building, 15

Vernacci, Giovanni, 242n

Vernica, 109

Verrocchio, Andrea del: apprentices of, 28; Colleoni monument, 46;

Verrocchio, Andrea del: *(cont.)*
Leonardo as apprentice of, 24, 26, 28–29; monetary problems of, 34; products of workshop of, 25; as sculptor, 46

Vespucci, Agostino: adding honorific to his name, 104; as assistant to Machiavelli, 64; description of battle of Anghiari, 2, 112; Leonardo's letter to d'Este in handwriting of, 152, 153, 167; Machiavelli's *First Decennale* published by, 166; in *Mona Lisa* commission, 227n; patrons of, 238n; on Pisan defeat of 1509, 169, 238n

Vespucci, Amerigo: on America as a new continent, 103, 120; and Giocondo, 227n; on inhabitants of the New World, 103–4, 121; investing in voyages of discovery, 102; Leonardo meets, 30; *Letter to Soderini* attributed to, 230n; and the Popoleschi, 64; voyage of 1499, 102–3, 226n; voyage of 1501, 103

Vespucci, Antonio, 63, 64

Vespucci, Bartolomeo, 68–69, 121, 122

Vespucci, Giorgio Antonio, 30

Vespucci, Giovanni, 239n

Vettori, Francesco: as ambassador to France, 184, 242n; infatuation with Costanza, 179; Machiavelli addressing as "Honored Patron," 238n; Machiavelli on problems of peace and war, 192; Machiavelli requesting papal position through, 177–79; and Machiavelli's *Florentine Histories*, 186; Machiavelli's letter of despair to, 180, 182; Machiavelli's letter on his reading, 56; Machiavelli's letter on his removal from office, 176; Lorenzo de' Medici's marriage negotiated by, 184; mission to Emperor Maximilian, 167, 168; as not trusting letters, 5; on *The Prince*, 180; requests Machiavelli's opinion on papal policy, 182; in Soderini's removal, 173, 239; Vespucci as secretary to, 238n; on why he has fallen in love, 5–6

Vettori, Paolo: Machiavelli's business commissions for, 185; and Machiavelli's letters to brother Francesco, 177; in Medici rule in Romagna, 182, 183; in plot to restore the Medici, 172, 239n

Vico, 109

Vinci, 7, 23

Vinci, Giuliano da, 153, 158, 235n

Vinci, Leonardo da. *See* Leonardo da Vinci

Vinci, Piero da (father of Leonardo), 23–24, 27–28, 31, 60

Virgin and Child with Saint Anne (Leonardo), 77, *78*, 154

Virgin of the Rocks (Leonardo), 35, 144, 217n

Vitelli, Paolo, 70, 222n

Vitelli, Vitellozzo, 79, 87

Washington, George, 208

Winter's Tale, The (Shakespeare), 198